X-MARKS

INDIGENOUS AMERICAS

Robert Warrior and Jace Weaver, Series Editors

Raymond D. Austin, *Navajo Courts and Navajo Common Law: A Tradition of Tribal Self-Governance*

Lisa Brooks, *The Common Pot: The Recovery of Native Space in the Northeast*

Kevin Bruyneel, *The Third Space of Sovereignty: The Postcolonial Politics of U.S.–Indigenous Relations*

Daniel Heath Justice, *Our Fire Survives the Storm: A Cherokee Literary History*

Thomas King, *The Truth about Stories: A Native Narrative*

Scott Richard Lyons, *X-Marks: Native Signatures of Assent*

Jean M. O'Brien, *Firsting and Lasting: Writing Indians out of Existence in New England*

Paul Chaat Smith, *Everything You Know about Indians Is Wrong*

Gerald Vizenor, *Bear Island: The War at Sugar Point*

Robert Warrior, *The People and the Word: Reading Native Nonfiction*

Robert A. Williams, Jr., *Like a Loaded Weapon: The Rehnquist Court, Indian Rights, and the Legal History of Racism in America*

X-Marks

NATIVE SIGNATURES OF ASSENT

Scott Richard Lyons

Indigenous Americas Series

University of Minnesota Press
Minneapolis
London

Published by the University of Minnesota Press
111 Third Avenue South, Suite 290
Minneapolis, MN 55401-2520
http://www.upress.umn.edu

Library of Congress Cataloging-in-Publication Data

Lyons, Scott Richard.
    X-marks : native signatures of assent / Scott Richard Lyons.
        p. cm. — (Indigenous Americas)
    Includes bibliographical references and index.
    ISBN 978-0-8166-6676-8 (hc : alk. paper) — ISBN 978-0-8166-6677-5 (pbk. : alk. paper)
    1. Indians of North America—Ethnic identity.   2. Indians of North America—Cultural assimilation.   3. Group identity—United States.   4. Self-determination, national—United States.   5. Identification (Psychology).   6. Race awareness.   7. Liminality.   I. Title.
    E98.E85L96 2010
    305.897—dc22

                                                                    2009016339

Printed in the United States of America on acid-free paper

The University of Minnesota is an equal-opportunity educator and employer.

17 16 15 14   10 9 8 7 6 5 4

For Leona Lyons

CONTENTS

I grew up on the border—literally and figuratively—of the Leech Lake Ojibwe Reservation in northern Minnesota and, as everyone already knows, life on an Indian reservation can be a hard thing to endure. The difficulties of Indian life are complicated by the shade and color of your skin, which in my case is fairly light. Sometimes during my youth I would speak as an Indian and in response be called a White Boy. Other times I would speak as a White Boy and be quickly reminded of my Indianness. This sort of liminality has long been theorized by Indian writers such as Mourning Dove, Louise Erdrich, Gerald Vizenor, Simon Ortiz, Leslie Marmon Silko, and others as the story of the "half-breed," "mixed-blood," and (most regrettably) "part-Indian" (never "part-white"), although today such hybrid terms are viewed as problematic by people who prefer to speak in terms of wholeness. But wholeness has never been my experience, at least not where identity is concerned. Liminality has always best defined me on the inside and perhaps on the outside, too, and I say that without trying to privilege the condition of in-betweenness even one little bit.

Some of my earliest memories are located in the Leech Lake Head Start building, where I was in the inaugural class. It was eventually the site of an AIM press conference, and I remember watching that press conference on television—seeing those large Indian men with their big bellies and big guns sitting in tiny Head Start chairs with their knees way up high and talking about revolution—and recalling at the time that our Head Start teacher had told us that we were Indians and should always be proud of who we are. There is a consistency here that I most certainly did not perceive in my youth: namely, that despite its fierce assimilationist agenda, my old Head Start program turned out to be a powerful source of Native identity in my life. Ironic, isn't it?

Leech Lake is decidedly rural, and since rural upbringings can be rather boring, I watched a lot of television. For years, probably until I was ten or so, I thought several leading men on popular shows and movies were Indians, even though most were not: Jack Webb from *Dragnet* (Jewish), Dennis Weaver from *McCloud* (actually, his father was Cherokee and Osage, but he never claimed it), Charles Bronson (son of Lithuanian immigrants), and of course Tom Laughlin, who created and played the role of the greatest cinematic Indian of all time, Billy Jack (completely white). Leonard Nimoy (Ukrainian Jew) was also on my list, but only when playing Mr. Spock, and please don't ask me why. After I entered public school in a border town that was predominantly white but acted as though it were exclusively so, I took comfort in the fact that Indian men could land leading roles on cool television shows and movies, and then one day I finally figured out the truth about my so-called Indian actors. In my own defense, let me say that they certainly looked like Indians to me, especially McCloud, who wore a cowboy hat and sheepskin coat and rode a horse in downtown New York. Though my perceptions turned out to be incorrect, I maintain that this example tells us something about how Indians look to Indians, even when we happen to be wrong.

Around the time of junior high I learned firsthand that Indians were a "problem" in the eyes of the whites who ran the world I lived in. AIM activists had made quite a splash, and there quickly emerged the sense that one should probably take sides. Naturally, this was impossible for me to do—as the half-breed/mixed-blood/part-Indian always asks, which side do I take?—and then the ambivalence of my identity took firm root. I was never given an adequate language to describe the experience of Being Me, racially speaking, and since all of my "Indian" TV shows had been canceled (plus they were all White Boys anyway), I ended up reading books as a way to avoid the incomplete map of my life. Absolutely none of those books were written by Indians, but I loved them anyway: Dickens, Melville, Tolkien, Poe, C. S. Lewis, Saki, *Dracula,* Shirley Jackson, Hemingway, Salinger, Updike, Alice Walker, Isaac Bashevis Singer, John Fitzgerald's *Great Brain* series, S. E. Hinton's young adult fiction, and everything written by, of all people, Judy Blume (literary historians take note: this may be the first time a Native, let alone a man, has ever acknowledged the great Judy Blume). It wouldn't go too far to say that literature, much of it written by proverbial Dead White Guys, helped me to survive some difficult times and consider a future that might allow for the transcendence of fractured roots.

Yes, there were difficulties, also fractures, and I'm afraid these must now be conveniently postponed. This book isn't about me. The only reason I'm starting with a preface that begins with my own liminality, misconceptions, and childhood reading habits is to introduce myself and locate this work, however provisionally, in a particular time, space, and range of discourses. To wit: raised during the Red Power years in a reservation border town that made me feel a little alienated on all sides, rescued in a way by certain books and authors (which I would later spend much of my graduate school years lumping together and condemning as "Western culture"), being the child of two (actually more than two) peoples and recognizing the conflicts that have historically attended those peoples, and especially being light-skinned—"white" in the eyes of most cabbies, clerks, and cops—I am, and have always been, brimming with contradictions. Most of the contradictory discourses that constitute "me" I have inherited, although some I sought out and others were just misconceptions like my childhood admiration of the Indian Jack Webb. At any rate, there is nothing very "pure" about me, and I wanted to lay that on the table straightaway.

This is because the book that you hold in your hands is extremely interested in impurities, contradictions, and misconceptions, and while it doesn't valorize liminality in the way of some other books (many of which, I believe, are generally accurate in their characterizations of our impure world and peoples), it does make the argument that there is no way around the hard fact that we live in mutually contaminating times. This is an age when non-Indian actors can appear Indian to Indian boys, who in turn draw inspiration from those actors, and this is a society where federal education programs that are designed to assimilate the "culturally disadvantaged" can ironically provide a grandstand for radical tribalists and Head Start teachers to talk about Indian pride. These modern times might well claim to be guided by Enlightenment, but I think we live under the Great Law of Unintended Consequences as much as anything else. Impurities, contradictions, misconceptions, mistaken identities, liminality, and irony: these are the prominent themes of my life and times, and, once again, saying it is not to celebrate it.

After all, what's to celebrate? Two other salient features of our age are violence and power, and these are experienced as very real indeed. Racism is real. Poverty is real. Suffering and hopelessness are real. These are not the products of liminality or irony but of violence and power, as I realized in my twenties when I consistently found myself serving not so much as a groomsman, as one might expect from a twentysomething man, but rather as a pallbearer. To address our historical moment honestly is not only to admit to our impurities but to connect ideas and events to the material conditions of daily life. So, coming back to the book that you hold in your hands, I have tried to honestly address the impurities, contradictions, misconceptions, slippages—the "postmodern" stuff—while at the same time upholding "modern" institutions and ideas that might hold promise as ways of addressing real material conditions. The "nation," for example, is a way to gather and organize resources that can help improve people's lives, so I say we should keep it around while de-essentializing it. The same goes for those legal fictions we call our "identities" and the many practices and beliefs known as "cultures": these too can be deployed in ways that might improve actual lives, problematic though they clearly are. The point, though, is to make things better.

In a manner of speaking, one might justly state that this project attempts to advance ideas that can be considered "modernist" and "progressive," and of course these are rather controversial terms in Native history. The modernists and progressives of yesteryear are usually opposed to "traditionalists," and at times, perhaps, the same sort of opposition might be found—and criticized—in my work. But, on the other hand, I would contend that today's traditionalists are not quite the same folks as yesterday's, and personally I would like to think of my ideas being opposed to villains of a more recent vintage—say, culture cops, fundamentalists, and political reactionaries. In any case, this work probably won't remind you of the "indigenous theory" that has been developing in the past few years (much of which I admire greatly); it may be more akin to what Arnold Krupat has called "indigenous cosmopolitanism" for the way it considers the tribe and the world in close proximity to and intimate relationship with each other.

Much of this text was written in the time between 9/11 and passage of the United Nations Declaration on the Rights of Indigenous Peoples in 2007, and it should be seen in the contexts of those rather different events. The Iraq War, an example of neocolonialism if ever there was one, was being waged as well, and the state of Israel tightened its hold on the throat of the Palestinians. The Native writer Ward Churchill was vilified in the mainstream media and even fired from his academic post for an essay he wrote on 9/11, and the Native press played its part by exposing him as an "ethnic fraud." The Red Lake Reservation in northern Minnesota, less than an hour from Leech Lake, became the site of the second-worst school shooting in American history. Vine Deloria Jr., who gifted me with friendship and mentoring late in his life, passed away, as did Paula Gunn

Allen and the great musician and activist (and my grandmother's cousin) Floyd Red Crow Westerman. Closer to my current home near Syracuse, New York, three different governors tried to impose sales taxes on Indian-owned smoke shops while I was working on this book, and they failed each time. My arguments for embracing modernity and resisting essentialism were developed during a historical moment that included these events and others that we could mention, many of them as liminal and ironic as your humble author. These may very well be contradictory times, but isn't that another way of saying it hasn't all been bad?

One last thing before I get to my acknowledgments. Do you want to know why I thought Leonard Nimoy was an Indian but only when playing the role of Mr. Spock? It was because of his demeanor. In real life, Nimoy is a happy and loud sort of fellow, the kind whose laughter is described as a "guffaw." By contrast, Mr. Spock had a dignified Indianish character about him, a stoicism that we all knew masked his hidden passions underneath. Spock was logical, yes, but also spiritual in a nontheistic way and incredibly passionate albeit very controlled. Of course, it also had to do with Mr. Spock's liminality as the child of a human mother and Vulcan father. He was often teased for that by Bones, Kirk, and even White Boys *of lesser rank* on the ship, and something about that struck me as completely accurate and morally wrong. Perhaps I saw Leonard-Nimoy-as-Spock as an Indian because at that time in my life I needed someone like him to be one. Perhaps one moral of this story is that the truths of our lives are not so because of any inherent qualities, but simply because we narrate them as truths based on our needs and desires. Perhaps another point is that Indians narrate Indianness in a lot of different ways and in a lot of different venues; this is unavoidable but ultimately a good thing in a world that always veers toward the contaminated and the contradictory. I'm not saying that Mr. Spock and the great Judy Blume are Indians; I'm saying that this particular Indian has Mr. Spock and Judy Blume as part of his interior landscape. That, if anything, serves as a fitting conclusion to my self-location, and if you are inclined to read on anyway, well, I'm much obliged.

This book was written after I started teaching at Syracuse University, located in the heart of Haudenosaunee country, and I am indebted to numerous Iroquois people who talked and argued with me about the issues discussed here, especially Robert Porter, Carrie Garrow, Freida Jacques, Regina Jones, Oren Lyons (no, we are not related), Eric Gansworth, Peter Jemison, Jeanette Miller, Kevin White, Tammy Bluewolf Kennedy, Justin

Schapp, and the Iroquois-by-marriage Meghan McCune. Since Nancy Cantor became chancellor in 2004, Syracuse University has become a wonderful place to work on Native studies. I am indebted to the English department for its support and collegiality, with special thanks to Gregg Lambert, Erin Mackie, Silvio Torres-Saillant, Crystal Bartolovich, and Monika Wadman (now at University of Richmond). Many thanks go out to my colleagues in the Native studies program, especially Richard Loder.

Although these ideas may have germinated at Syracuse, they were planted during my time at Leech Lake Tribal College between 1998 and 2002. I fondly remember many productive discussions with Ginny Carney, Leah Carpenter, Henry Flocken, Duane "Dewey" Goodwin, Bob Jourdain, Adrian Liberty, Bennie Tonce, and most of all Michael Price. I became closely involved with traditional ceremonial life in those days, and for that I extend my sincere gratitude to George Goggleye for his friendship and instruction. Those were also the days of shaking my feathers on the pow-wow trail, and for that I fondly remember Jeff Harper and Jonie Johnson, traveling buddies. Since this is apparently turning out to be my Leech Lake paragraph, it seems a good place to offer my gratitude and good wishes to David Treuer, Anton Treuer, and my entire family back home.

I am very grateful to my editors Robert Allen Warrior, Jace Weaver, David Thorstad, Laura Westlund, and Jason Weidemann at the University of Minnesota Press, and I express special gratitude to Arnold Krupat, who has been a wonderful mentor and friend to me and who offered truly valuable advice and encouragement as this writing progressed. My thanks and love go out to Dana Nichols for being both sounding board and patient soul, and also to Nina, Equay, Josephine, Randa, and Mia, for keeping it real. Finally, this book is dedicated to my grandmother, Leona Lyons.

S. R. L.
Geneva, New York
January 2010

Migrations/Removals

An x-mark is a treaty signature. During the eighteenth and nineteenth centuries it was a common practice for treaty commissioners to have their Indian interlocutors make x-marks as signifiers of presence and agreement. Many an Indian's signature was recorded by the phrase "his x-mark," and what the x-mark meant was consent.

An x-mark also signified coercion. As everyone knows, treaties were made under conditions that were generally unfavorable to Indians, and as a result they were often accompanied by protest. Treaties led to dramatic changes in the Indian world: loss of land and political autonomy, assent to assimilation polices, the creation of quasi-private property on communal lands, and much else. Natives knew it and sometimes resisted it. At treaty councils individuals retained a right to withhold their x-marks, and many did. But most did not. Most made their x-marks.

An x-mark is a sign of consent in a context of coercion; it is the agreement one makes when there seems to be little choice in the matter. To the extent that little choice isn't the quite same thing as no choice, it signifies Indian agency. To the extent that little choice isn't exactly what is meant by the word *liberty*, it signifies the political realities of the treaty era (and perhaps the realities of our own complicated age as well).

An x-mark is a sign of contamination. There were no "treaties" before the arrival of the whites, no alphabetic writing or "signatures" at all, although there were practices of making formal agreements between different communities (wampum belts would be one example). Before the arrival of the whites, communities dealt respectfully with each other in a way that encouraged different peoples to retain their ways of life, while at the same time establishing territorial boundaries, conditions of trade, and what would now be called "diplomatic relations." Treaties were different. When made with Europeans—and especially later when made with Americans—treaties increasingly introduced new and unfamiliar concepts that situated peoples, parties, lands, and relationships between them differently. Treaties compelled Indians to change how they lived. They addressed the parties who signed treaties in a new way, too—as "nations"—thus bringing to bear a platonic character that wasn't necessarily there before.[1] Smaller groups became larger, more nominative, and more abstractly defined as political entities, assuming a "soul" or "spiritual principle" that in all likelihood did not exist—at least not in the way we think of such things now—prior to the arrival of the whites and their strange ways of doing things.[2]

Edmund Danziger writes of the first treaty council between the Ojibwe and the Americans at La Pointe on Madeline Island (offshore present-day Bayfield, Wisconsin, on Lake Superior): "Jealousy and ill will between the lake and Mississippi River bands threatened to break up the council at La Pointe. The Mississippi bands would not even talk to their cousins from the east, much less agree to sell any mutually held lands."[3] This was 1854, a period when the Ojibwe had "ripened into independent communities whose only sense of tribal unity came from language, kinship, and clan membership."[4] Up until the eighteenth century the Apostle Islands and Chequamegon Bay region had been the center of Ojibwe power, and Madeline Island was the penultimate stopping point of the Great Migration; but the fur trade compelled Ojibwe people to continue migrating to places as far-flung as southern Michigan and western Minnesota, and any political ties that may have once existed had long since atrophied. Still, the La Pointe treaty characterized these groups as a single political entity, and since treaties are by definition contracts between nations, it turned them into a "nation." Article II established "territory," Article III created "allotments," Articles IV, V, and VI promised "annuities" (including monies, agricultural implements, education, blacksmiths, and assistance with paying off debts owed to traders), and these promises resulted in the arrival of new technologies, cultural practices, beliefs, and ways of living. These things are sometimes characterized as signs of "colonization" and "assimilation"—as well as "Civilization" in the parlance of the mid-nineteenth century—but they can just as well be described as characteristics of modernity. They contaminated the lifeworld of Ojibwe who made their x-marks, so Ojibwe cultural purity (if such a thing had ever actually existed) would exist no more.

The x-mark is a contaminated and coerced sign of consent made under conditions that are not of one's making. It signifies power and a lack of power, agency and a lack of agency. It is a decision one makes when something has already been decided for you, but it is still a decision. Damned if you do, damned if you don't. And yet there is always the prospect of slippage, indeterminacy, unforeseen consequences, or unintended results; it is always possible, that is, that an x-mark could result in something good. Why else, we must ask, would someone bother to make it? I use the x-mark to symbolize Native assent to things (concepts, policies, technologies, ideas) that, while not necessarily traditional in origin, can sometimes turn out all right and occasionally even good.

The First Remove

If anything can be considered an enduring value for Ojibwe people, it has got to be migration. The legend of the Great Migration passed down through the oral tradition begins in a time when *anishinaabeg* were living as one large, undifferentiated group (we would probably call them Algonquins today) along the eastern seaboard of the United States and Canada. Seven prophets emerged to tell the people to move westward or risk their lives. A woman dreamed about standing on the back of a turtle, and it was decided that a turtle-shaped island would be the place where the people would go. The first stopping point of the Great Migration was likely an island near Montreal in the Saint Lawrence River, but that was only the beginning of their journey. The people followed a vision of a Sacred Shell, the *miigis* shell, which compelled them to keep moving. The second stopping point was Niagara Falls, but the Haudenosaunee objected and fought with the people. Eventually, a pipe was shared and peace was made, and the people moved farther westward to the third stopping point: a place described as "a river that slices like a knife," in all likelihood near the Detroit River where Lake Erie and Lake Huron connect. We are told that it was there that the Three Fires—Potawatomi, Odawa, and Ojibwe—emerged and took their leave of one another. The Great Migration continued, always leaving in its wake new peoples and new communities scattered along the Saint Lawrence and the Great Lakes. The fourth place was found after a boy had a dream revealing stepping stones in a river; these led to islands along the north shore of Lake Huron, of which Manitoulin Island was the largest, and for a time it became a great Ojibwe seat of power in the region. The fifth stopping point was Sault Sainte Marie, which would eventually become a fur-trading center. From the Sault the Ojibwe divided into two parties taking different paths around Lake Superior—one to the north, the other traveling south, both groups leaving a record of impressive rock paintings that survive yet today—eventually meeting at Spirit Island, a sixth stopping point where a *miigis* emerged, near Duluth, Minnesota. It was there that another prophecy was fulfilled, as this was a place "where the food grows on water," referring to *manoomin* or wild rice. *Manoomin* is now both a nutritional staple and a sacred food for the Ojibwe. The Sacred Shell rose on one last occasion, leading the people to the seventh and final stopping point: Madeline Island, a turtle-shaped island, and the same place where the Ojibwe eventually made that fateful treaty at La Pointe. The people had arrived at last, the ancient prophecies were fulfilled, and the Great Migration seemed complete. Well, at least for a moment.

The Great Migration probably started around 900 CE and took some five hundred years to finish—if it really can be said to have "finished" at all, for in fact the Ojibwe kept moving, sometimes by choice, sometimes by following the seasons, and sometimes because other people said it was time to move. But even before the era of colonization, migrating had become a primary cultural value. The Ojibwe were a people on the move. The Ojibwe envisioned life as a path and death as a journey; even *Ojibwemowin,* the Ojibwe language, is constituted by verbs on the move. What does migration produce? As we can see in the story of the Great Migration, it produces *difference:* new communities, new peoples, new ways of living, new sacred foods, new stories, and new ceremonies. The old never dies; it just gets supplemented by the new, and one result is diversity. What was once undifferentiated is now represented by many different fires, not only the new peoples who emerged from the Great Migration—the Potawatomi, Odawa, and Ojibwe—but those who stayed behind as well. The Abanaki, for example, get their name from a word that refers to both "east" and "morning"—*waaban*—while *aki* signifies their homeland. *Waabanaki,* as the story goes, are the daybreak people of the east who decided to remain and as a result differentiated into a people distinct from Potawatomi, Odawa, and Ojibwe. Migration produced a sense of movement and diversity as worthy values unto themselves; stagnation was always impossible in a people on the move. Yet the Great Migration also speaks of *home.* There was always a destination in view, oh yes, but the wondrous thing is, it kept changing! One moment the Great Migration had come to an end; the next moment people were telling stories about the last two, three, four stopping points they encountered. Home is a stopping point, for there is no sense in the migration story that there will be only one home for only one people forever. That was what the Great Migration was all about: a moving away from an undifferentiated singularity that had existed in the time long ago toward a more localized differentiation of the new. Finally, migration tends to privilege *the small*: not great warriors whose names are long remembered in tribal epideictic, not glorious monuments to conquest and victory, but the power of little things—a shell, a food that grows on water, the dreams of a woman or a little boy. The Great Migration not only included these humble things but followed them as guiding visions. Diversity, home, stopping points, and the power of the small: these are the lessons of the Great Migration insofar as it reveals something we might call the "spirit of a people."

This faith in migration as a value is what Gerald Vizenor has called transmotion: a "sense of native motion and an active presence" that is recognized by "survivance, a reciprocal use of nature, not a monotheistic, territorial sovereignty." It's a "*sui generis* sovereignty" that is reproduced in "creation stories, totemic visions, reincarnation, and sovenance," and honored in stories. "Native stories of survivance are the creases of transmotion," writes Vizenor.[5] "Stories keep us migrating home," writes Kimberly Blaeser.[6]

The Second Remove

In the late summer of 1889, three federal commissioners traveled to the woods of Minnesota to negotiate an allotment and removal treaty with Ojibwe. The Nelson Act is Minnesota's variant of the Dawes Allotment Act of 1887, which required Indian people to abandon communal lands for the adoption of new individual allotments: "private property." The stated goal was the transformation of Indians into agrarian capitalists. Based on a somewhat superstitious belief in the magical civilizing powers of private property, the Nelson Act was designed to assimilate Indians while opening up "surplus land" for settlers, lumber companies, and the U.S. government. (It had also been planned to remove all Ojibwe to a single reservation, White Earth, but that goal was never realized.) Henry Rice, Martin Marty, and Joseph B. Whiting were the commissioners entrusted with the negotiations to be held at Red Lake, White Earth, Gull Lake, Leech Lake, Cass Lake, Lake Winnibigoshish, White Oak Point, Mille Lacs, Grand Portage, Bois Forte, Vermillion Lake, and Fond du Lac, and they reported the results of their work to President Benjamin Harrison.

Rice, Marty, and Whiting met with the White Oak Point band that lived along the Mississippi River near present-day Federal Dam, Boy River, and Bena on four occasions during September 1889. It was the rice-making time, when the food that grows on water is harvested and processed for consumption over the following year. Deliberations were recorded, translated, and published in Rice's report, which opens with a note of concern regarding the poor state of the people as he found them: "The condition of the Indians at White Oak Point is described as beyond hope of improvement, they being dissipated and dissolute, but they still have intelligence enough to ask that whiskey may be kept from the country and that missionaries and schoolteachers be sent them."[7] Their troubled state was the result of the Americans dishonoring treaties they had previously made and the confinement of Ojibwe to a tiny parcel of land that prohibited effective hunting and gathering. The United States had failed to pay them the annuities and goods they had been promised in exchange for earlier land cessions, and reservoir dam projects had flooded huge sections of hunting and gathering territory. In a startlingly short period of time, quality of life at White Oak Point had plummeted from prosperity to impoverishment; their sad condition reflected it, and Rice acknowledged that it was the Americans' fault.

The first council was held on September 4 at Payment Point on the Mississippi River. Rice complained in his report, and apparently at the meeting as well, that the council had to be conducted "in the open air, there being no settlement of any kind at this place," to which Kah-Way-Din, an elder and leader in attendance, responded with a history lesson: "There was a promise made to the Indians here at White Oak Point that there should be a schoolhouse, and if it had been here, you could have talked in that schoolhouse."[8] Kah-Way-Din was referring to an earlier treaty made in 1867 that had gone unfulfilled by the Americans, the disappointment and bitter frustration of which was leading Kah-Way-Din to consider withholding his x-mark this time around:

> There was a mill promised for this place too, but we never saw it.
> They told us that whenever the whites wanted to saw anything, we
> could allow them to saw their lumber in the mill, and that the whites
> would pay us. And there was cattle promised to us then, and now
> this same promise is repeated. You say the truth when you say these
> Indians are poor. You see the rents in my nails; if I wanted to hold
> something, I could not do it because my fingernails are torn. If the
> cattle had not died on the road that had been promised us in the name
> of the Great Father, maybe our young men would be able to use those
> cattle in their work. That is the reason I speak to you on behalf of my
> friends here, not to sign until we have made up our minds to sign.[9]

Torn fingernails are a sign of malnutrition and possibly starvation; the White Oak Point Ojibwe were suffering badly and it was the Americans' fault. The council continued on with Rice presenting an "extended explanation" of allotment, Whiting following with a speech on the value of industriousness, and Marty concluding with the promise of a church. The Nelson Act was signed by most people at White Oak Point, including Kah-Way-Din, and the Ojibwe got on with the task of making rice. As a result of the Nelson Act, the White Oak Point band was consolidated with several other bands into what is now called the Leech Lake Band of Ojibwe; and as another result, Leech Lake controls only 5 percent of its original treaty-established land base today.

Such grim results are often blamed on an impoverishment of Indian life caused by the treaties and assimilation policies, but perhaps the more urgent lesson is simply a cautionary tale about the risks of dealing with people who don't keep their word. Kah-Way-Din threatened to withhold his x-mark not because he thought it would initiate the arrival of the new, but because his previous experiences had taught him to distrust the Americans. Once bitten, twice shy. He signed anyway, but only after making the federal commissioners squirm.

Another White Oak Point Ojibwe who signed the Nelson Act agreement (signature 68) was a young man named Nay-Tah-Wish-Kung, soon to be renamed John Lyons. He was my great-great-grandfather, the first Lyons, and the first in my lineage to write in the English language. What he wrote was the letter X.

Indian Time

Native people have a lot to forgive. When Columbus came there were around ten million people living north of the Rio Grande; by 1900, only 250,000 Natives survived in the United States. They died from disease, yes, and also from war, but by the turn of the twentieth century Indians were mostly dying from utter poverty. The assimilation period was especially bad, as Natives lived on reservations run like refugee camps and children were no longer being raised in their communities but in boarding schools. (Truly, a community without any children can be a dangerous and volatile place.) Treaty-established reservations were whittled away by allotment policy; between 1887 and 1934, Indian landholdings shrank from 138 million acres to 48 million.[10] Indian languages were attacked by teachers, and religions were attacked by missionaries and policy makers.

We are still living the legacies of this history. American Indians live below the poverty line at twice the rate of the general American population—more than 25 percent.[11] Natives are twice as likely to die young as the general population, with a 638 percent greater chance of dying from an alcohol-related disease, an 81 percent greater chance of being murdered, and a 91 percent greater chance of committing suicide.[12] Native teens are fully three times as likely to kill themselves as are other teenagers.[13] Our heritage languages are in decline. No fewer than 45 out of a presently spoken 154 languages in the United States face an imminent extinction, with another 90 predicted to go silent by 2050.[14] To get a sense of how immediate this language decline is, consider that in 1950 the U.S. Census Bureau recorded no fewer than 87.4 percent of American Indians speaking heritage languages as first languages; by 1980 that had plummeted to 29.3 percent; and by 2000, only 18 percent spoke languages other than English at home.[15]

These grim statistics are not the result of Native migrations but more the consequence of "removalism." Removal was a federal policy established in 1830 by President Andrew Jackson, and it would now go by the name of ethnic cleansing. Removal is to migration what rape is to sex, and while the original political policy was concerned with actual physical removals like the Trail of Tears, the underlying ideology of removal in its own way justified and encouraged the systematic losses of Indian life: the removal of livelihood and language, the removal of security and self-esteem, the removal of religion and respect. Bit by bit, change by change, loss by ever-exacting loss, removalism has been as much a legacy of our history as migration, and colonialism was its cause.

Americans are no longer pursuing removalism, and reversing our losses is now up to us; nonetheless the gaping wounds of history are still visible and will remain so as long as the relationship between Native and newcomer is defined by past betrayals and present inequalities. But what of those promises made? I refer not only to the commitments made by whites to Natives but also to the promises made by Natives to themselves and their future heirs. X-marks were commitments to living a new way of life, not only in the immediate present but "for as long as the grass grows and the rivers flow." How do they appear to us now? *They only signed treaties because they were forced to sign.* No one was forced to sign a treaty. *They did not understand what the treaties meant.* Were the Natives not intelligent? Does the historical record not show that they understood rather clearly what was at stake? *It's ancient history.* Is that not what antisovereignty groups say when arguing that treaty rights are of little consequence because Natives no longer live in wigwams or hunt the buffalo? I am interested in the promise of the x-mark insofar as it still stands, or more precisely as the promise moves through *time, space,* and *discourse.* Let's consider these three contexts more closely.

The time of the x-mark might as well be called "Indian time." This multi-layered expression has several different meanings, the most prominent being a Native version of the ubiquitous "c.p. time" ("colored people's time"), a racist stereotype that emerged in the colonies to characterize the colonized's ostensible lack of punctuality. This sense of Indian time is only slightly altered when appropriated by Native people as an excuse for our own lateness (e.g., "Sorry I'm so late. I'm running on Indian time"). As with all appropriations of racial slurs (the n-word is another example), it both defangs the slur and creates new problems. An older meaning of Indian time seems to capture a sense of doing things when the moment is right. Ceremonialists use the expression in this way to describe a certain spiritual rightness, but it could also describe a natural or seasonal tempo-rality. From this sense, running on Indian time means knowing precisely when to start harvesting wild rice: not too early (it must be ripe) and not too late (it must still be on the stalks and not at the bottom of the lake). Finally, we've all heard the stereotypical line that Indian time is "circular" rather than "linear," a characteristic we apparently share with Disney's *The Lion King.* I object to that particular variant on the grounds that Indian time isn't any more circular or less linear than anyone else's sense of time, and why would we expect it to be? Shape is a characteristic of space, not time.

X-marks are made in a different kind of Indian time that must be characterized in some potentially problematic ways. First, I distinguish between traditional and modern time, clocking the supplanting of the for-mer by the latter at around 1492, or really when the treaties were made. This should be understood as a revision of the older imperialist measure-ments of time according to misguided teleologies of Progress, particularly the ethnocentric chronology of Savagism to Barbarism to Civilization.[16] Where treaties say "Civilization" we can substitute "modernity" with-out losing the basic spirit of what is usually described—schools, science, churches—yet shedding the unkind connotations of ethnocentrism, supe-riority, and progress that no one would defend now. This is likely how the treaties appeared to the Natives who gave them their x-marks: as promises of a new way of life, not the removal of "savage" or "barbaric" qualities (the latter always being imperialistic obsessions and not Native concerns). My distinction between the traditional and the modern must also be understood as a challenge to the stereotype of Indian time as simplistically circular and cyclical and "natural."

The most problematic aspect of a modern/traditional distinction is, of course, its binary-oppositional character: that is, those things we identify as modern can often be discovered in what we call the traditional, and vice versa. Everything is relative and exists on a continuum that does not carve neatly into two separate and oppositional wholes. There are no great leaps in the story of human history, only differences and definitions made in contexts of power that have often proven to be ethnocentric at best and genocidal at worst. I would be the last to disagree with that general objection. At the same time, I think the distinction is often useful as a way to understand the various discourses regarding time and change that Indian people advanced. We need a way to characterize the dramatic changes of life that treaties authorized and initiated. That language used to be *savage/civilized,* but it never served us well and won't be revisited anytime soon. Nativists tend to prefer *native/white,* but the obvious objection there is that time does not recognize racial binaries. My preference for *traditional/modern* comes not from a deep-rooted admiration on my part for the Enlightenment but rather from my conviction that the original x-marks were pledges to adopt new ways of living that, looking backwards, seem most accurately described as modern.

Nativists, or what we will call traditionalists, seek to undo the grim legacies of history by proclaiming the primacy of traditionalism; in so doing, they sometimes engage in battle with a removalism that no longer exists, or, worse, a removalism "internalized" by a self-defeated population. Traditionalists do not deconstruct binaries so much as flip the script: now "white" or "Western" time is corrupt and only pure traditionalism can save us from further losses. It is in opposition to this way of thinking that my x-mark is made; for while I clearly have no truck with the traditional, the x-mark is never made out of fear of corruption. It simply works with what we have in order to produce something good. X-marks are made with a view of the new as merely another stopping point in a migration that is always heading for home, always keeping time on the move.

But what exactly do we mean by the terms "modern" and "traditional"? Let us begin with tradition, which is not a traditional Native notion but an inheritance from Europe and the English language. Raymond Williams considered "tradition" a "particularly difficult word" to understand for its inconsistent and selective meaning; that is, not every old thing gets called traditional (much less exalted as such), but when it does, it tends to demand "our respect and duty" in keeping with the original meaning of its Latin root word *(tradere)* signifying "surrender or betrayal."[17] The original word also implied a sense of "handing down" or "delivering," which is how traditionalists always deploy the concept. But sometimes one's surrender to tradition entails a betrayal of something else that is good, and that's where problems can emerge in traditionalist discourse. Surrendering a good in the name of tradition would have made little sense to migrating peoples and prophets.

There is also the problem of how the modern world generally views "traditional societies." As the African philosopher Achille Mbembe has argued, three features tend to characterize the idea of traditional societies in discourses that emanate not only from "the West" but to a startling degree from traditionalists. First, *facticity and arbitrariness,* the idea that traditional people do not "examine" something from their world; rather, "the thing *is . . .* there is nothing to justify."[18] *It came to meet us. It was always there.* This idea attributes to traditional societies the ostensible habit of always using myth and fable "in contrast to reason in the West" to denote order and the passage of time: "there is little place for open argument; it is enough to invoke the time of origins," hence "such societies are incapable of uttering the universal."[19] The second feature is even worse: "these societies are seen as living under the burden of charms, spells, and prodigies" and are thereby perceived as "resistant to change."[20] Time "is supposedly stationary: thus the importance of repetition and cycles."[21] Third, "the 'person' is seen as predominant over the 'individual,' considered (it is added) 'a strictly Western creation.' Instead of the individual, there are entities, captives of magical signs, amid an enchanted and mysterious universe."[22] Mbembe attacks the myth of the traditional society as little more than a racist stereotype that functions to keep Africans in the realm of what he calls "nothingness," but in fact these tendencies are not only the habits of racists or anthropologists; they also appear in the discourse of traditionalists (albeit with the script flipped). The Indian time initiated by an x-mark, by contrast, does not deny or discount traditional time. Rather, it moves beyond it.

As for modernity, I have in mind a general sense of the new, a feeling regarding one's life in "modern times" that can be distinguished from "the way we used to live." In fact, this was the original meaning of the word. Hans Robert Jauss locates the first use of the Latin *modernus* in the fifth century to distinguish the Christian present from the Roman, pagan past, and ever since the word has been used to characterize a sense of some great epochal change underfoot.[23] Today's understanding of the modern has an additional twist to it, one that is more, well, modern, as Anthony Giddens explains:

> At its simplest, modernity is a shorthand term for modern society or industrial civilization. Portrayed in more detail, it is associated with (1) a certain set of attitudes towards the world, the idea of the world as open to transformation by human intervention; (2) a complex of economic institutions, especially industrial production and a market economy; (3) a certain range of political institutions, including the nation-state and mass democracy. Largely as a result of these characteristics, modernity is vastly more dynamic than any previous type of social order. It is a society—more technically, a complex of institutions—which unlike any preceding culture lives in the future rather than the past.[24]

This understanding of modernity has been attacked by traditionalists, postmodernists, and fundamentalists of all stripes, but I follow Jürgen Habermas in seeing modernity as neither inherently negative nor positive; it is, rather, "an incomplete project" that "still depends on vital heritages, but would be impoverished through mere traditionalism."[25] The particular x-marks I am interested in—identity, culture, and the idea of the Indian nation—are historically contingent concepts, and my analyses of them should be understood as serving the larger project of developing functional modern institutions in Native America; that is, I see the modernization that was initiated by treaty signers as an unfinished project that can and should be pursued further. I want more of it, not less. The idea of the Indian nation, as only one example, is a modern idea that I believe was invented precisely at the moment of treaty, hence my call for more modernization is simultaneously a demand for greater nationalization. Now, many thinkers today are deeply invested in traditionalism and this is not necessarily a problem. It can become a problem, however, when the traditional is transformed into a fetish, loses its realism, denies the actually existing diversity of Indian life, and/or confuses modern practices and institutions with the assimilation of a "white" or "Western" identity. There's a baby here and some bathwater too, and we must be careful about throwing things out.

The idea of an x-mark assumes that indigenous communities are and have always been composed of human beings who possess reason, rationality, individuality, an ability to think and to question, a suspicion toward religious dogma or political authoritarianism, a desire to improve their lot and the futures of their progeny, and a wish to play some part in the larger world. Surely, these characteristics are not the exclusive property of "white" people or the "West," and to the extent that any of them can be characterized as "modern" (not all of them can, to be sure), they seem associated with the passage of time, not identity. Yet it is also the case that since modernity's onset in Native America—a process that happened by way of conquest and colonization—there has always been a great number of different, interlocking "epochs" or *durées* at any given moment: multiple modes of production, diversities of belief, contending memories, and competing future visions—in other words, different times unfolding in common space. This has given us the businessman living next door to the medicine man, both trapline and assembly line, and the power of a Great Spirit competing with "ardent spirits." It is nearly impossible to speak with much accuracy of the times before or after colonization (although we must try to do so anyway in order to analyze history); nor can we imagine migratory times unfolding in a linear progression with everyone marching in lockstep toward a new order (although dominant orders do come and go). Indian time tends to move like a people migrating home: in fits and starts, with false beginnings and many fulfilled endings, always looking to both past and future, always producing diversity. If the expression "Indian time" means anything, it should signify this history of temporal multiplicity. For far too long Natives have been discussed exclusively in the past tense, and for far too long modernity has been discussed as if it were strictly a Western imposition. It is time to acknowledge not only our continued presence in history, but also the reality of Indian time on the move.

The Third Remove

My grandfather always enjoyed telling exciting stories to his grandchildren about his grandfather—"a real old-time Indian"—whom he characterized as living in a traditional manner, sometimes wearing buckskin clothes, always speaking Ojibwe, and typically using his old birchbark canoe to hunt and fish. I have a photograph of John Lyons taken several years after the Nelson Act's passage that depicts him sitting with a dignified group of Ojibwe leaders in Bemidji, Minnesota. In the photo, he appears to be a large man with dark skin and a serious expression, yet also with laugh lines at the corners of his eyes and mouth. He wears a nice suit for those days (dark wool, not buckskin) and what appears to be a bowler hat. The photograph was given to me by my great-uncle Ernest Lyons, who was ninety-three at the time. We were sitting at his kitchen table. When I asked him who was John, Uncle Ernest said, "the man with the X over his head." There it was: a shaky little X in black ink scrawled long ago, presumably so that we might not forget.

John married Josephine, formerly Pah-Gwah-Bin-Dig-O-Quay, and today they are buried in the Lyons plot of the old Bena cemetery overlooking Lake Winnibigoshish. In the late 1990s I was told by an elder that Josephine Lyons was the last to see the spirit from which Leech Lake derives its name *(Gaa-zagaskwaajimekaag)*, literally, "the place where there are a lot of leeches." "She was just a girl and she saw large ripples and a wake in the water," explained this elder, "and then she saw its large, black back." Josephine Lyons had children before marrying John and is remembered by many Leech Lakers who claim her as an ancestor. Being a woman, she was never asked for her x-mark by American treaty commissioners, but she is still honored today in a tribal and familial consciousness.

John and Josephine gave birth to Bill Lyons, my great-grandfather, and he became mayor of Bena, an old logging town of some two hundred residents located near railroad tracks, tall trees, dams, and Highway 2. In April 1899 the *Cass Lake Independent* wrote, "The land near Bena is mostly covered by allotments. The town is quite centrally located on the reservation and is the proper point at which to locate the Agency buildings. Bena is also the shipping point to the Winnibigoshish Dam."[26] Incorporated as a formal town in October 1906, Bena's population swelled from two hundred residents to near eighteen hundred during the timber boom initiated by the Nelson Act. (Bena has since resumed its former population.) A Civilian Conservation Corps camp was built in Bena in May 1933 and operated until 1942, after which it housed German prisoners of war until 1945. In its economic heyday, Bena reportedly had five saloons, five hotels, a "sporting house," and other sundry businesses that one would expect to find in any boomtown. In 1922 a Native American Church (NAC) was established at Ryan's Village just outside of Bena, bringing the syncretic peyote religion from the plains to the north woods. Different times were on the move in Bena during the first half of the twentieth century and Indians both benefited from and were dispossessed by the economic order initiated by the Nelson Act. (It depends on which Indians we're talking about.) As for religious expression, Bena had all kinds: NAC peyotists, Catholics, Episcopalians, sinners of various stripes, and participants in Mike Rabbit's Midewiwin lodge, which eventually went dormant during the 1940s.

The second half of the century was unkind to Bena. Gerald Vizenor, whose relative Clem Beaulieu lived across the street from my grandparents and father, wrote in *Interior Landscapes* (1990) that Bena had developed "the reputation of being the 'Little Chicago' of the north woods," having the worst crime rate in the state of Minnesota and no fewer than 10 percent of its population serving hard time for felonies. Clem "said it was true what they said about his town. Bena was wicked, and the town was like no place in the world, but . . . it made it a great place for stories." As for Vizenor himself, "I wrote about that wicked town but the town was never wicked to me."[27] Bena provided source material for the village called Poverty in David Treuer's novel *Little* (1996). I have relatives living in Bena who are unequivocal that the town is going to hell in a handbasket, but who say nonetheless they wouldn't dream of living anywhere else.

Bill Lyons was mayor during the boom years, and he and his brother established a fishing-guide service called Lyons Landing that operated from 1932 to 1950, the first of its kind on the east end of Lake Winnibigoshish. It was wildly successful, and people still remember the long trains of parked cars along Highway 2 signaling that the Lyonses were out fishing with their customers. Most were out-of-state tourists; in 1936, more non-resident fishing licenses were sold at Bena than at any other agency in the state, more than eleven hundred in all.[28] Bill and Charles Lyons hired their children and other relatives to help the business grow, including Art Lyons, who, on August 28, 1957, set the Minnesota state record for the largest muskie; it weighed in at fifty-four pounds and was nearly as tall as he was. Mafia men were among their early clientele as they allegedly operated stills in the woods during Prohibition. One family story tells of a supposed run-in between Bill and Al Capone, but it has a suspiciously mythological quality that has always made me wonder. Lyons Landing closed in 1950 when Bill's youngest son, my great-uncle William "Billy Boy" Lyons, became a bank robber in the Twin Cities and rang up so many legal bills that it broke the family business. Things fall apart. Yet to this day topographical maps of Lake Winnibigoshish still identify reefs and bays that were named (in English) by my (bilingual) great-grandfather Bill and his brother Charles. They made a lot of x-marks in those days—mayor, businessman, fishing guide, bank robber—in the ever-shifting spaces of Bena.

Indian Space

Everyone knows what Indian space is like. It is circular, communal, and never near a cosmopolitan center. (Even when it is, it's not.) It is always pungent: smoky and sagey in a manner that evokes the past. Things are organized in fours. It is spiritual and stoic, quiet like a Quaker service, yet always with dogs around (and they always stay in the background). Indian space is dark and warm, not at all unpleasant, but then again it is not very exciting either. Women work quietly with children at their sides while the men are always just returning. A pot of food is simmering and people's tones of voice seem to be hushed. This space is poor, economically speaking, and therefore to be pitied; at the same time it is an honor to inhabit this space, if only for a moment. Friends of the Indian will note a pristine natural beauty. Indian haters will note the litter strewn in the ditches, the diapers and bottles and Styrofoam cups: tragic contradictions. Stuff hangs in Indian space; it may be drying, it may signify some religious meaning, or maybe it is just hanging. Indian space is not well maintained in the sense of interior decoration (Indians are unconcerned about such trivial bourgeois matters); rather, these spaces are "organic," "practical," and above all "communal." They are also secretive: hidden away, hard to find, closed to outsiders. When an outsider manages to enter Indian space, the emotion experienced is exhilaration: *I cannot believe I am here.* Indian space feels eternal and deep. Yet because of its communal quality and proliferation of good-natured humor it can also feel like the most casual space in the world. Above all, it is slow. Time creeps like the turtle in Indian space.

This is a stereotype, but persistent to say the least. Thinking historically means seeing different Indian spaces invented in different times and social contexts, and in fact our spaces have been imagined in many different ways since the first x-marks were made. At first, Indian space was isolated and always on the move; its image was the *camp.* On occasions when Native and newcomer had to meet, the space for doing so was a *frontier.* The frontier was traditionally conceived as the line where Civilization meets Wilderness, the latter as yet untamed by the former, so the concept is inseparable from imperialism. In 1890, the U.S. Census Bureau famously declared the frontier closed, leading Frederick Jackson Turner to advance his "frontier thesis" at the 1893 World's Columbian Exposition in Chicago. Jackson thought the significance of the frontier was its transformation of old Europeans into new Americans, a process that must have happened at the frontier line, as it produced characteristics that seemed specific to American identity: individualism, self-sufficiency, distrust of authority figures, lack of culture and arts, and a propensity for violence. As for the Indians imagined on the wild side of the line, they would either stay in their camps and vanish or evolve into someone who might yet live on the civilized side of time and space. Such was the logic of a world cut in two by imperialism.

At precisely the same time the frontier was declared closed, federal policy gurus were changing the logic of Indian space by delineating and distributing allotments. These divisions of communal land into individual parcels of private property not only created an abundance of "surplus land" offered to speculators and settlers, but also forged a new category for describing overlapping legal jurisdictions in Indian country: the *checkerboard*. Space imagined as a checkerboard means different people are ruled by different sovereigns at different times. Today at Leech Lake, for example, you can be issued a speeding ticket by tribal police, but only if you are a Leech Laker. If you are a non-Native, or an Indian hailing from elsewhere, you fall under the jurisdiction of the state of Minnesota, in keeping with Public Law 280. Should you commit a major crime at Leech Lake, you will fall under a third jurisdiction, that of the federal government, in keeping with the 1885 Major Crimes Act. Checkerboarded space can feel schizophrenic (as one imagines tribal police know all too well, given their task of having to visibly ascertain not only who is Indian, but if that Indian is from Leech Lake or someplace else, before putting on the siren). The world was still cut in two during the allotment era, but space was imagined in such a way that it put those two worlds into extremely close proximity. Practicality was never a goal of the spatial invention of the checkerboard.

In fact, the checkerboard has always been bogus anyway. From the perspective of the federal government, Indian space has been, simply, *Indian country* since 1790 when the phrase was invented.[29] A federal statute imagines this space as follows:

> "Indian country" . . . means (a) all land within the limits of any Indian reservation under the jurisdiction of the United States government, notwithstanding the issuance of any patent, and including rights-of-way running through the reservation, (b) all dependent Indian communities within the borders of the United States whether within the original or subsequently acquired territory thereof, and whether within or without the limits of a state, and (c) all Indian allotments, the Indian titles to which have not been extinguished, including rights-of-way running through the same.[30]

A clearer description of a colonized territory could scarcely be found anywhere. To live in Indian country is to live under the jurisdiction of the United States as a "dependent." Indeed, if Indian space is a checkerboard, the idea of Indian country reveals who is actually playing the checkers. It's worth mentioning that this same expression is used by the American military—yes, even today—to describe enemy territory.[31] Taken together, the two meanings of Indian country suggest an enemy territory under control, making that "dependent" an effective prisoner of war.

Sometimes old Indian space is reimagined in a new way. Roughly a century after its announced closing, the frontier made a comeback. In *Being and Becoming Indian* (1989), James Clifton defined frontier as "a culturally defined place where peoples with different culturally expressed identities meet and deal with each other."[32] In his book *Ethnocriticism* (1992), Arnold Krupat likewise reclaimed frontier as a metaphor for discursive space but sagely observed that "the two cultures which met and dealt with each other at the various frontiers . . . were almost never two cultures of equivalent material power."[33] In *Mixedblood Messages* (1998), Louis Owens advanced the idea of "'frontier space,' wherein discourse is multidirectional and hybridized." This would be "the zone of trickster, a shimmering, always changing zone of multifaceted contact within which every utterance is challenged and interrogated" using "appropriation, inversion, and abrogation of authority." Owens's frontier space would stand "in neat opposition to the concept of 'territory' as territory is imagined and given form by the colonial enterprise in America":

> Whereas frontier is always unstable, multidirectional, hybridized, characterized by heteroglossia, and indeterminate, territory is clearly mapped, fully imagined as a place of containment, invented to control and subdue the dangerous potentialities of imagined Indians. Territory is conceived and designed to exclude the dangerous presence of that trickster at the heart of the Native American imagination, for the ultimate logic of territory is appropriation and occupation, and trickster defies appropriation and resists colonization.[34]

Behind these reinventions of frontier space—as culturally different, politically unequal, and discursively slippery—there was an assumption that Indian space was inherently resistant, "mixed," guided by tricksters, and generally in dialogue with whites.

Naturally, there was a reaction to this line of thought as the notion of a territory defined nationally reasserted itself after a long slumber. Postmodernists like Owens fell into the disfavor of scholars like Elizabeth Cook-Lynn, Craig Womack, Robert Warrior, Jace Weaver, and others waving the flag of nationalism who immediately called foul on any reinvention of Indian space as essentially "unstable, multidirectional, hybridized" or in some other way less than politically coherent. The space of any nation must be by definition stable, unidirectional, and whole (or at least that's the basic idea), so it's not much of a surprise that related figures—mixed-bloods, tricksters, cosmopolitans—were likewise condemned by the nationalists. There was a bit too much mixing going on during those days, and not only in Native discourse, as mestizas, nomads, border-crossers, and just about everything falling into the general category of the transnational became positively ubiquitous by turn of the millennium. It all appeared to conspire against the idea of the Indian nation as a viable political category in the twenty-first century, one with its own securely bounded and bordered senses of sovereignty.

It wasn't only Indians who reacted against porous postmodern metaphors and arguments for a politically unbounded and transnational sense of space. Michael Hardt and Antonio Negri's *Empire* (2000) took global indigenous movements seriously and characterized them as a form of "subaltern nationalism" defined by two ambiguous functions. First, the subaltern nation "serves as a line of defense against the domination of more powerful nations and external economic, political, and ideological forces. The right to self-determination of subaltern nations is really a right to secession from the control of dominant powers."[35] In their analysis, subaltern nationalisms tend to advance a political content that can subvert the nationalisms of more powerful nations, because the cultures from which indigenous nationalisms emerge are defined by different value systems. Second, the subaltern nation "poses the commonality of a potential community."[36] Community becomes overcoded by the idea of the nation (the result of "modernizing," according to Hardt and Negri), and the effect is, as remarked earlier, the creation of a larger group where once there had been the many and the small.[37] As for the ambiguous aspects of subaltern indigenous nationalism, there are two: first, the danger of any nationalism suppressing a community's actual diversity in the name of cultural unification; and second, the contradictions that always emerge when the nation becomes the only way to imagine community. (These are also the concerns of this book you hold in your hands.) As for all of that postmodern mixing—so often characterized as automatically progressive or resistant just by virtue of its claim to impureness—Hardt and Negri identify its probable, if not all that inspirational, source:

> Many of the concepts dear to postmodernists and postcolonialism
> find a perfect correspondence in the current ideology of corporate
> capital and the world market. The ideology of the world market has
> always been the anti-foundational and anti-essentialist discourse par
> excellence. Circulation, mobility, diversity, and mixture are its very

conditions of possibility. Trade brings differences together and the more the merrier! Differences (of commodities, populations, cultures, and so forth) seem to multiply infinitely in the world market, which attacks nothing more violently than fixed boundaries: it overwhelms any binary division with its infinite multiplicities.[38]

In other terms, that dashing, hybridized, polyglot, rebellious trickster figure could very well be a souvenir from Epcot Center, just as frontier space can create rather favorable conditions for a trendy new ethnic marketplace.

X-marks have been made in every Indian space imagined since 1492 and they are now being made in the space of the *nation*. Indeed, the very idea of an Indian nation is, I argue, an x-mark. But because nation is such a large and unwieldy abstraction, too large and abstract to sustain a real community, Indian space is now being imagined in a much smaller domestic locale: the *kitchen table*. "The fires of Cherokee nationhood still burn," writes Daniel Justice, "around the kitchen table."[39] "What if we want to have a conversation just among ourselves over a cup of coffee at the kitchen table?" asks Jace Weaver.[40] And it's not just the Cherokees, or for that matter the boys. "I remember well the experience of sitting at Chief Homer St. Francis's kitchen table," writes Lisa Brooks. "Many years later . . . I found myself at a lot of kitchen tables, all over Indian country."[41] Question: what explains this curious preoccupation with kitchen tables?

Perhaps the kitchen table is not so unlike a camp. After all, this space is circular, communal, and located far from cosmopolitan centers; it is pungent, warm, and slow; it is a space where people are nourished. Joy Harjo poetically memorialized this Indian space in *The Woman Who Fell from the Sky*: "The world begins at a kitchen table. No matter what, / we must eat to live" (yet she also ominously added: "Perhaps the world will end at the kitchen table").[42] As a new Indian space (if that is what this is), the kitchen table is not so very quiet or spiritual but in fact actually seems to be a noisy site of conflict, "where everyone would be fed but that didn't mean you were safe from confrontation. Many a fight broke out at the table, many a man was challenged."[43] The kitchen table is no longhouse or tribal council chamber, but decisions and community are made in this democratic space, and in that regard it might have something in common with spaces invented by peoples migrating home in traditional time.

As symbolic of Indian space, the kitchen table may require a double hermeneutic. On the one hand, it appealingly attests to the noble and democratic desire to keep power and decision making in an everyday communal site, where men, women, children, and elders can meet for fellow-ship and debate without stuffy formalities or imposing architectures. On the other hand, the image of a common kitchen table could erase class differences that exist in real Indian spaces. The kitchen table isn't only a feminine or domestic image, after all; it is above all a working-class image, and as such runs the risk of being romanticized. Do I really sit at the same table as my cousin just released from jail, or the homeless, or the addicted? The image of a kitchen table suggests that we do, but sitting here in my comfortable university office, I'm really not so sure about that.

I suspect that the word *rezzy* is now deployed in a similar manner to conflate ethnicity and class in a way that risks nostalgically erasing class difference "on the rez." To be rezzy is to be tacky but in a humor-ous, endearing way. Lovable losers are rezzy, and so are cars stuck in reverse. No one has aestheticized the rezzy better than the always rezzy Sherman Alexie. It is funny but problematic, that rezziness, and the same can be said of those kitchen tables. I suspect it's going to be a real chal-lenge to imagine nations that are just as democratic and inclusive as our old-fashioned conversations at the kitchen table without acknowledging, erasing, or romanticizing social differences like class. Nonetheless, I think the image of a kitchen table is an x-mark well made.

X-marks operate in a time understood as neither linear nor "circular" but multiple and always on the move. In similar fashion, the space of the x-mark has a multiplicitous quality, having been variously invented over many years as camp, frontier, checkerboard, Indian country, subaltern nation, and rezzy kitchen table, and still others we haven't even mentioned (like "Fourth World"). Indian space is always overlapping with other kinds of space, and sometimes it will contest them as well. Any consid-eration of an x-mark should contend with this intractable multiplicity of Indian space. Further, we must always admit that space can be modern-ized. Indian space is never defined by tradition or culture alone because Native people migrate in modern times as well. Like it or not, X marks the spot of Indian space.

The Fourth Remove

One of Bill Lyons's best fishing guides, according to my late grandfather Aubrey Lyons, was my late grandfather Aubrey Lyons. "Aub," as he was known, was warm and gentle with children, and he was lightning fast with a joke. The first Lyons to receive American citizenship—in 1924—Aub attended an off-reservation boarding school at Flandreau, South

Dakota, from age six to fourteen and ran away four times. He had been sent there by Bill, not only because Bill wanted his children to be educated but also because Sarah, Aub's mother, had died young and left Bill with children he could not raise alone. Such was a common Indian story during the early twentieth century, because tuberculosis had raged through many Native communities in northern Minnesota and hit Bena as well. As he used to tell it, the first time Aub ran away it was because a little bird told him to do it (he never elaborated on the bird). The second and third times he brought his little sister Tootie, who wasn't older than eight. The fourth and final time was after he was cruelly whipped with a leather strap in front of a school assembly "to make an example out of me." It took him several days to make the nearly four-hundred-mile journey from Flandreau to Bena, and he was helped along the way by white people he called (with no insult intended) "hobos": homeless travelers during the Great Depression who treated an Indian kid with kindness. Aub walked and hopped trains all the way to Bena, and each time he did, save the last, his father sent him back.

No aspect of Native history has been more maligned in contemporary discourse than the boarding-school experience, or, as the historian David Wallace Adams names it, "education for extinction."[44] This story is very well known: federal authorities removed Indian children from their homes and families and sent them to harsh institutions far away, where they had their mouths washed out with soap for speaking their languages and had even worse forms of abuse inflicted upon them. This discourse is powerful. The narrative is unshakable. I remember a few years ago inviting three older Native women to speak to a class on their boarding-schooling experiences, thinking they would complicate the typical narrative of victimization. In fact, they reproduced it faithfully, to the point of breaking down into tears while recounting the awful abuses that they had to endure. Naturally, my class was horrified, as was I. Yet, during the Q & A it was revealed that the abuses the women had described did not happen to them. One who claimed she had been punished for speaking her language confessed that she actually never spoke that language, and another admitted to never having attended a boarding school at all ("but my brother did"). The narrative, it seems, had colonized the women's own personal experiences. Whether this was because of a desire to produce a certain critical discourse in the Indian space of my classroom, or to the return of a repressed historical trauma, is impossible to say. In any case, despite new scholarship on boarding schools that complicates greatly the discourse of victimization—I am thinking here of Tsianina Lomawaima's *They Called It Prairie Light: The Story of the Chilocco Indian School* (1995), Brenda

Child's *Boarding School Seasons: American Indian Families, 1900–1940* (2000), and Amanda Cobb's *Listening to Our Grandmothers' Stories: The Bloomfield Academy for Chickasaw Females, 1852–1949*, as well as other recent histories describing the boarding-school experience as multiple, mixed, and diverse—it will probably be a while before the boarding schools receive more complex treatment in the realm of public memory.

Complex treatment was exactly the last thing I had on my mind during my college years when I interviewed my grandfather about his classically grim experience. All of us grandkids interviewed him for paper assignments at one point or another, and we always did well on our papers. No one ever wanted to interview Aub's wife, Leona, my Dakota grandmother from the Lower Sioux Indian Community (Morton), who attended the same school ten years after my grandfather and loved it completely. "Flandreau gave me a lot at a time when I needed it," Leona told us, "and where else would I meet so many friends?" Now eighty-eight, she is still in touch with several of those friends. My grandmother was the first in my line to receive not only a high school diploma—she graduated valedictorian—but also the first higher education, attending a teacher's college and eventually becoming one of Leech Lake's first Indian teachers. Leona has been a devout Christian since childhood and was never much fun to talk to about tradition. "Indian spirits are demons!" she often warned, and literally believed. That sort of talk gets one called assimilated; on the other hand, who but an Indian would ever take Indian spirits so seriously? I spent years living with my grandparents, and for the most part Leona was strong, strict, judgmental, and sometimes absolutely authoritarian. She was the matriarch and everyone knew it. Yet she was also extremely encouraging to her grandchildren, especially when it came to educational matters. She reviewed all of my writings and attended all my school events, and she was never judgmental about any of that. She was critical in that constructive way that helped me learn. People from all over Leech Lake say that about her (and nearly everyone between the ages of thirty and sixty had to take her at some point or another). My grandfather sure had the better story when it came to the boarding schools—and his story was doubtless true—but it was my grandmother who put us kids on the path to education.

Talking Indian

We have looked at the time and space of an x-mark; we must now consider a third context—discourse—understood in the way of social scientists, Foucauldians, and lit-crit theorists: as discursive formations, or ways of speaking that are traceable to institutions, the state, and dominant cultural understandings, and always associated with power and hierarchies. To the extent that one's freedom fighter is somebody else's terrorist (to evoke a frequently evoked example), discourse wields the great power of definition by literally setting the terms of debate. X-marks are always made in the political context of discursive formations that never emanate from organic indigenous communities. I am saying this even in the so-called age of "self-determination"; even now our discourses of Indianness are generated by institutions, the state, and the market (although it is true that more Natives than ever before can be found in these particular sites). The subaltern never speaks, because once it does, it is no longer subaltern; so we should all probably disabuse ourselves of ideas to the contrary. It is not the end of the world to admit it, but this does need admitting, especially in these tribal-nationalistic times. Let me explain.

When Columbus arrived to what quickly became the New World, he lacked a point of reference for understanding the people he saw—these folks being something of a great surprise, as we know—so he drew upon existing discourses that were already in use in Western Europe, for example, concepts and words like heathen, infidel, *indio,* and so on. Early visual representations of Natives by Theodorus de Bry and other engravers exemplified how existing discursive formations influenced what could be said and known about Indians. De Bry never visited the New World himself, but he did make numerous illustrations of Native people that simultaneously drew upon and contributed to the new discourses of Indianness. De Bry's subjects were naked, dancing, primitive, smaller, cannibalistic, and enthralled by a pagan spiritual order, all of this stereotypical knowledge dependent upon other portraits and descriptions by people like Columbus and Thomas Harriot, and all of it generated by someone who never saw his subjects with his own eyes. That didn't make his engravings "inaccurate." It made them a part of a powerful discourse that for centuries has gone by the name of "Indian."

As a discursive formation, "Indian" connected to another powerful discourse, that of savagism and civilization, which set the terms of debate regarding Indians for a very long time. Yet this binary opposition was never stable, as we learn from the work of Roy Harvey Pearce, who distinguished three basic periods in which the savagism of Indians was construed a bit differently each time. First, from 1609 to the 1770s Indians were generally described as the same as other people, as capable of sin and seduction by Satan as anyone else, and just as open to God's salvation and grace. As Krupat has written regarding this period, "The Puritan aim, then, was to transform the Indian, to improve him as land might be improved, lifting him up from the wild state of nature to civilization and to God."[45] Yet, around the time of the American Revolution, the attitude changed. As Pearce remarks, "The problem, then, became one of understanding the Indian, not as one to be civilized and to be lived with, but rather as one whose nature and whose way of life was an obstacle to civilized progress westward."[46] In the third period, starting in the removal years and ending, I would suggest, in 1890—when the frontier was closed, thus eliminating the need for a savage—Indians were described in a manner that Krupat describes as the "Zero of human society": not a changeable sort of person deserving civilization, nor even a savage that might be usefully romanticized, but simply as a sign of noncivilization: "so the Indian must vanish, for noncivilization is not life."[47]

It was always within the context of these kinds of discursive formations that real Natives spoke, and, beginning with Samson Occom at the end of the eighteenth century, wrote. To understand these Native texts requires a vigilant awareness of the discursive formations that created their contexts, as early Native writers were always acutely aware of their rhetorical contexts and addressed them accordingly, sometimes through challenging or appropriating the dominant discourses of their day. Hence, during the removal era when the dominant discourse promoted an increasingly racialized notion of Indian unchangeability, writers such as William Apess and Elias Boudinot constantly represented changeable Indians in their narratives. Likewise, at the turn of the twentieth century, when the dominant discourse dependably portrayed Indians as the "Zero of human society," sentimentalist writers such as Charles Alexander Eastman and Gertrude Bonnin tenderly depicted Indians as extremely human indeed. Discourses can always be appropriated and challenged, even if you have to don regalia to do it (as the latter two often did), but they cannot be ignored. When the Indian speaks, it always speaks as an Indian, and it must do so in a discursive context that, thanks to colonization, is never of pure Native origin. This is why all Indian texts are x-marks.

This is also why some traditional people devise harsh restrictions regarding the writing of certain stories, songs, and other cultural fare. Perhaps this is not so widely known, but there are serious writing taboos on reservations having a strong cultural foundation, so serious in fact that people are sometimes warned to keep what I'll call the "tribal private" private, lest the lives of their children be taken by the spirits. The tribal private does not enter Indian space. It is hidden away where it can be defended by taboos, elders, and culture cops; and the reasons for it are purely protective. People who are invested in the survival of the tribal private are justifiably wary of discourse formations appropriating, mutilating, or in some other way destroying knowledge that has existed "since time immemorial." Time moves very slowly in the space of the tribal private, and people generally don't want what happens there to be recorded as a text. It would be a mistake to make too much of the line existing between Indian space and the tribal private, however. Although the idea that today's postmodern world destroys all distinctions between inside and outside probably goes too far—there are still places in which such distinctions make sense, the tribal private among them—it nevertheless seems true that inside/outside is delineated by a dotted line at best. Things get out and things come in, and there seems to be absolutely no way to prevent that. So, if there is a "door" to be imagined between public Indian space and the tribal private, it would be best envisioned as a screen door. The goal of a cultural sovereignty movement should not be the forging of stronger doors—that would be illusory—but rather to insist that, whenever possible, one's doors should be opened from the inside.

All Indian texts are x-marks, all texts contend with discursive contexts, and Indian space is where this all gets played out. What discourse formations set the limits of Native intellectual discourse today? For starters, the savagism/civilization binary is no longer a factor, speaking Indians are no longer a curiosity, and writing Indians are no longer seen as an inherent contradiction. This we can all take as the good news. The bad news is, given the logistics of our peculiar technological age (globalization, late capitalism, mass media, the Internet revolution, the global village, multiculturalism, etc.), and considering what the postmodernists have identified as a general lack of faith in the grand narratives of emancipation and enlightenment, what we would seem to be left with is a call to perform our roles as ethnic spectacles, and the greatest of these is always ethnic discontent. Rey Chow has argued that ethnicity has transformed from a modernist paradigm defined by imagery of captivity, alienation, and struggle for rights to a postmodern commoditized spectacle. Global capitalism is the culprit here, as it has spent the last several decades dismantling boundaries, shattering essences, and obliterating binary oppositions in order to open markets and put ethnic identities up for sale. What is called "diversity" and "multiculturalism" also happens to function as a "niche market" from another point of view, and this new ethnic market is the machine that now produces most of our dominant discourse formations. Dominant among these is what Chow calls (with apologies to Weber), the "protestant ethnic":

In this context, *to be ethnic is to protest*—but perhaps less for actual emancipation of any kind than for the benefits of worldwide visibility, currency, and circulation. Ethnic struggles have become, in this manner, an indisputable symptom of the thoroughly and irrevocably mediatized relations of capitalism and its biopolitics. In the age of globalization, ethnics are first and foremost protesting ethnics, but this is not because they are possessed of some "soul" and "humanity" that cannot be changed into commodities. Rather, it is because protesting constitutes the economically logical and socially viable vocation for them to assume.[48]

Capitalism has never been opposed to resistance or protest; much to the contrary, it has actually been driven by them. So the protestant ethnic serves an invaluable function: namely, justifying capitalism by demonstrating its openness and ability to self-correct. Like filling out a comment card at a restaurant, the spectacle of ethnic protest provides an example of global capitalism's undying belief in free speech, hence protest becomes both job and divine vocation, because "the more one protests, the more work, business, and profit one will generate, and the more this will become a sign that one is loved by God."[49]

"We belong to this land," writes Daniel Heath Justice in a 2004 essay, "Seeing (and Reading) Red: Indian Outlaws in the Ivory Tower," adding, "we're not guests of the Invaders, to be given access at their whim. The knowledge of Native peoples is the voice of Turtle Island that speaks closest to all humanity. This is our inheritance."[50] Two years later in *Our Fire Survives the Storm* (2006), Justice characterized white Oklahoma settlers as "lawless border trash" and himself as a "Ross man," referring to Chief John Ross, who resisted removal.[51] In most Cherokee histories, Ross is typically opposed to the Treaty Party who illegally signed a bogus treaty authorizing the Trail of Tears, and the familiar story about resistant Ross and the traitorous Treaty Party is retold once again in this book. But Justice takes it in a new and dramatic direction: "When I read, years ago, that I might be related to three of the men suspected of killing John Ridge for his part in the Treaty, my heart swelled with pride and Cherokee patriotism."[52]

However one might characterize the killing of the Treaty Party (which included the writer Elias Boudinot)—that is, as either a murder or an execution—it is a hard fact that there was never a trial for the victims, never a chance to face their accusers and the charges against them; so the men who make Justice's heart swell would today be called vigilantes or a death squad. Do we really wish to celebrate that sort of thing? But there's more: in 2007, Justice published another essay (coauthored by Debra K. S. Barker) in the journal *Profession*, titled "Deep Surveillance: Tenure and Promotion Strategies for Scholars of Color." Here are a few excerpts: "Honestly evaluate your areas of potential strength and improvement."[53] "Be proactive, and be professional."[54] "Be a professional and respectful departmental citizen."[55] "Begin organizing your tenure dossier from the first year of appointment."[56] Finally, "you may expect that you need to establish a sustained record of excellent scholarship as well as a national or international reputation in your discipline. Institutions appreciate it when their faculty members gain increased visibility."[57]

Truer words were never spoken, but a question is raised: might there be a slight contradiction in the body of Justice's written work, moving as it does from the decrying of white "Invaders" and "trash," through a Cherokee patriot's history siding with an assassination squad, before finally arriving at what is basically a self-help manual for how to get tenure? (Try picturing Frantz Fanon or Aimé Césaire publishing an essay about seven easy steps to advancing a university career, and you'll catch my drift.) On second thought, there may be no contradiction at all when viewed through the lens of the protestant ethnic; indeed, from that point of view Justice's oeuvre is refreshingly clear insofar as it reveals the logical trajectory of the spectacle of ethnic discontent as it now seems to move through academe: namely, from "Indian outlaw in the ivory tower" to a tenured professor in that same tower. To be clear, I'm not saying that Justice or any other ethnic who protests is somehow being insincere or inauthentic. As with de Bry's engravings, there is no question that accuracy is sometimes achieved (and sometimes not) in any discourse formation, and certainly the same can be said for the personal sincerity of those who produce it. What I am saying is that our dominant discourse is governed by the spectacle of the protestant ethnic, which means that dishing on the white man or cursing one's state of oppression is not necessarily or automatically an act of "resistance." To the contrary, it can actually get you tenure. Institutions do appreciate it, after all, when faculty members gain increased visibility, and in our world today few things shine so brightly as the shimmering spectacle of ethnic discontent.

All is not lost. Admitting one's participation in the present discourse formation of the protestant ethnic does not require succumbing to cynicism or pessimism; to the contrary, protestant ethnics can sometimes achieve good things for the groups and movements they inevitably represent, although these things will usually be small and changes will be incremental at best. Consider the role of what I call the "professional

Indian." Professional Indians are people who look and speak the part and almost always represent the traditional in Indian space (but not the tribal private). They are hired by museums, schools, and universities to speak on subjects regarding history, politics, and related matters, even though in nearly every case they lack a university degree (which puts them in an exclusive class, to say the least). Professional Indians can make decent money doing this work, even at times a living, and I think we would be hard-pressed to find an example of a professional Indian who did not produce some benefit to the people she or he represents. This benefit may be visibility or something more tangible, such as a new fellowship or a grant. Professional Indians work the protestant ethnic to their advantage to get what they want, and this is not necessarily a problem.

The problem with the protestant ethnic as a discourse formation is the limitation it places on other Indian speakers, writers, and texts. All discourse formations place limitations on possible speech, so obviously we are not seeking some sort of "limitless" linguistic power here. It is more a question of which limits are in place and how they function in the public. For example, Indians may not produce prophetic discourse, by which is meant language that warns of some imminent retribution for past or present injustices. No Native jeremiads will be tolerated, for instance, referring to a prophetic discourse that has characterized a great deal of African American rhetoric (e.g., works by David Walker, Malcolm X, and Amiri Baraka), as well as the writings of Ward Churchill. Churchill's case was particularly instructive, as it showed in the most literal way imaginable how movement away from protestant ethnic discourse toward a more prophetic discourse can not only destroy a career but actually remove one from Indian space altogether. Churchill wasn't simply fired; he was actually transformed into a non-Indian before our unblinking eyes. An additional problem has existed since Samson Occom's day: can the Indian utter the universal, or does ethnic protest set the limit of our speech? If the latter is true, the Indian who speaks still speaks as an Indian, and no matter what the given topic at hand, the Indian will be expected to say something about the following: *culture, tradition, heritage, land, the circle of life, colonization, resistance, suffering at the hands of the white man, whether or not gaming is good thing,* and/or *whether or not mascots are a bad thing.* In such a limited context as this, uttering the universal is going to be a bit difficult.

The thing to do given our present discourse formation is probably to follow the lead of our predecessors who were faced with their own daunting rhetorical contexts and limitations but spoke the universal anyway.

Apess, Boudinot, Eastman, Bonnin, as well as a host of other Native writers, always assumed the roles of public intellectuals in ways that made sense in their particular times. Sometimes it worked best to don a suit and tie and employ a Christian discourse. At other times, wearing regalia and invoking the Great Spirit seemed appropriate. But no matter what their particular occasions or adornments, Native intellectuals resisted and appropriated the dominant discourses of their times and uttered the universal anyway as a means of forcibly entering the public sphere. Another thing to do is to revisit those old "trickster" linguistic games and highlight through irony, humor, and explicit subversion the invisible presence of the dominant discourse and thereby the visible absence of the Indian who speaks. Few have done this as well as the comedian Charlie Hill, the writer Gerald Vizenor, and the artist Jaune Quick-To-See Smith; what they share is a wry commentary on discourse carrying a powerful critical pedagogy (even though the political potentials of this kind of speech are sometimes missed). Finally, while all discourses are linked to sundry other historical structures, from economy to politics, one should never forget that it is always possible that discourses can change, fail, or be outmaneuvered by accident or chance. The Indian still speaks as an Indian, yes, and this is a limitation, to be sure; but every so often an x-mark can be seen escaping from the prison house of dominant discourse.

The Fifth Remove

My grandfather Aub and his brother Ray became police officers and patrolled the reservation in search of thieves, drunks, and Red Power activists. When I was in my late twenties, Mutt Robinson from Cass Lake showed me a side of my grandfather I had never seen. "He and Ray were pretty mean to us," Mutt said, referring to his old activist days. "Sometimes it seemed like they enjoyed roughing us up." When I first met Dennis Banks during my thirties, he smiled and said, "I knew your grandfather." "No doubt," I replied. I remember hearing a lot about Dennis Banks, AIM, and Red Power when I was a boy, and nearly all of it was bad. According to my grandparents, the "AIMsters" were radicals and ne'er-do-wells who would have been better served getting haircuts than occupying public spaces like my old Head Start classroom. Leona and my great-aunt Joyce went to a single rally on the reservation and, as they told the story, stood up and exhorted male AIM leaders to "start fathering some of the children you've made with all of these young girls."

Oh, how I used to cringe when hearing that story! It was even worse than Leona's telling me that Indian spirits were demons. I detested their use of the word *AIMster,* how they laughed scornfully at the silly idealism of it all, and I hated the way they dependably trotted out another story about my grandmother's cousin who tried to live like "a real old-time Indian" in the 1970s, selling everything he had and erecting a tipi in the woods but lasting only six months before the Minnesota cold compelled him to seek modern refuge. I hated that sort of talk, because, you see, I loved AIM. I remembered those young Indians with their long hair and horses—also guns—speaking a discourse that sounded more like pride than anything I had ever heard from Indians before. I wanted to get a horse of my own and ride with them to wherever it was they were going next (as it turned out, Wounded Knee).

I was too young to ride with AIM, but my father and his two brothers were not. My father spent the Red Power years raising his family and working various jobs before going to college on a scholarship when I was in elementary school. I remember well his old Smith-Corona electric typewriter tap-tap-tapping late into the night while I drifted off to sleep. He attended Bemidji State University (where one of his professors was Gerald Vizenor), and he graduated with a bachelor's degree in industrial education. Neither of his brothers finished high school; them I remember spending the Red Power years playing softball for the Minnesota Chipps, a championship team with a formidable reputation on the national Indian softball circuit. I loved watching my uncles play with the Chipps, and especially when they played white teams. Most of the Chipps had long hair and big guts and couldn't run for squat, but they sure could hit. And they always beat the white team.

My dad's youngest brother Vern socialized with Red Power activists like Mutt Robinson but never really joined them. I have never been clear as to why. "Too busy" is what Vern tells me, although memory tells me otherwise. "I never had any problem with those guys. They did some really good things." Vern is a master of the woods and lakes, having made a meager but survivable living as a trapper, hunter, fisherman, and wild rice harvester throughout his youth. He learned those skills from my grandfather, and as a form of knowledge they reach far back in time to an age when all Ojibwe men made their living that way. We no longer live in that time. Market forces eventually compelled Vern to take a job with the tribe, and now he goes to the woods and lakes when he is not too busy.

Whatever one thinks about the characters or contradictions involved with the Red Power movement, it is undeniable that it changed Indian life significantly. Such changes, as summarized here by Alvin Josephy, Joane Nagel, and Troy Johnson, would include the following:

> a proliferation of native newspapers, organizations, and associations supporting American Indian interests and representing Indian communities, a series of landmark tribal land claims and reservation resource rights, decisions that have reaffirmed Indian treaty rights, a legislative and judicial reaffirmation of tribal rights to self-determination and sovereignty that has opened the way for tribal economic development including casino gambling, a blossoming of cultural and spiritual renewal on many reservations and in urban Indian communities, an emerging intertribal urban Indian culture and community in U.S. cities, and an upsurge in the American Indian population as more and more Americans assert their native ancestry.[58]

Every one of these developments can be characterized as modern, and we might as well call them progress. They improved the lot of Indians, and Red Power activism was their agent.

My grandparents never gave enough credit to those young people who fought racism and injustice to make a better Indian world, even though it is also true that the Red Power movement had contradictions that should not be overlooked. Although they were too busy to get involved, my father and uncles benefited from Red Power too, my dad in the form of education funding, and my uncle through a career made possible by increased federal funding for tribes. Red Power benefited me as well, not only thanks to the new educational opportunities it engendered, but also for the way it brought me to a traditional culture I did not know before. For a time in my youth I reveled in that culture and rejected everything else, but now I see it as part of a vast historical complex in the Fourth World, a structure that also must include my grandmother, grandfather, uncles, dad, Joyce, Mutt, Dennis, me, and the Minnesota Chipps. Since that irreducible tribal diversity needs a name, I wrote this text.

Make Your X-Mark

This book argues for a greater recognition of the actually existing diversity in Native America, and it further posits the suggestion that indigenous people have the right to move in modern time. That means, first, acknowledging differences that already exist in the Fourth World, and, second, seeing those differences as by-products of modernity, hence nothing to be ashamed of. Native shame is rarely justified. We require a little self-forgiveness for being the people we are, and we should remember that the flip side of forgiveness is a promise. Our ancestors promised that their descendants would be part of the modern world while continuing to maintain that activist sense of community that Jace Weaver has called "communitism."[59] Sometimes that means adopting new ways of living, thinking, and being that do not necessarily emanate from a traditional cultural source (or, for that matter, "time immemorial"), and sometimes it means appropriating the new and changing it to feel more like the old. Sometimes change can make the old feel new again. Sometimes a removal can become a migration.

I use the x-mark to symbolize Native assent to the new, and to call into question old ideas of "assimilation" and "acculturation" (at very least they get the scare quotes). The sites that most interest me are the ones that are most controversial: identity, culture, and the idea of an "Indian nation." These are sites where x-marks are now being made; hence they are spaces where the old guards of reaction are most likely to be found. Chapter 1 examines the current proliferation of Indian identity controversies and reads them as a signifier of a larger identity crisis. Chapter 2 deals with culture and how it gets used by parties who feel the need to police its boundaries. Chapter 3 takes the idea of an Indian nation—and the nationalism that always produces that idea—seriously. Chapter 4 considers the prospects of indigenous citizenship as a force to be reckoned with in modern times. Each chapter attempts to unpack its subject by locating it in time, space, discourse, and, whenever possible, in *Ojibwemowin*.

I wrote this book because I found myself increasingly dissatisfied with the ways in which terms like *identity, culture,* and *nation* are used, which is to say, "naturally," ahistorically, and with a large measure of essentialism. While it may be true that Native essentialism has been politically expedient for the way it resists incorporation into the dominant culture and settler state, and while it may be equally true that essentialism is open to readings (by highly educated cosmopolitan intellectuals like me and probably you) as "strategic," it is also the case that the conditions of life that essentialism tries to sustain are often retrograde and unjust. When an Indian nation purges a population in its jurisdiction on grounds that it lacks certain characteristics, people actually lose their homes. When a Native religious movement that has existed for nearly five centuries is deemed unauthentic or nontraditional because its name is Christianity—even though it might well enhance the lives of the Indians who follow it—then we require a discussion about what we mean by "traditional."

This book is interested in these sorts of issues, as you'll soon see, and it follows a question that I have long asked myself: is it possible today to envision the survival of indigenous identity, culture, and nationalization in a nonessentialistic manner?

Perhaps the thing to do is to see essentialism as part of our history, appreciate its function at certain critical junctures, but then recognize that recent indigenous gains on the world stage might well signal a new time now when Native essentialisms should be discarded, because, after all, as "ahistorical truths" they are always illusory and usually harmful. Politically, this investigation will be nobody's manifesto. To the extent that it resembles theory, it is clearly more polytheistic than monotheistic. Nevertheless, I have tried to call it as I see it, and what I usually see when I look at Native America and the indigenous world—indeed, when I look into the mirror—is an x-mark.

CHAPTER ONE

Identity Crisis

It was the last night of the powwow, and my twelve-year-old daughter was walking around with her girlfriends, or, more precisely, walking back and forth in front of a group of boys their age. This was during that awkward but sweet time of life when formerly distinct groups of girls and boys start to merge, and my daughter and her friends were justifiably feeling pretty in their colorful regalia. Yet it was also during that unbelievably petty time when adolescents can become exclusive and mean, leading to rejection and possible self-esteem issues. So you can imagine the twinge in my gut when I overheard a boy, not dressed for dancing but just hanging out, call my daughter a "white girl."

Yes, it was meant as an insult, which tells you something about the present state of things. Yes, my daughter is fair-skinned and light-haired, the genetic inheritances, one might suppose, of her blonde Norwegian mother (and who knows, perhaps something of me as well). Yes, I suspect that in some weird preteen way that boy's comment was his way of flirting; but if that was the case, it did not produce the desired response in my daughter.

What it produced was a forceful assertion of identity. My daughter replied quite indignantly in sharp *Ojibwemowin:* "Gaawiin, nind Anishinaabekwe! Ogiimaabinesiik indizhinikaaz, awaazisii indoodem, Gaa-zagaskwaajimekaag nindonjibaa! Ginisidotam ina?" She had just completed a week at our reservation's language immersion camp and apparently felt pretty fluent, pointedly telling him that she was in fact an Ojibwe girl with a name, a clan, and a nation, and asking if he understood, which he obviously did not. "Then why don't you speak for yourself!" shouted Ashley, my daughter's darker-skinned girlfriend visiting from

Red Lake, before the entire group of girls danced giggling back into the circle, leaving the boy looking sheepishly dejected and probably a little less inclined to police the identities of others. I'm guessing he felt a little less Ojibwe too.

That was an Indian identity controversy, and on that particular occasion my daughter resolved it to her benefit. Using language to trump phenotype, wielding one authenticity over another, and with the important support of her uncontroversially Indian girlfriends, she spoke for herself and redefined that thing we call Native identity in the very heart of Indian space. Two years later, however, I overheard my daughter referring to herself as a "white girl." Two years after that she started calling herself "multiracial." I have always told her that she is Ojibwe, and an Ojibwe person is a complicated thing to be. As she enters her adult years and begins raising a daughter of her own, she suddenly seems more inclined to believe me. I'm just waiting to see what happens next.

The Perennial Question

The most nagging question in Native intellectual discourse happens to be its most basic: who is an Indian? Or, as Louis Owens put the question in 1992,

> *What* is an Indian? Must one be one-sixteenth Osage, one-eighth
> Cherokee, one-quarter Blackfoot, or full-blooded Sioux to be
> Indian? Must one be raised in a traditional Indian culture or speak
> a native language or be on a tribal roll? To identify as Indian—or
> mixedblood—and to write about that identity is to confront such
> questions.[1]

The difference between who and what is significant, insofar as the former refers to a person while the latter signifies a thing. Yet when we confront the question of Indian identity, we are in fact dealing with both people and things. People may be people, sure, and obviously most folks don't enjoy thinking of themselves as "things." But definitions of identity are not people; they are in fact things, things used to describe people, and always the invented fabrications of human beings. They are, to invoke that most ubiquitous of buzzwords, "constructions."

Indian identities have been viewed as constructions, as more nurture than nature, at least since 1826 when Elias Boudinot became the first Indian to ask the now-perennial question: what is an Indian? In "An Address to the Whites," a speech given at the First Presbyterian Church of Philadelphia during a terrifying moment in history when his people were facing the prospect of ethnic cleansing, Boudinot made the then-unfashionable argument that Indians were human beings like anyone else:

> What is an Indian? Is he not formed with the same materials with yourself? For "of one blood God created all the nations that dwell on the face of the earth." Though it be true that he is ignorant, that he is a heathen; that he is a savage; yet he is no more than all others have been under similar circumstances. Eighteen centuries ago what were the inhabitants of Great Britain?[2]

Boudinot's description of Natives as ignorant heathens and savages suggests that he wasn't much of a multiculturalist, but hardly anybody was in those days, and neither would you likely press the issue if your people were in similar straits. Boudinot's rhetorical charge, quite literally a matter of life and death, was to convince the whites that Indian identity was no more than the product of one's environment, that underneath our circumstances humans were essentially the same as God's children and made of the "same materials." As an early Indian identity theorist, one who at the time happened to be staring down the Trail of Tears, Boudinot was by urgent necessity both a universalist and a constructivist.

Between Boudinot and Owens the concept of universalism fluctuated in terms of its popularity, but surely the key role played by "circumstances" in the construction of identity is something on which we can all agree. Indian identities are always historically produced: constituted in writing and laws, on tribal rolls and employment forms, through social relationships and perceptions of phenotype, and of course in the inner recesses of one's sense of self. They are sometimes fashioned at your local powwow grounds, sometimes at ceremony, and often worked over in books. They appear in movies, during halftime, and on the packaging of butter. Identities always serve particular interests, and that's probably the most important thing to figure out: just whose interests do they serve? Within reason, all identities can be challenged and redefined; a successful assertion of identity depends mainly on its recognition by someone else. This is because identity is intersubjective, which means I can be whatever I want to be so long as you agree that I am what I say. And if you don't recognize my identity, especially if you are that thing I claim to be (or maybe you're just bigger than me and saying no), well, then it's hard to argue that I really am that thing. Things become definitive when there are lots of you, or lots of "us," weighing in on the matter, because identity is ultimately a communal thing. Identities are neither natural nor divine nor self-evident;

they are communal constructions of meaning inseparable from language. Indeed, on this view every Indian would be a "man made of words,"as the Kiowa bard said (and we assume he meant women too).[3] Finally, these constructed, intersubjective, language-mediated things—these linguistic definitions of humanity that give meaning to an individual body or community of people—can lead to material results, among them rights, responsibilities, privileges, discriminations, stereotypes, citizenships, and the ways you might be treated by the police, the state, or teenage boys. In other words, to more things.

One thing leads to another because while Indian identities may be constructions, they are not just imaginary things playing games in the kingdom of meaning. Identities connect deeply to our material, political world. As Linda Martín Alcoff and Satya Mohanty have written, "identities are not our mysterious inner essences but rather social embodied facts about ourselves in our world; moreover, they are not mere *descriptions* of who we are but, rather, *causal explanations* of our social locations."[4] A "social location" is, among other things, your place in a hierarchy and the vantage point from which you watch the world go by; and it can predict how your identity will likely be interpreted and treated by others. Note the logic of identity in Winona LaDuke's foreword to Andrea Smith's *Conquest: Sexual Violence and American Indian Genocide:* "as a Native woman, you always know that you will be viewed as a woman of color, hence your politics will be race based, your analysis marginalized, and your experience seen as limited."[5] Providing a host of hard examples of how Native women are generally perceived and treated in our world— from being seen as a novelty, to being ten times more likely than white women to die a violent death (and "the National Guard will not spend hours of manpower scouring for your missing body"), to suffering from "ethno-stress" because you know that *you are no longer a priority*"[6]— LaDuke reveals the implacably political nature of Native female identity, as well as how one's Indian identity can intersect with other axes of identity, such as gender, sexuality, and class. Despite the commonality of our "same materials," identities are rarely treated in the same way. In this way, identity can function like a cage.

On the other hand, identity can also feel like freedom itself. Native people aren't the only social group in the world who have fought to keep their identities intact or used them to provide the foundation for political movements, and this persistent embrace of Indian identity becomes all the more meaningful when viewed in the historical context of assimilation policies. From the 1680 Pueblo Revolts, to the nineteenth-century resistance movements of Tecumseh and Tenskwatawa, to the Red Power activism of the 1960s and 1970s, and right up to the global indigenous people's movement of our present day, identity has always been of paramount value to Native people and not something most are willing to trade in exchange for other desired things. That is not to suggest that identity politics has been pursued at the expense of other worthy political movements such as economic or environmental justice (as critics like Walter Benn Michaels and Todd Gitlin contend); it is simply to acknowledge that tribal or Indian identity has long been viewed as a value all its own, one that should be protected alongside other kinds of rights.[7] For example, the Red Power activist Clyde Warrior's famous 1967 speech "We Are Not Free" was a critique of American political paternalism and repeatedly referred to economic problems like Indian poverty, but embedded in Warrior's words was a strong defense of Indian identity. Indians should not "integrate into American society and economy individually," he said, "but enter into the mainstream of American society as a people, and in particular as communities of people."[8] A just incorporation into the economy should not require peoples to check their collective identities at the door.

Indians want to keep their communally constructed, intersubjective identities for the same reasons other people do. Identity orients you in space and time, connects you to the past, helps you develop a vision for the future, and provides you with a story. Indian identity stories can be particularly powerful in this regard. My daughter's story goes a little like this: *Long ago our people migrated from the eastern seaboard of Canada down the Saint Lawrence River to a place a prophecy foretold: "where the food grows on water." It was this place, and this is one reason why we harvest and eat wild rice. Your Ojibwe name, Ogiimaabinesiik, was given to you by your great-great-aunt, and it was given to her by her grandmother. That means your name has been in our family at least since the nineteenth century and perhaps even longer than that. See here, this headstone marks the resting place of Josephine Lyons, your great-great-great-grandmother, who was the last person said to have seen the spirit from which Leech Lake derives its name. See here, a map of Lake Winnibigoshish; all of these reefs and islands were named by your great-grandfather and his father and all those Lyons men who were fishing guides. Your dance moccasins were made for you by your great-grandmother; she beaded a traditional floral design into the brain-tanned deer hide just as our people have done for a long time, and you should remember this and be grateful each time you dance at our powwows.*

That story was quickly erased when that boy called my daughter a "white girl," but she reinscribed it by contesting his definition and asserting Indian identity by other means. Her argument was that Ojibwe identity is more about language than phenotype—a claim often made by elders and speakers of *Ojibwemowin* as well—and her example reveals a most powerful manner by which Indian identities are intersubjectively constructed today: namely, through *arguments* over what properly constitutes the materials for the making of Indian identity. Similar Indian identity controversies have increasingly appeared in the form of public spectacles, and like those questions asked by Louis Owens above, they highlight the different materials from which Indian identities are forged. For Owens, those things were blood quantum, culture, language, and tribal rolls, but there have been other materials used in the past, and new ones are in use today. That these things are rarely the same things is evidence of history's hand at work.

What were those older materials? What new ones are offered up now and why? What is at stake in the intersubjective construction of Indian identity? This chapter is about these kinds of questions, and it assumes that Indian identity is a prime site for the making of x-marks: contaminated, coerced signs of consent made under conditions not of our making but with hopes of a better future. That means from the outset that there can be no possibility of purity, no dream of disconnection, at the site of Indian identity. All we can do is think consciously about the materials out of which our identities are made—their origins, logics, and implications—and make the best calls we can during those moments when identity controversies beg for authentication. Indian intellectuals are increasingly asked to weigh in on such crises and the result is often contradictory, with one writer talking about blood over here, another arguing for the vital importance of language and culture over there, and nearly everyone quietly troubled about the colonial roots of tribal rolls (which in every case were assembled by Indian agents and not Indians per se). Lost in these disputes is the recognition that Indian identities are constructed; that they do not come from biology, soil, or the whims of a Great Spirit, but from discourse, action, and history; and finally, that this thing is not so much a thing at all, but rather a social process. Indian identity is something people do, not what they are, so the real question is, what should we do? This chapter does not advance an authoritative definition of what I think Indian identity is or should be; it does not offer an ultimate answer to the perennial question. It simply considers some of the historical meanings of Indian identity and the possibility of making good x-marks.

I'll start with a quick review of a few Indian identity controversies, then consider the increasingly privileged realms of language and tradition, and finally propose a model for critical analysis that examines Indian identity not for what it *is,* but more for what it *does.*

Indian Identity Controversies

Hardly a moon goes by without some big controversy erupting over who is a "real Indian," and not just between teenagers at powwows. At the site of every Indian identity controversy, x-marks are made and identity is (re)defined. Some of the biggest have focused on people who faked their Native identities (which is really to say little more than that their constructions proved unconvincing). In 1984, Hank Adams outed a writer who had long spoken as an Indian but had no apparent Native ancestry: Jamake Highwater.[9] In 1996, a self-described Ojibwe was criticized for not disclosing that, although raised by an Ojibwe adoptive father, she possessed no Indian blood: Shania Twain.[10] In 1999, it was finally confirmed that the "crying Indian" of the famous 1970s Keep America Beautiful ad campaign was of pure Italian-American extraction: Iron Eyes Cody.[11] In 2006, *LA Weekly* published an exposé (titled "Navahoax") revealing that a memoirist of who claimed to have been born in a hogan and raised by migrant workers was in fact a white man named Timothy Barrus who grew up in relatively cushy suburban digs: Nasdijj.[12] Such revelations are not really new. In 1906, a Briton named Archibald Stansfeld Belany moved to Ontario, assumed an Ojibwe identity, renamed himself Grey Owl, and became a well-known conservationist.[13] In the 1970s, Asa Carter, founder of the North Alabama White Citizen's Council and a speechwriter for George Wallace, proclaimed himself a Cherokee named Forrest Carter and wrote novels with Indian themes, including *Gone to Texas: The Outlaw Josey Wales* (1973) and *The Education of Little Tree* (1977).[14] Finally, who can ever forget the tragic story of silent-screen star Sylvester Long, aka Chief Buffalo Child Long Lance, who, after his ancestry was revealed to be of African and not Indian origin, took his own life at the age of forty-one?[15]

These sorts of Indian identity appropriations received a name during the 1990s—"ethnic fraud"—invented by Native intellectuals who had gained access to institutional power and noticed that non-Indians had apparently been sneaking into their identity category to take unfair advantage of economic perks. Declaring Indian identity in need of protection, they developed new policies. In 1990, U.S. Senator Ben "Nighthorse"

Campbell (R-CO) guided passage of the Indian Arts and Crafts Act, which established a review board to determine authentic identity for the purpose of controlling what could be marketed as "Indian art."[16] In 1993, the Association of American Indian and Alaska Native Professors (AAIANP) issued a "Statement on Ethnic Fraud," extending the same logic to university hiring procedures and suggesting that universities require "documentation of enrollment in a state or federally recognized nation/tribe" from job applicants.[17] Critics of ethnic fraud policies have called them overly restrictive, inconsistent, essentialist, alien to traditional tribal thought, and objectionably in the business of "numbering and registering" Indians.[18] Proponents have countered that such policies finally recognize the sovereignty of indigenous nations and grant Indians important say-so over the meanings of their own identities.[19] Anticipating the objection that not all legitimate Indians would be enrolled in federally recognized nations or tribes, the AAIANP "Statement" wisely recommended a "case-by-case review process for those unable to meet the [enrollment] criterion."

That the AAIANP "Statement" has generally not been implemented as policy by most institutions of higher learning is mostly owing to the thorny legal questions it raises for wary campus administrators, who have long operated under the assumption that self-identification and visibility are the most reliable indicators of ethnicity. For its part, the Indian Arts and Crafts Act, which is now law, immediately had the humorous effect of compelling Indian craftspeople who sold their wares at powwows to start prominently posting their enrollment numbers on their booths, especially in cases where the artisans had ambiguous phenotypes. In other words, these policies may have had the ironic effect of making phenotype and self-identification more and not less important to the way we think about Indian identity, despite efforts to the contrary.

According to these two ethnic fraud policies, being Indian means being an enrolled member of a federally recognized nation. What matters most is the tribal roll. That said, every one of our examples above was uncloaked not because they lacked enrollment but because they lacked "Indian blood." Nothing else is quite so important as that: not phenotype (Cody had it), nor language (Belaney had it), nor even an Indian family (Twain had it). Enrollment rarely comes up. In fact, in every single ethnic fraud case to date, the outing was justified by the blood. Thicker than language and culture, blood is the only recognized material that will always protect you from allegations of ethnic fraud; if it didn't, we might see even more celebrity Indian identity controversies than we already do. (Heather Locklear, anyone? Wayne Newton? How about that silver-haired elder Bob Barker from *The Price Is Right*?)

It's worth mentioning that ethnic fraud policies, and more specifically the "Statement on Ethnic Fraud" produced by the Indian professors, emerged in response to what the statement called "documented instances of abuse." That is to say, the problem is real, especially in academe, where it has become common for non-Indians to fabricate Indian identities for the purpose of landing jobs at institutions attempting to diversify their ranks. No one I know uses the phrase to refer to legitimate Indians who lack tribal enrollment because they don't meet stingy blood quantum or clanship requirements; indeed, the AAIANP statement makes a concerted effort to account for people who fall through the cracks in such ways. Rather, ethnic frauds are people with no demonstrable blood connection to indigenous communities beyond what they imagine or just assert. In such cases, when they check that box on a job application, they are treated as minority applicants, receiving affirmative action preferences and sometimes market-driven higher salaries reserved for (still very rare) Native faculty members. Who loses in such situations? Legitimate Indians who don't get the job for one. Native communities that are henceforth represented by outsiders for another. The beleaguered idea of affirmative action loses too, because ethnic frauds are usually outed at some point and thus pour fuel on fires that are already raging. Finally, institutions that "think they hired an Indian," as Cornel Pewewardy has put it, lose out as well, since they do not get the Indian they thought they hired.[20] Who wins? No one, it seems, but the ethnic frauds themselves. Non-Indians win.

Inventing a bogus ethnicity in order to receive favorable employment treatment is probably best considered identity theft, because ethnic fraud is pursued for the same reasons that identity thieves fish through other people's trash for personal information like Social Security numbers: that is, for the money. It is dishonest and not at all waved off by arguments like the one saying that Indian identity is constructed. To be perfectly clear, Indian identities are not *personally* constructed; they are *socially* constructed. Legal fictions, identities are always at least as real as your bank account or credit report, so policies designed to prevent dishonest appropriations of them remain necessary and justified as a way of protecting people from those who abuse the system for unearned personal gain.

Indian identity wars aren't only waged against "wannabes" these days. To the contrary, we are now witnessing the rise of a new identity controversy produced in the most indisputably Indian of contexts: reservations and tribal government chambers. "Disenrollments" and "banishments"—legal decrees that strip people of their tribal citizenship and all of the rights that come with it—have recently taken place at Las Vegas Paiute (Nevada); Mille Lacs, Grand Portage, and Bois Forte Ojibwe (Minnesota); Oneida and Tonawanda Seneca (New York); Lummi and Sauk-Suitattle (Washington); Narragansett (Rhode Island); Sac and Fox (Iowa); and among several small California tribal nations (Maidu Barry Creek Rancheria, Redding Rancheria, Enterprise Rancheria, the Pechanga Band of Luiseno Indians, the Chukchansi of the Picayune Reservation, the Viejas Band of Mission Indians, and Santa Rosa Rancheria). Disenrollment is the removal of a citizen from the tribal rolls, and more often than not it happens in the context of (a) acrimonious political conflict, (b) new casino profits, or (c) both. Banishment is just what the word suggests—the physical removal of people from the community, on top of disenrolling them—and it should be understood as a policy conceived in a social climate marred by increasing rates of crime. Neither disenrollment nor banishment can remove your color, culture, or self-concept, but they do diminish your right to call yourself a member of the tribe, thus making you for all legal intents and purposes a non-Indian.

These cases are now far greater in number than the more widely publicized ethnic fraud spectacles. Unlike the latter, which tend to be open-and-shut cases about blood, they also deal in more complex definitional criteria and initiate other kinds of discussion. Disenrollments and banishments raise questions about traditional modes of punishment and the meanings of community membership, they lead to allegations of draconian crime policies, greed, and politically motivated identity assassinations, and they often initiate debates over the proper reach of tribal and federal governmental powers. In almost every case, they feature some connection to new influxes of casino cash (a point that has not gone unnoticed by the enemies of tribal sovereignty), although David Wilkins has argued that they are not reducible to money so much as to the wielding of power by new Indian elites.[21] These controversies are always fiercely contested, yet growing in number.

The lines drawn by proponents of banishment are found not in the realms of blood but in behavior. Losing your Indian identity is now a possible consequence of committing a crime. For its part, disenrollment has transformed Indian identity into a political tool that might be wielded by elites against political enemies, so identity has become a question of sovereignty: who has the right to strip someone of his or her identity? I don't think I am overstating these issues. Disenrolled or banished people, after all, would not be seen as Indians according to existing ethnic fraud policies because they would lack enrollment. (Blood, of course, would say otherwise.) Further, these new policies are often justified by the claim that they constitute some traditional tribal practice, but we might note their resemblance to a peculiar modern logic that has solidified connections between behavior and identity. As Michel Foucault often observed, before modernity people could commit theft or engage in "perverse" sexual practices—be judged and possibly punished for them—but that did not necessitate the acquisition of an identity in the process. In modern times, however, one doesn't simply break a law but is henceforth a "criminal"; one doesn't merely sleep with a member of the same sex but becomes a "homosexual"; and in our neck of the woods, a wayward Indian doesn't just receive restoration or healing after committing a transgression; he or she can now be legally transformed into a "non-Indian."

I think banishment is less the revival of traditional forms of social control and more a predictable reaction to the systemic disempowerment of tribal jurisprudence. The Major Crimes Act of 1885 unilaterally granted legal jurisdiction to the United States, but it has not had a positive effect in Native communities. Major crimes often go uninvestigated, as charged in a 2007 Amnesty International report showing how sexual assaults are not only widespread in Native America but sometimes ignored by federal authorities who assumed responsibility for them in 1885.[22] In a context where crime is common but law enforcement lacking, it makes sense that something like banishment would emerge. But what, we should ask, is the long-term political effect of making Indian identity seem as revocable as a driver's license?

Finally, on top of ethnic fraud, disenrollment, and banishment, there is another Indian identity controversy emerging in our time and ending up in court with increasing frequency. As I write, a federal lawsuit filed by the Minnesota Mdewakanton Dakota Oyate (MMDO), a federally unrecognized community based in Minnesota, has formally accused the Shakopee Mdewakanton Sioux Community (SMSC) of pulling off what the Sioux anthropologist (and MMDO Chief) Barbara Buttes calls "the great Mdewakanton identity heist."[23] According to Buttes's research and federal court documents (Wolfchild v. United States), the MMDO alleges that most SMSC members aren't Mdewakantons at all but rather usurpers of Mdewakanton identity who have (thanks to the unsightly collusion of the Bureau of Indian Affairs) ridden their bogus identity all the way to the bank.[24] SMSC's casino, Mystic Lake, located near the Twin Cities, is one of the most lucrative gaming institutions in the United States, and for years its profits have been shared by a tiny (fewer than two hundred) and wealthy (estimated one million dollars per capita per annum) group that has long been charged with inconsistent and unconstitutional enrollment practices. The MMDO won its first legal round in October 2004 when Judge Charles F. Lettow of the Court of Federal Claims found the United States in violation of its trust responsibility—that is, he agreed that the United States bungled precisely as charged—and the MMDO now awaits damages that could amount to billions. This case might result in a dramatic reorganization of the Dakota communities in southern Minnesota and could very well change everyone's understandings of what Mdewakanton identity means.

This story goes back, as such cases often do, to the nineteenth century. In 1851, the United States signed a treaty with Sioux Indians in Minnesota reserving a ten-mile strip of land on either side of the Minnesota River for the Dakota to live on. Land was exchanged for money that never arrived, leading to an armed rebellion in 1862. Under the care of Bishop Henry Benjamin Whipple, 208 Mdewakanton Dakota pledged not to fight the Americans and even protected white settlers in exchange for individual eighty-acre parcels of land on the Minnesota River tract, a deal that earned them the unsexy moniker "Loyalists." After the fighting subsided, new censuses were taken, land certificates were issued, and in 1917 the Mdewakantons actually paid for their own lands using the treaty monies promised back in 1851. But the deal was never completed: no land, no recognition, no resolution. After decades of languishing in the limbo of unresolved Indian litigation, the matter was finally addressed in 1969 and again in 1980 when the BIA finally placed the lands under the sovereignty of alleged non-Mdewakantons: in other words, the wrong Indians. According to the lawsuit, the SMSC is comprised of Sioux from other bands, and even allegedly some non-Indians, who are now claiming the sovereign right to exclude the real Mdewakantons on whose lands they operate the formidable Mystic Lake Casino.

This lawsuit has something in common with another Indian identity controversy whose discontents have made a federal case out of it. In December 2006, a federal court ruled against Cherokee Nation of Oklahoma for stripping black "Freedmen" of their tribal citizenship, a case also reaching back into the nineteenth century.[25] Some Cherokees kept slaves until 1866, when a treaty with the Americans freed them and made them citizens of the Cherokee Nation. By then many Freedmen had already embraced the culture, learned the language, intermarried with other Cherokees and reproduced with them, and for more than a century were more or less treated as equals (at least in theory) until 1983 when Principal Chief Ross Swimmer noticed during an election that most Freedmen were supporting a rival candidate. Swimmer introduced legislation requiring Cherokee citizens wanting to vote to carry a Certificate of Degree of Indian Blood (CDIB) card, a document available to anyone who could trace their lineage to the 1906 Dawes Roll, a census that excluded the Freedmen, who were listed on their own separate roll. After two decades of conflict over the matter, the Freedmen were prevented from voting again in 2003, sued and won, but then faced a 2007 referendum introduced by Principal Chief Chad Smith to revoke the Freedmen's citizenship in the Cherokee Nation. It passed, and as I write the United States is considering reprisals for Cherokee Nation that look a lot like termination. Smith's rationale will now sound familiar: "Is it really such an outlandish thing to think that Native American tribes and nations would like their citizens to have Indian blood?"[26]

There's that blood again. But of course Smith wasn't really talking about blood so much as *lineage,* saying that Cherokee citizens should be able to trace their ancestry to the 1906 rolls that excluded the Freedmen. As contemporary Freedmen like to point out, however, those rolls weren't written by Indians in order to establish an eternal source of Cherokee blood identity; they were written by the U.S. government to distribute land allotments during the assimilation era, and they were administered by whites using the old "eyeball test" of racial identity; that is, if you "looked black" to the agent who held the pen, you were listed as a Freedman. Another objection is that Smith's proposal would abrogate the 1866 treaty that made the Freedmen full citizens of the nation in the first place, raising concerns about a new round of tit for tat in the realm of Indian treaty rights. On this view, the Freedmen don't need to be considered Indians at all; rather, they are *citizens* of the Cherokee Nation who are now in the process of being ethnically cleansed.

That these two cases will likely prove to be historically significant is obvious, to say the least; for our purposes, we must understand what they suggest about the making of Indian identity. To wit, on top of blood, enrollment, and behavior, these cases present another material used for the intersubjective construction of Indian identity: the historical fact of American participation. It was no one but the Americans, after all, who distinguished "Loyalists" from "Hostiles" during the 1862 Dakota War, and it was those same Americans who set forth two separate rolls on which Cherokee identities were recorded on the basis of perceived phenotype. American fingerprints can usually be found at the scene of Indian identity controversies, whether in the form of identity-establishing documents like tribal rolls or in materials whose meanings speak more of "Western" values and beliefs than traditionally indigenous ones.

Let us try to capture the big picture here. I have been saying that Indian identity controversies highlight and problematize the materials out of which Indian identities are fashioned and subsequently recognized in people by others. They are sites for x-marks to be made. In cases of ethnic fraud, during the 1990s Indian policy makers attempted to make tribal enrollment the most meaningful criterion for the public recognition of Indian identity, but that particular definition has been consistently trumped by the idea of Indian blood. In cases of disenrollment and banishment, the formal recognition of Indian identity has become linked to behavior and—I don't know how to say this without sounding a bit cynical—political favoritism: criteria that speak more of the logic of modernity and the exercise of power than of traditions, despite claims to the obverse. Finally, tribal identities are now literally on trial. The Mdewakanton and Cherokee controversies reveal the impossibility of establishing definitions of Indian identity without taking into consideration the fact of American involvement. The upshot is that this thing we call Indian identity is never unitary, organic, or uncontested, and never unattached to power, but increasingly a public spectacle revealing a very wide range of impure materials in use. All of these spectacles are addressed in the same basic manner as my daughter's identity controversy on the powwow grounds: through arguments over what should constitute the meanings of Indian identity proper. What is an Indian? Why, the argument that wins the day.

Indian identity controversies make one thing clear: today's tribal communities are intractably marked by diversity and contest within. The Loyalists and Freedmen are only the most visible examples today of subgroups within the category of tribe who can claim to be denied, and this fact is significant for reasons that have to do with the social process by which Indian identity is made; that is, when we study the intersubjective construction of Indian identity, we must always ask which materials count and who gets to recognize. Power is at play in every Indian identity controversy, and critics should acknowledge the involvement—and probable fates—of winners, losers, silent partners, and those who get to make the final call. That means acknowledging what is at stake in the outcome of any successful definition. But we must begin by admitting an uncomfortable truth: long gone are those fabled days when the world seemed to be neatly and understandably divided between Indians and non-Indians. Such clean-cut Manichaean divisions no longer exist. Today belongs to the x-mark.

What can we make of these Indian identity controversies if we view them as a single historical formation? I think this: Indian identity is in crisis. By "crisis" I mean no more than a state of instability and a turning point, both a danger and an opportunity, a fork in the road with divergent paths in view. I am saying that older meanings of identity are losing (or have already lost) their foundations, while new meanings present themselves as legitimate. It is not my intention to express undue alarm over this matter, only to point to a condition of crisis that has actually been with us for quite a while. What created this identity crisis? Lots of things, but it is essential that our analysis remain situated within the larger historical context of colonialism, for it is to colonialism that we can attribute both the general state of uncertainty undergirding Indian identity controversies and nearly all of the criteria that are advanced to resolve them. Natives didn't invent assimilation or concepts such as "enrollment" and "banishment" (even less "Loyalist" and "Freedmen"). We didn't establish blood and race as useful indicators of identity. We aren't responsible for stereotypes or the systemic poverty that has made casino economies so attractive. It was colonialism that gave us those kinds of things and Indians who had to live with their consequences. Today's identity crisis is a predictable result of political policies and their aftermath whose original purpose was actually to destroy Indian identity, so coming out of this history we should probably find ourselves amazed that people still call themselves Indians at all. Colonialism left Indian identity in tatters: fragmented, uncertain, endlessly questioned, and something people squabble about. (And not just squabble; as we've seen, sometimes these things are matters of life and death.) Today's controversies might be compared to the ways bombing survivors fight over clean water: the more threatened the resource, the greater the conflict. But it wasn't Indians who dropped this bomb.

The attempted obliteration of Indian identity has its historical roots in assimilation policies, including off-reservation boarding schools that attempted to turn Indian children into whites by replacing their languages with English and "savagism" with "civilization," and allotment programs that attempted to turn their parents into private property–owning entrepreneurs. That said, our identity crisis today is primarily nurtured by a great race for dwindling, and sometimes surging, resources. Money is increasingly at stake in identity controversies, and that should not surprise anyone who has ever tracked Indian poverty rates. Colonization not only attacked Indian identity; it created poverty too; and if respite from grinding poverty can be glimpsed on the other side of a tightening definition, there lies a certain rationality. But if cultural and linguistic elements of identity are to survive, perhaps something other than money should be privileged as a reason to be an Indian.

The historic challenge before us now is to speak responsible new answers to the perennial question, what is an Indian? At stake is more than mere musings about who is "more Indian" than someone else. One important outcome will be rights: to claim tribal citizenship and land, to market Indian art or check a box for job preference, to practice a religion or adopt children, even to pass a legitimate identity on to your descendants (what is usually called a "birthright"). Another outcome is recognition, the way we validate an Indian person or group; this one reaches into the innermost depths of one's self-concept and it means a great deal. Another issue is racial difference: can Indians be black? White? Or will Indian identity itself continue to be thought of as a "race"? Finally, the recovery of those things we've lost—language, culture, worldviews—is also at stake. To what extent will ethnicity inform our future definitions of Native identity? Rights, recognition, racial difference, and recovery are all up for grabs, so the way our identity crisis plays out will not only redefine Indian identity, it will also affect the quality of Indian life as we know it. Our goal should be the development of definitions of Native identity that would keep "Indians" viable for at least seven generations, strengthen existing communities, enhance our political independence, and provide the greatest degree of happiness for the greatest number of Indians (whatever those things turn out to be). This is a much more daunting task than speaking Ojibwe back to a kid at the powwow grounds, but the basic argumentative logic doesn't really differ in kind. The meanings and materials out of which indigenous identities are fashioned are now open for debate—Indian identity controversies are our public venues—and our age will be remembered by a great battle of authenticities. While most policy makers will doubtless cling to the idea of blood as the most reliable carrier of identity, some Native intellectuals have been saying that tradition should trump all else when it comes to answering the perennial question. Let us now enter that shadowy realm of tradition to see what might lurk there in the way of ascertaining the meanings of Indian identity.

The Turn to Tradition

In *Real Indians: Identity and the Survival of Native America,* Eva Marie Garroutte posits "radical indigenism" as the proper foundation for theorizing Indian identity. Her use of the word *radical* is meant to signify not a Ward Churchillesque ideological stance, but rather a sense of the Latin word *radix* meaning "root," as in the roots of traditionalism. Reclaim your *radix,* Garroutte suggests, for what you will discover is a definition of identity that she summarizes as follows: "individuals belong to [Indian] communities because they carry the essential nature that binds them to The People and because they are willing to behave in ways that the communities define as responsible."[27] Let us note the primary components to Garroutte's definition of Indian identity: "essential nature" and "responsible behavior." Garroutte understands the first component as kinship and the second as action: "one must literally *be* a relative, and . . . one must also *act* like one."[28] Garroutte's is a admirable attempt to develop a theory of Indian identity that not only privileges traditionalism but also values inclusiveness and change, and for that alone it should be applauded. One can also appreciate her explicit highlighting of the materials used in Indian identity definitions, for instance, "biology," "culture," and "self-identification" (these are the topics of her chapters). Yet, despite her book's many strengths, I suspect Garroutte's definition of Indian identity might actually exacerbate, not resolve, our Indian identity crisis. To make this argument, let me first try to answer her call for radical indigenism by examining the roots of Ojibwe culture and language to see how my own *radix* has conceived of Indian identity.

In philosophical discourse, "identity" refers to the state of two things being alike. What the other things have in common is "difference." How have the Ojibwe discerned identity and difference in the past? According to David Beaulieu, during the eighteenth and nineteenth centuries Ojibwe "classified a person Indian if he lived with them and adopted their habits and mode of life."[29] These habits and modes included language use, customs, worldviews, religious beliefs, and, rather importantly, dress. This was the age before blood and enrollment, when identity was simply established according to observed everyday phenomena. Back then, if it talked like you, acted like you, hunted and cooked like you—if it believed in the things you believed in, and most of all if it lived with you—then chances were, it was just like you. You shared a mutual Indian identity.

Even after the introduction of cross-cultural mixing, when Natives and whites started intermingling and producing that third, straddling class of identity—the métis or mixed-blood—observed lifestyle remained the sole marker of identity. Take, for instance, the importance placed upon dress. As Beaulieu explains, "Indians wore breechcloth and had braids in their hair whereas mixedbloods wore hats and pants."[30] Indians were held to be different from mixed-bloods, who were in turn seen as different from whites. The identities were changing but the basic criteria used to discern them were not; people were deemed such and such on the basis of observable cultural lifestyle markers like hairstyle and dress. It wasn't only about your looks, however; in fact a whole range of lifestyle distinctions established identity and difference. In the late nineteenth and early twentieth centuries, Ojibwe families distinguished Indians from mixed-bloods, and certainly Indians from whites, by observing the types of housing they lived in and the kinds of music they liked. White and mixed-blood "frame houses" had pianos or fiddles playing inside, while the wigwams (later, tarpaper shacks) occupied by Indians served as venues for traditional drum music. Cooking served as an important marker of identity as well: mixed-bloods and whites prepared their food inside, whereas Indians preferred to cook over an open fire outdoors. These sorts of life practices were all basically cultural in nature, as people read signs like proximity and the reproduction of daily life as reliable markers of identity. Indians were people who lived with and like Indians; it was as plain as the nose on your face (which itself had absolutely nothing to do with identity).

Such commonsensical cultural standards used by traditional Natives for the determination of identity also appear in tribal languages. As we can see by examining *Ojibwemowin*, Ojibwe not only made distinctions between Natives, non-Natives, and mixed-bloods, they also distinguished between various kinds of Natives and different types of whites. Ojibwe have long referred to themselves as *anishinaabeg*, meaning original or indigenous people in the plural. Beyond that, there have been many different kinds of *anishinaabeg*, what Europeans called "tribes," based upon cultural or linguistic particularities. For instance, some have suggested that the word *ojibwe* means something "puckered up" in reference to the distinctive style of moccasins that Ojibwe folks wear, so the term would seem to name those particular Indians who wear puckered up moccasins: *anishinaabe ojibwe*.[31] Sioux can also be called *anishinaabeg*—because they are also an original people—but they are further referred to as *bwaanag* or "roasters": *anishinaabe bwaanag*. The origin of *bwaan* is a bit unclear, some insisting it referred to the Sioux burning people alive, others suggesting it was a reference to the traditional dog feast. All etymologies aside, the crucial point is that Ojibwe have long spoken of both *anishinaabe ojibwe* and *anishinaabe bwaanag*, identity markers classifying both Ojibwe and Sioux as original or indigenous people, but different kinds, and we can see how these identity distinctions were based on cultural criteria.

The same holds true for the language used to describe non-Indians. The Ojibwe word for the color white is *waabishkaa*, but it has never been used to talk about people of European origin. Rather, "white" people have long been called *gichimookomaanan* or "big knives," signifying the swords the Ojibwe saw carried by the first whites they met (and probably the power and potential violence they signified too). Since contact there have been many different kinds of big knives to discern. *Wemitigoozhi* signifies French descent, "one who wears a piece of wood," just like those crucifix-wearing Jesuits they met long ago; while *agongos,* or "chipmunk," describes a person of Scandinavian descent. Why chipmunks? Perhaps their sod houses struck the Ojibwe as comparable to the dwellings of rodents. In any case, both *wemitigoozhi* and *agongos* are *gichimookomaanan,* but as with the different types of *anishinaabeg,* not all long knives are cut from the same cloth. A French person was one who lived like French people, a Scandinavian was one who lived like the Scandinavians (and chipmunks). What made them different from each other was culture and lifestyle, and these were things that you could actually see.

Identities never come into existence until there are perceived differences in one's midst; at the dawn of colonialism new identities were created on both sides of the divide. The Europeans became "white," yes, and the original people became "tribes." But it also happened that *wemitigoozhi* and *agongos* became *gichimookomaanan,* while *ojibwe* and *bwaanag* became *anishinaabeg.* From a Native point of view, these identities emerged not from earth, biology, soul, or social-science discourse, but rather from the perception of visible cultural differences: language, religion, hairstyle, dress, or what people now call ethnicity. There were no "essences" implied, and the groups were not ranked in any particular order. People were simply given names that established identities, the names were indicative of a worldview on the part of the namer, and this process was guided by perceptions of how people lived their lives. In a manner of speaking, at least from the pragmatic perspective of the traditional world, Indian identity followed this ironclad law: you are how you eat.

One of the best ways to capture this entirely constructivist and ethnic manner by which traditional Natives distinguished Indian, tribal, and non-Indian identities is through examining the words that describe mixed-bloods. These words are particularly instructive because they provide us with a sense of how new or ambiguous kinds of people were similarly identified in cultural or ethnic terms. For example, the Ojibwe word used to signify persons of mixed ancestry is *wiisaakodewininiwag* or "diluted men." What is diluted is not specified, but it seems telling that one would not use the word *wiisaakode* when mixing something with water or some other liquid; that's *ginigawin.* If not that liquid called blood, what exactly is "diluted"? One elder I asked about this term, Bob Jourdain of Leech Lake, told me that *wiisaakode* referred to the dilution of "Indianness." When I pressed him about the possibility of blood being the thing that is at least implicitly diluted in the word *wiisaakode,* he just laughed, shook his head, and said, "No. *Wiisaakodewininiwag* might be *deluded,* but they're not *diluted.*"[32] A mixed-blood would be one whose identity is the product of mixed cultures. Now, this manner of thinking is rather at odds with dominant cultural notions of mixed identity, for when Europeans began describing people of mixed ancestry, they drew upon the language of blood and breeding—"mulatto," "half-breed," and so on—metaphors that were derived from animal husbandry and that not only characterized the mixed but by fiat circumscribed two locations of parental purity as well. By contrast, Ojibwe speakers have played a different language game regarding mixed identity, dealing in "Indianness" and not blood or breed when discerning one's degree of "dilution."

These Ojibwe assessments of Indianness seem to resonate with similar standards held by the Lakota people, whose language hails from an entirely different language family. Consider the similarities between Ojibwe's *wiisaakodewinini* and Lakota's word for a person of mixed ancestry, *iyeska,* or "speaks white."[33] Like our diluted man, "speaks white" marks an identity known not by its blood or breeding but by the manner in which a person speaks. Granted, on one level *iyeska* probably just refers to the speaking of English, but as the Lakota writer Elizabeth Cook-Lynn has remarked, this word carries an additional connotation indicating which social group the *iyeska* seems to politically and culturally align with. *Iyeska,* she writes, "is not generally regarded as a complimentary term" because people of mixed backgrounds "were and probably still are seen by native peoples as those who were already converts to the hostile and intruding culture."[34] Speaking white is a sign of conversion or allegiance to the white world. You are what you speak, on this view, and what you speak reveals your standpoint. It is a political statement.

This political understanding of identity is similarly articulated by another Lakota commentator, Mary Moore (formerly Mary Crow Dog), in her autobiography:

> being a fullblood or breed [iyeska] is not a matter of bloodline, or
> how Indian you look, or how black your hair is. The general rule is that
> whoever thinks, sings, acts, and speaks Indian is a skin, a fullblood,
> and whoever acts and thinks like a white man is a half-blood or breed,
> no matter how Indian he looks.[35]

Here a person who "speaks Indian" doesn't need to possess a certain degree of blood or conform to a particular phenotype to be considered a "full-blood." The truly important things are mind-set and action, which themselves indicate political allegiance.

Mind-set, action, and allegiance were all connected to identity by the American Indian Movement (AIM) during the 1973 establishment of the Independent Oglala Nation (ION) at Wounded Knee II. AIM consciously allied itself with the traditional people it defended, and the ION reflected traditional understandings of identity. Its foundational precepts were a rejection of federally controlled tribal governments, the restoration of the nation-to-nation treaty-making relationship, and a renewed affirmation of Indian rights as delineated in the 1869 Fort Laramie Treaty; in short, the ION sought meaningful political independence and diplomatic relationships with other nations, governments, and peoples around the world. In keeping with this assertion of nationalism, they created a citizenship roll. According to a press release dated March 16, 1973, 394 Wounded Knee occupants were sworn in as citizens of the Independent Oglala Nation, including 160 "Indians and chicanos of other tribes" and "seven whites and blacks."[36] Clearly, in this "enrollment," blood and race were deemed so irrelevant to Oglala national identity that they played no role at all in the making of its citizenry. What mattered most at Wounded Knee, when the lines between insiders and outsiders were made all too clear, was political allegiance.

"It's too bad assimilation didn't go the other way," my friend Michael Wassegijig Price likes to say. The ION's multiracial citizenship roll came awfully close. In fact, this small historical event nearly realized Marge Piercy's imagination of Indian nations in her classic sci-fi novel *Woman on the Edge of Time* (1976), about a Chicana from our own day who time-travels to both utopian and dystopian future worlds. On the utopian side of time, Connie finds that the Wampanoag Nation has become strong and healthy because they "broke the bond between genes and culture, broke it forever," as the Wampanoag (but phenotypically black) character Bee explains:

> "We want there to be no chance of racism again. But we don't want the melting pot where everybody ends up with thin gruel. We want diversity, for strangeness breeds richness.
>
> "It's so . . . invented. Artificial. Are there black Irishmen and black Jews and black Italians and black Chinese?
>
> "Fasure, how not? When you grow up, you can stick to the culture

you were raised with or you can fuse into another. But the one we were
raised in usually has a . . . sweet meaning to us."[37]

Wampanoag culture, identity, and nationhood survive in the book (but
only in the utopian future, not in the dystopian one Connie also visits)
because culture and biology have been separated. "We're all a mixed bag
of genes," Luciente tells Connie when she can't believe she is actually
among Wampanoags ("You're what? Blond Indians?").[38]

Other novels written by Native authors imagine political landscapes
where culture and biology have been disconnected in the realm of identity
in order to promote cultural survival—the "genome pavilion" in Gerald
Vizenor's *The Heirs of Columbus* (1991) and Leslie Marmon Silko's multiracial tribal revolutionaries united against the "Destroyers" in *Almanac
of the Dead* (also 1991) both come to mind—and in each case the authors claimed indigenous traditions as source material for their writing
and ideas. Would it be too much to suggest that the same basic logic of
identity played a role in the ION's establishment of a multiracial Indian
citizenry, if only for a moment, and despite its immediate destruction by
state repression? Might this separation of meanings from blood actually
resemble a traditional Indian logic?

Whether discovered in heritage languages, historical descriptions, or in
futuristic fictions, my evidence suggests that traditional notions of Indian
identity have generally used culture, ethnicity, language, and allegiance—
and not blood, breeding, or biology—as the determinants of Indian identity
and difference. Traditional Natives did not distinguish an Indian "race"
from other versions, although they did recognize different cultural groups.
There is nothing in Ojibwe language that evokes biological notions like
blood quantum or other essentialist traffickers of identity. Rather, Indians
have simply discerned "big knives" from "original people," "puckered-
ups" from "roasters," and "wood-wearers" from "chipmunks." They distinguished "deluded" from "diluted" and "talking white" from "speaking
Indian." An Indian was someone who lived with and like Indians: it was
about the proximity, practice, and principles that people lived by.

If we can take this quick account of history and language as revealing something meaningful about the roots of Indian identity recognition,
then it would seem to follow that Garroutte's definition might well describe the way we think and talk about Native identity today, but probably not yesterday, not in heritage languages, and subsequently not quite
"traditionally." Remember, for Garroutte Native identity came down to
the recognition of an "essential nature" and "responsible behavior": one

must literally be a relative, and one must act like one. I would submit that these particular criteria do not reflect traditional understandings of identity so much as modern ones; that is, they seem less indicative of a *radix* and more symptomatic of our present identity crisis.

Take "essential nature," which Garroutte understands as kinship but which two-thirds of Native America's tribal enrollment offices—and the dominant culture at large—continue to interpret as blood. The non-Indian *radix* of blood quantum has been much interrogated[39]—including by Garroutte[40]—but the idea of kinship too has a genealogy that winds its way through modern academic discourses such as anthropology. What is kinship? At its most basic level, kinship refers to the ways social groups and roles are organized. It was invented by Lewis Henry Morgan, and ever since anthropological discourse has addressed kinship in implicitly biological terms, as David Schneider argued in *A Critique of the Study of Kinship* and other works revealing how anthropologists constructed kinship studies based on ideas of human reproduction as understood in their own Euro-American culture.[41] Given its biological connotations, we shouldn't be surprised that the idea of kinship often beats a path to essentialism, because "relatives" ultimately rest upon the idea of a single original ancestor. Garroutte's view is that "indigenous essentialisms [are] quite different from the biologistic, social scientific varieties," because many Indian communities made people their kin through adoption ceremonies; so, while the end result may be a sense of identity that might feel like a family, Indian essentialism is not actually essentialist. One can insist upon "ancestry" while recognizing its social construction.

This is a clever argument, and one wishes to cheer Garroutte for arguing that "people of any race [could theoretically be brought into] kinship relations through the transformative mechanism of ceremony."[42] But if we actually wish to revisit the *radix* of Ojibwe culture, why use modern academic concepts like kinship in the first place? The word has no clear Ojibwe correlate, I suggest, because it is not really a traditional idea. It is a modern anthropological concept. Traditional Ojibwe recognized other Ojibwe by their proximity and the way they lived, including but not limited to their family relations. What they recognized as themselves—what they saw when they saw an Ojibwe—always had the potential to change and incorporate new ideas, and even incorporate new people, but this act of recognition did not rest entirely upon familial relationships. If it does so today, perhaps that says more about our present relationship to anthropology than it does about our connections to tradition; and if it leads to essentialism (as I think talk about kinship inevitably does), we should admit that this too is a modern concept and not a traditional value. If essentialism is to be defended, it really shouldn't happen on the backs of people who are not responsible for it.

Garroutte's second criterion for indigenous identity is "responsible behavior," which means adhering to certain principles like reciprocity and caring for others. One gets the sense that what Garroutte calls responsible behavior is in fact a universal human longing for functional communities, and the particular behaviors she discusses (caring, sharing, helping, being honest, etc.) are certainly worthy of esteem. Further, on first glance it seems as though this particular criterion of identity is even less essentialist and more inclusive than kinship, since it concerns action not being. But the question before us is not whether the criterion is valuable; the question is whether it is traditional, and I would suggest that this standard is not. Ojibwe identity words *describe* certain behaviors but they do not *prescribe* them. They do not speak of *ethics*. They speak of *ethnics*. If identity were prescriptive in an ethical sense, then it would logically follow that people would lose their identity because of bad behavior, and there is little indication in Ojibwe history that that ever happened—at least not until now: the age of banishment.

Neither appropriate behavior nor essential nature are traditional ideas in Ojibwe culture, at least not historically or linguistically, although both concepts have appeared on the stage of late. But this appearance too, I would suggest, is no more than a symptom of the larger historical issue: Indian identity in crisis. Essential nature soothes the stress of crisis by presenting a stable, timeless, originary point from which Indian identities can be understood to flow; appropriate behavior makes a similar move by connecting identity to socially circumscribed behaviors and possesses the additional benefit of enforcing proper standards of conduct. Both concepts present themselves as traditional answers to modern problems—problems that are very real and pressing, no doubt—but on closer inspection I think these answers seem more modern than traditional.

Perhaps we have come to expect too much from tradition these days, as if it alone could possibly provide answers for all of the complicated problems we face. For reasons that have much to do with the logic of the global market, tradition has become an attractive rallying cry. But perhaps we should acknowledge that whenever we talk about tradition what we are really discussing is culture, thus asking culture to solve problems that are not always cultural in nature. Most of our problems today, including the crisis of identity, have economic, social, or political dimensions that might be lost when we frame them as primarily cultural issues.

Identities, for example, are linked to global operations and flows of capital and information—to casino economies, satellite television, university presses, and more—and they will prove resistant to change by cultural exhortation alone, no matter how innovative those exhortations might be (and Garroutte's work is extremely well-intentioned and thoughtful in this regard). One just doesn't resolve a historical crisis through the use of a few well-placed Ojibwe words.

I don't mean to disable the uses of tradition, which I obviously have a tremendous respect for and interest in preserving; nor do I mean to throw up my hands and suggest that we all sit on our *diiosh* while there's a crisis afoot. What I want to suggest is that a *radix* is awfully difficult to import into the modern world. Traditionalism has long been cloaked in shadow, it retains an undeniably religious veneer, it doesn't easily translate into nontraditional languages like English and rarely fits seamlessly into modern locales like academe. In my upcoming chapter on citizenship, I will humbly suggest that tribal nations throw themselves headlong into modern, not traditional methods of establishing national identities; doing so could promote tradition in ways that academic traditionalists like Garroutte might appreciate. But rather than using tradition to define identities, I would suggest making it work the other way around: defining our identities in ways that promote tradition. Tribal citizenship criteria are the best technologies we have to make that idea a reality, because nations can require what they want to produce. But let's not get ahead of ourselves. We're still in crisis, and if radical indigenism can't point our way out of it, what can?

From Being to Doing

Perhaps the first thing we should do is stop asking the perennial question, what is an Indian? The query itself seems symptomatic of the crisis and probably just reproduces the problem. I would suggest that for analytic purposes we turn our attention instead to the social processes that create intersubjective Indian identities. This would mean a move away from conceptions of Indians as "things" and toward a deeper analysis of Indians as human beings who *do* things—things like asserting identity, defining identity, contesting identity, and so forth—under given historical conditions. One benefit of this shift, which might be characterized as a move from being to doing, would be an opportunity to finally put the question of essentialism behind us. No longer would we feel pressured to defend the unscientific idea that Indians are a "race," or even "kin" related by "blood." Indians would simply be people seen as Indians by other Indians, all definitions intersubjectively produced, all open to scrutiny and debate. Another potential benefit would be a deeper awareness of the historical imperatives leading to the ascendance of particular definitions over others. This historical consciousness might well extend into the future, as scholars and policy makers would more readily consider the long-term consequences of any given definition—for instance, one's grandchildren or the survival of traditional languages and cultures—things not often considered when we ask what an Indian "is." Finally, another benefit could be a counterattack to the genocidal implications that are always inherent in the notion of Indian identity as timeless, stable, eternal, but probably in the minds of most people still "vanishing." Being vanishes. Doing keeps on doing.

Abandoning the question of what an Indian is, we would ask instead what *kinds* of Indian identities are in production during a given historical moment and what is at stake in their making. "It is easy to agree on the fact that . . . all identities are constructed," writes the sociologist Manuel Castells. "The real issue is how, from what, by whom, and for what."[43] In *The Power of Identity*, the second of his three-volume work *The Information Age*, Castells defines identity as "the process of construction of meaning on the basis of a cultural attribute, or related set of cultural attributes, that is/are given priority over other sources of meaning" (6). His thesis is that he "who constructs collective identity, and for what, largely determines the symbolic content of this identity, and its meaning for those identifying with it or placing themselves outside of it" (7). That is to say, our old perennial question is not nearly as important as ascertaining which "cultural attributes" or "sources of meaning" come to define an Indian, who gets to do the selecting, and why some terms become definitive over others. It's about analyzing the controversies and arguments that produce Indian identity and assessing the interests that are served in the process.

Influenced by the great sociologist of social movements, Alain Touraine, Castells identifies three basic types of political identity that are operating around the world today. First, "*legitimizing identity:* introduced by the dominant institutions of society to extend and rationalize their domination *vis à vis* social actors" (8). This kind of identity supports the political status quo because its content legitimizes the parties who are responsible for producing it (for example, the BIA and federally recognized tribal governments, both of which answer to the American government). This is the identity that no one in power has much of a problem with, because it supports their interests. Second, "*resistance identity*: generated by those actors in positions/conditions devalued and/or stigmatized by the logic of domination" (ibid.). Resistance identities define themselves in opposition to the mainstream because the status quo somehow oppresses the people who hold them ("identity politics" comes to mind here). Power usually attacks resistance identity because its content tends to deny its legitimacy. Finally, Castells points to "*project identity*: when social actors, on the basis of whatever cultural materials are available to them, build a new identity that redefines their position in society and, by so doing, seek the transformation of the overall social structure" (ibid.). Project identities emerge when people transcend their local struggles and set their sights on changing the whole world (feminism and environmentalism would both be examples). This identity grows out of resistance identity and almost always becomes an "ism."

Castells believes that all identities are one of these three types, thus all identities are "political," and not simply because they are controversial. They are political because identities are sources of meaning that can be—and always are—placed into the service of power relationships. This is no less true for Native identities than any other, which is to say that we can never speak of Indians as just one thing or apolitical. The same holds true for tribal identities, like "Cherokee" or "Mdewakanton"; these too serve given agendas and take the same three forms. Following Castells, the best we can do is ascertain the extent to which a given assertion of identity—a claim, definition, policy, and so on—resembles a legitimizing, resistance, or project identity, based upon the character of its content, then consider its political and ideological implications. We have to analyze the argument, that is, asking who wins and who loses whenever Indian identity is made.

Legitimizing identity, for example, would not only be the province of the BIA and federally recognized tribal governments—those institutions that authorize Indians to be Indians—it would also include mainstream representations of Indians, for instance, stereotypes in schoolbooks or old Hollywood films. Yes, your typical tribally enrolled, phenotypically correct Indian automatically shares something meaningful with Disney's Pocahontas: a political function. As two sources of Indian meaning, both federal recognition and stereotypes produce the kinds of Indians that the dominant society ultimately approves of, because both in turn legitimize the dominant institutions in our society. Maybe you think that's a perfectly fine thing and maybe not; it really depends on how content you are with the status quo.

Legitimizing Indian identities were articulated in early writings and speeches by Natives such as Elias Boudinot, Sarah Winnemucca Hopkins, Charles Alexander Eastman, plus a host of white reform groups, who all pursued assimilation as a goal.[44] Consider these lofty words of the Ojibwe George Copway from his 1850 book *The Traditional History and Characteristic Sketches of the Ojibway Nation:* "Education and Christianity are to the Indian what wings are to the eagle. They elevate him; and these given to him by men of right views of existence enable him to rise above the soil of degradation, and hover about the high mounts of wisdom and truth."[45] This is saturated with "Indian" imagery—eagles soaring around mountains of truth—invoking a "Native" aesthetic while simultaneously calling for assimilation. But it was no contradiction. Copway's invention wasn't any less real or authentic than any other identity; it was the making of a new legitimizing identity for Natives, one that did in fact come into widespread existence and reinforced American imperialism. Imperialism needed Indians to assimilate, and it legitimized them—and was in turn legitimized by them—when they did.

Castells believes that identities always produce something else in society, and in the case of legitimizing identity, civil society is the thing that's made. It is indeed interesting to note how most nineteenth- and early-twentieth-century Native writers and orators were supported by numerous American civic associations, from church congregations to the Lake Mohonk Conference to the Society of American Indians, although I'm guessing Castells might think it more accurate to suggest the obverse: that Native writers and orators actually produced these groups (think of Elias Boudinot's Philadelphia church audience, listening to him, feeling moved, sympathizing, forming an organization . . .). Is this a bad thing? Again, it really depends on your perception of the status quo, but we can see that one troubling characteristic of civil society—as seen in the work of Gramsci, Althusser, Foucault, Weber, and others who have described its propensity for internalized domination—is its tendency to uphold the status quo by serving as a release valve for social pressures that always build in contexts of obvious inequality.[46] On this view, groups like the Lake Mohonk Conference, totally earnest and well-meaning reformers who agitated tirelessly for Indian justice, can in fact legitimate a system of Indian injustice by demonstrating through their dissent that society is ultimately just. The civic organizations that supported Indian boarding schools would be another example—all of those well-intentioned associations formed in part under the leadership and rhetorical vision of Indian advocates like Copway, who was without question an Indian, not in spite of his assimilationism, but ironically because of it.

Radical resistance to political hegemony doesn't happen until a group formulates a resistance identity. In Indian history this form of identity would characterize not only the participants of the Ghost Dance and other pan-Indian cultural resistance movements but also the Red Power groups of the 1960s and 1970s. One leader of the American Indian Movement, Dennis Banks, illustrates the logic of a resistance identity in a statement that in a roundabout fashion answers Copway. Remember, for Copway assimilation was a means of helping Indians soar like the eagle. For Banks, by contrast,

> An eagle is an eagle, still practicing the ways of its ancestors. . . . The buffalo still teaches its young and the salmon still travels the thousands of miles to spawn its future generations. If we Native People are to survive as a cultural species, then we must follow the way of our ancestors. We must continue to sing the songs and have ceremonies to welcome each day. Like the eagle . . . we must never abandon our old ways. Those ways have been good to us and they will provide us with direction for our future generations. Like an eagle flying high, we are who we are. Still strong![47]

This is no argument for assimilation but its exact opposite: a resistance identity speaking back to the dominant society. It works with the same imagery that Copway employed—soaring Indian eagles—but now they are very different birds. Both are Ojibwe "eagles," however, both are Indian identities, yet doing different political work in different eras: one legitimizing the status quo, the other resisting it. Both are "Indian."

Unlike legitimizing identities producing civil society, resistance identities produce communities. Thus we recognize not only the many community-based occupations of the Red Power years—from Alcatraz to the "Native American Embassy" to the Independent Oglala Nation—but also the hard demographic fact that since Red Power urban Indians have been returning to their reservations. Usually removed by a generation or two, these reservation returnees have spent the past few decades developing tribal colleges, starting language revitalization programs, reviving old ceremonies, and pursuing other kinds of community renewal, making not revolution so much as a significant transformation of their homelands. These initiatives are usually grassroots to the core, legitimizing not the status quo but radical change, including a desire to create a traditionalist society. What's more, these community activists pursue this work not as civic do-gooders but *as Indians*. It's a way of being who they want to be and resisting the legitimizing identities that drove many away from reservations in the first place. There is probably no better example than the Los Angeles–born, Jewish-Ojibwe activist Winona LaDuke, who upon her graduation from Harvard moved home and established the visionary White Earth Land Recovery Project.

Finally, recent years have witnessed the development of an emergent project identity. Project identity produces a subject—"the collective social actor through which individuals reach holistic meaning in their experience"[48]—which we find in that growing global movement called indigenism. Subjects transcend the local and seek to transform the world. Promoting indigenous culture in opposition to neoliberalism and "settler culture," indigenism seeks a life where power is decentralized and people live in harmony with the natural world and each other. It focuses on ecological sustainability, collective land rights, the primacy of Native ways of knowing and indigenous values, and the political virtues of "respectful coexistence."[49] Articulated by Evo Morales of Bolivia, Rigoberta Menchú of Guatemala, Oren Lyons and the late John Mohawk of the Haudenosaunee Confederacy, and others around the "indigenous world" (the phrase itself is evidence of indigenism), the indigenist subject argues that two irreconcilable worldviews are at war—quoting LaDuke, "indigenous or industrial . . . land based or predator"[50]—and seeks to dismantle neoliberalism and imperialism on a planetary scale. It does not seek secession from settler states, but it does pursue sovereignty and self-determination for the many tribal peoples who constitute the concept.

The face of indigenist identity is not brown or in any other way associated with phenotype or skin. Its most persistent image has been a black ski mask. We have seen these masks at Oka and other sites of indigenous struggle as well as every mass protest against economic globalization to date, but nowhere has this face become more iconic than among the Zapatistas of Chiapas, Mexico, when donned by their enigmatic leader Subcomandante Marcos. Who is Marcos? As the masked man himself put it in 1995,

> Marcos is gay in San Francisco, a black in South Africa, Asian in Europe, a Chicano in San Isidro, an anarchist in Spain, a Palestinian in Israel, an indigenous person in the streets of San Cristóbal, a gang member in Neza, a rocker on campus, a Jew in Germany, ombudsman in the sedana, feminist in political parties, Communist in the post–Cold

War era, prisoner in Cinalapa, pacifist in Bosnia . . . Marcos is every undulated, oppressed, exploited minority that is resisting and saying "Enough!"[51]

This is project identity: historically ambitious, globally connected, radically inclusive, and passionately geared toward justice and social change. Naturally, people invested in the world as it is will attempt to delegitimize this subject by shifting identity back to safer ground, just as the Mexican government tried to do in 1995 when it "outed" Marcos as a bourgeois white man who came not from the mountains but actually from a comfortable university professorship. It didn't work. In response to this revelation (which isn't quite the same thing as American-style ethnic fraud given the absence of a personal economic motive), thousands of Indians and indigenist sympathizers descended upon Mexico City wearing ski masks and shouting *"¡Todos somos Marcos!"* "We are all Marcos!"[52]

Indigenism is identity politics of a different sort and needs a different face. As the Subcomandante once explained, "Marcos does not even have a face . . . if they kill me, someone else can put on the mask and say they're Marcos. This way there will always be a Marcos."[53] There will always be Indians too, but this identity might assume a different character. In 1995, Antonio Hernández Cruz, a Tojolabal Indian and secretary-general of the State Indigenous and Campesino Council of Chiapas, interestingly observed, "there is more awareness of our identity. Many people now— even those that are not Indian—call themselves Indian people."[54] *It's too bad assimilation didn't go the other way.* It's worth noting that Cruz was tortured by the Mexican military for supporting the Zapatista uprising, not because he was an Indian—for that he was merely disdained—but because he was an indigenist and thereby thought to possess a dangerous new consciousness. This same consciousness might also explain Cruz's apparent lack of prejudice concerning "new" Indians, as if in his view more Indians would actually be the merrier.

These three forms of identity—legitimizing, resistance, and project— undergird all identity politics, and they deserve attention as we study assertions of Indian identity. One implication of this model is the recognition that Indian identity is never static or singular but always dynamic and multiple. Another is the possibility of rapid transformation from one identity to another. (Remember that old joke about Tonto and the Lone Ranger being surrounded by hostile Indians? The Lone Ranger says, "Well, Tonto, it looks like we've finally reached the end of our road," to which Tonto replies, "What do you mean we, paleface?" Sometimes the transformation can be as rapid as that.) A third implication is that there is a dialectic between political desire and Indian identity, the one influencing the other in a relationship that is rarely if ever mutually exclusive. However, I do not want to suggest that any of these identities is inherently positive or negative. It would be a bad mistake to assume, say, that legitimizing identities are always stodgy endorsements of all that is bad in one's society, for they also legitimize the things that people enjoy about the status quo. Similarly, resistance identity has no inherent value other than the fact that it opposes the status quo, and that opposition can emerge in the form of reaction as much as resistance; after all, "white power" groups and religious fundamentalists are resistance identities too. And the same can be said for project identities, a rubric that captures not only indigenism but also the missionary zeal of Christianity, the "white man's burden" of Civilization, and imperialist tendencies of Soviet-style Communism. One should be careful not to be swept away by an identity that seems cooler than another simply because it defines itself against the status quo. That said, this model is useful to the extent that it allows us to have these discussions in the first place, distinguishing political desires and actions from each other rather than talking about an identity that supposedly "is" and by implication must always be. Sorting out the good from the bad in all three categories will be an important task for intellectuals to pursue in the future.

"Indian"

Shifting scholarly analysis from being to doing requires us to disabuse ourselves of another idea whose critical potential has most likely run its course: the notion that, as Robert F. Berkhofer Jr. articulates it in *The White Man's Indian* (1978), "the *Indian* was a White invention and still remains largely a White image."[55] This lesson guides thinkers as diverse as the postmodernist Gerald Vizenor and the nationalist Taiaiake Alfred, and it offers a valuable historical perspective while making a fine pedagogical point; that is, it is true that *Indian*—a category reducing tremendous cultural, linguistic, and geographic diversity to a single, all-encompassing word—was Columbus's great misnomer. In those days *India* was a synonym for all of Asia east of the Indus River, and *Indios* referred to the peoples of Asia. After Columbus, *Indios* was applied generally to the peoples of the New World; "for so caule wee all nations of the new founde lands," wrote Gonzalo Fernández de Oviedo y Valdés in *De la natural hystoria de las Indias* in 1526.[56] As is clearly revealed in Berkhofer's classic treatise, the idea of the *Indian* came with a tremendous amount of European baggage and set into motion some persistent themes: "(1) generalizing from one tribe's society and culture to all Indians, (2) conceiving of Indians in terms of their deficiencies according to White ideals rather than in terms of their own various cultures, and (3) using moral evaluation as description of Indians."[57] *Indian* rode on the back of another set of European ideas—savagism and civilization—which increasingly provided content for the term. The English called the Natives "savage" (or "salvage") until the seventeenth century and the French employed *sauvage* until the nineteenth (and indeed I was called a savage to my face by a French person less than a decade ago, and it was not intended as an insult). Savage, *sauvage, salvaticho,* and other variations all descend from the Latin word *silvaticus,* referring to someone who lived in the forest and retained a kind of "animalistic" lifestyle: a primitive person, or a *wilder Mann* in German parlance. By the time Americans arrived on the scene, most everyone in the white world understood what *Indian* meant. It meant savage, not civilized, not part of civilization, and not white. *Indian* represented the lack of things that defined civilized whiteness: reason, democracy, science, enlightenment, literacy, law, and a true religion. It wasn't good to be an Indian, regardless of how "noble" one may have been, because *Indian* was defined by deficiency.

Thus we should not be surprised that people called Indians today often resent the term, preferring instead to use their own particular names to describe themselves: Ojibwe, Cherokee, Mdewakanton, or at least when it seems appropriate to do so. Folks will argue over terms like "Indian," "Native," "American Indian," "Native American," "indigenous," and "aboriginal" in an effort to best characterize pan-Indian or pan-indigenous identities, and I have no particular stake in that ongoing debate. (I generally use the words *Indian* and *Native* when referring to indigenous peoples of North America, *Native* and *indigenous* to refer to the Fourth World in a more global sense, and tribal names to refer to specific communities and cultures.) The reclamation of tribally specific names and debates over the best English words for describing pan-Native populations are indicative of our desire to free identity from old European understandings that defined it by deficiency. It is a reasonable desire, and Native intellectuals have advanced sophisticated theories to put it into action. As his term implies, Gerald Vizenor's "postindian" conceives of the *indian* (he never capitalizes the word) as a white theoretical concept, while the "post" indicates what comes after the white invention. "The postindian arises from the earlier inventions of the tribes only to contravene the absence of the real with theatrical performances," he writes; "the theater of tribal consciousness is the recreation of the real, not the absence of the real in the simulations of dominance."[58] Indian identity is always a performance, and a postindian inflects his or her performance with either "survivance" or "dominance." In a rather different discourse, Taiaiake Alfred argues against what he calls "aboriginalism," "the ideology and identity of assimilation" by which Native people accept an identity that is no more than "a legal and social construction of the state" and thus amounts to a "silent surrender" of one's "real" identity: "The acceptance of being aboriginal is as powerful an assault on Onkwehonwe existences as any force of arms."[59] Although their politics couldn't be farther apart, Vizenor and Alfred theorize from the same basic starting point: the idea that *Indian* (or "aboriginal") is a white invention that any good warrior should try to evade. For Vizenor, that's achieved through simulating survivance, not dominance; for Alfred, it happens through active resistance to assimilation and the strong reclamation of traditions. Both would agree that *Indian* is not an Indian idea. It's a discourse that lands in Indian space but does not emanate from what I earlier called the tribal private.

Denying the Indianness of *Indian*—or, to put it another way, asking Indians to stop being *Indians*—is the sort of argument that makes a great deal of sense in theory but runs into great difficulty when attempting to put it into practice. It is hard, if not impossible, to find an Indian who does not use the term to describe himself or herself from time to time, and the same holds true for specific tribal communities as well. "Indigenous" as a globalized political term for the peoples of the Fourth World received a significant shot of power in 2007 when the United Nations passed the Declaration on the Rights of Indigenous Peoples, a document largely drafted by "indigenous" people and lacking signs of the sort of state-sponsored assimilation that concerns Alfred. (Vizenor, I'm guessing, appreciates its simulations of survivance, not dominance.) Insofar as we don't wish to say that *Indian* identities as they are claimed and lived out by actually existing people—and have been for more than five centuries—are no more than a script written by colonizers, we might want to hesitate before protesting too much than *Indian* is a white invention.

More to my point, I want to suggest that *Indian* was not an exclusively non-Indian invention. There is an entire history, albeit largely obscured and oral, of commentary on this particular term on the Indian side of the equation, and it started as soon as Europeans began arriving to the New World. As Roger Williams writes in "A Key into the Language of America" (1643), local Indians "often asked me, why we call them Indians, natives, etc. And understanding the reason, they will call themselves Indians, in opposition to English, etc."[60] From the Indian point of view, *Indian* seems to have been an acceptable word to adopt in order to distinguish themselves "in opposition to English, etc." and lacking the ideological weight of the English meaning of the word.

Those etceteras in Williams's text seem important as well, because they suggest the sense of larger identities growing out of smaller ones. Williams says as much in his "Key," which opens with "names": "First, those of the English giving: as natives, savages, Indians, wildmen (so the Dutch call them *wilden*), Abergeny [aboriginal] men, pagans, barbarians, heathen." These are standard fare in discussions of the white man's *Indian*, but Williams also tells of "two sorts of names" the Natives used for themselves: "First, general, belonging to all natives, such as Nínnuock, Ninnimissinnúwock, Eniskeetompaúwog, which signifies Men, Folk, or People. Secondly, particular names, peculiar to several nations, of them amongst themselves, as Nanhiggannêuck, Massachusêuck, Cawasumsêuck, Cowwesêuck, Quintikóock, Quinnipiêuck, Pequttóg, etc."[61] There were names for smaller local ethnic groups, and there were names for larger groups that emerged from the smaller. As with *anishinaabeg*, *Indian* signified people who were not new to this land. As with *ini(i)wag* (an Ojibwe cognate to "Nínnuock" meaning "men" and sometimes "people"), there was another understanding of "Men, Folk, or People" generally. Meanwhile, the names "peculiar to several nations" had their meanings as well. One can imagine the sorts of discussions that would emerge from there—and we will have to imagine them—but however they played out, they were contributions to the meaning of *Indian*, at least for Indians. In any case, it seems inaccurate to say that *Indian* was *purely* a white invention. This is not to contest Berkhofer, Vizenor, Alfred, or anyone offering a critique of the damaging *Indian* idea that emerged in 1492, only a reminder that it was never a stable signifier and Indians played a role in its making. I'd call it an x-mark.

Why Don't You Speak for Yourself?

That Indian identity is in crisis should surprise no one, given all that's transpired since 1492. That Indian identity conflicts are so fraught with acrimony and divisiveness seems symptomatic of a wide array of problems, from personal insecurities to the decline of tribal languages to conflicts over dwindling (or surging) resources, but these too must be understood as products of history and not a death knell for Native identity. This crisis isn't genocide. We fight over identity because we know that the meanings of Indianness—those all-important "cultural attributes"—are not only human inventions but irreducibly slippery, unstable, and always open to contest. Saying so is not to diminish their worth; to the contrary, it attests to the creative possibilities that exist in our own historical moment, and in ourselves, to make good decisions. Future definitions of Indian identity should (and will) be made by Indian people. In this time when pretensions to purity and dreams of disconnection have become both impossible and undesirable, those definitions will be x-marks, and the identities will be too. So make your x-mark, and make it a good one.

What does it mean to make a good x-mark in the realms of Indian identity? For one, I hope the day has passed when Indians will always be held in contempt of culture for thinking about identity in terms that are not always traditional. It seems logical and fair, for example, to allow for characterizations of Indianness as a "racial" identity, even though it seems just as logical and fair to remark on the scientific fact that "race" doesn't exist in any biological sense. To speak of race as socially constructed means more than saying that it's not really real; it means its existence is a social construction. I see no reason why Indians can't use this European concept as a means of recognizing Indian identity in this race-obsessed society (even though that means ushering in a whole new set of potentially icky issues). Now, this should not be misinterpreted as an endorsement of nineteenth-century scientific racism, nor, for that matter, an endorsement of the strange Nike N7 Air Native (supposedly the first shoe designed for "the Native American foot").[62] And this is definitely not an argument for blood quantum, which is one of the most fraught ideas operating in Indian country today. All I'm saying is that it seems fair game to claim the idea of race—or blood, or phenotype, or enrollment, and so on—as a definition of Indian identity, just as it is equally fair to adamantly object in the name of traditionalist standards (ethnicity, proximity, political allegiance, etc.). None of these meanings or materials is any purer than any other, although some are clearly older. All are constructions; all can be legitimizing, resistance, or subject identities depending on their particular contexts and uses. Making an x-mark means more than just embracing new or foreign ideas as your own; it means consciously connecting those ideas to certain values, interests, and political objectives, and making the best call you can under conditions not of your making. So, the next time some Indian identity controversy rears up and someone asks you for an answer to the perennial question, consider what's at stake and make the best x-mark you can.

On our worst days, when the Indian identity wars take their heaviest ca-
sualties, we would do well to recall how far we've already come. After all,
it wasn't so long ago, just 1962, that Frell Owl, Eastern Band Cherokee, a
lifetime BIA employee and former superintendent at Fort Hall, could define
Indian identities in such a problematic manner as this (from an article titled
"Who and What Is an American Indian?"):

> A tribal member is an "enrolled Indian." An Indian who is not a
> tribal member is a "non-enrolled Indian." A non-Indian is a person
> who does not possess Indian blood. "Full-blood" means pure Indian.
> One who is part Indian and part non-Indian is a "mixed-blood" or
> "breed." An Indian is generally regarded as a "ward" of the United
> States. An Indian who can manage personal affairs without help of
> Government workers is a "competent Indian." One who needs help
> in managing personal affairs is "incompetent." "Reservation Indian"
> may indicate residence on a reservation or it may indicate the degree
> of acculturation attained by an Indian. A reliable, honest, industrious
> person is a "good Indian." One who is unreliable and constantly
> in trouble with the law is a "bad Indian." A person who has been
> converted to Christianity is a "Christian Indian." One who adheres
> to native religious ceremonies is a "pagan" or "heathen" Indian.
> Prior to 1924, a "citizen Indian" was a member of a special group
> of Indians. The President of the United States is "Great White Father."
> A "White Indian" is a person whose degree of Indian blood is small.
> An acculturated Indian may also be called a "White Indian."[63]

There may be no better example of a legitimizing Indian identity. Yet this
paternalistic discourse was doomed from the very moment of its utterance, for around the very same time young Red Power activists began
articulating a new resistance identity, and from that emerged a powerful
new indigenist identity still in the process of articulation today. If one
conclusion to be drawn is a sense of relief that Indian identity is no longer
stuck in old imperial ruts, surely another is the importance of speaking
for yourself. That's what my daughter did on the powwow grounds, and
it made a difference.

CHAPTER TWO

Culture and Its Cops

In 1961, 420 Indians representing sixty-seven nations held a small but historic conference at the University of Chicago. The American Indian Chicago Conference discussed numerous aspects of Indian life, formed policy resolutions, established work committees, set agendas, and catalyzed the creation of the National Indian Youth Council, an early Red Power group. One important product of the Chicago conference was its "Declaration of Indian Purpose," a little manifesto that anticipated— perhaps launched is a better word—what we now recognize to be an indigenous cultural revival. Boldly asserting the "right to choose our own way of life," the declaration defined Indian life in cultural terms and proclaimed its need of protection: "Since our Indian culture is slowly being absorbed by the American society, we believe we have the responsibility of preserving our precious heritage." As is often the case with such daunting responsibilities, this one came with an "inherent right":

> We believe in the inherent right of all people to retain spiritual and
> cultural values, and that the free exercise of these values is necessary
> to the normal development of any people. Indians exercised this
> inherent right to live their own lives for thousands of years before the
> white man came and took their lands. It is a more complex world in
> which Indians live today, but the Indian people who first settled the
> New World and built the great civilizations which only now are being
> dug out of the past, long ago demonstrated that they could master
> complexity.[1]

Notice in this statement how the right to protect culture is understood to be inherent, but the culture itself is not. What hath been given can easily be taken away, or "absorbed," or maybe just forgotten, because culture is assumed to be a vulnerable social construct. Notice as well that culture is described not in terms of specific practices or ceremonies but as "values." This wasn't an exhortation of religious principles or a call for converts, just a general defense of ideas that Native societies considered good, right, and desirable. Finally, notice how these unspecified values were deemed to be necessary for normal human "development," a condition assumed to be shared by all people but the "free exercise" of which was impeded for Indians. Characterizing culture in these ways, the "Declaration of Indian Purpose" situated its defense within the universal discourse of human rights. No longer would Native culture be treated nostalgically like some relic teetering on the edge of history's ash can. No, culture was a signifier of "complexity," proof positive of "great civilizations" past, but in need of active protection.

Written during a historical moment we can locate between global decolonization movements on the one hand, and the American civil rights era on the other, and marking the transition of federal Indian policy eras (from Termination to Self-Determination), the "Declaration of Indian Purpose" was an early example of a particular line of reasoning that would be articulated by Natives for decades to come: namely, that indigenous cultures are good, but endangered, thus in need of protection. From that point forward, armed with inherent rights in one hand and precious cultures in the other, Indian activism, including that of the National Indian Youth Council and other Red Power groups, marched vigorously throughout the turbulent sixties and seventies and brought everyone (some kicking and screaming) into the Indian movement. For all our talk today about ancient tribal traditions and the purported powers of the past, we should acknowledge that it was mainly political activism, not some inherent staying power in culture itself, that gave birth to our cultural revival.

After all, traditional culture was on the ropes. As my father recalls it, during the fifties Ojibwe culture at Leech Lake was widely discredited and nearly dead: "We were told that ceremonies were places of devil worship or drug taking. No one really wanted to be Indian." Charles Trimble has written about kids "in the Indian boarding school I attended and in my home village on the Pine Ridge Reservation through the 1940s and '50s [who] wished sometimes that we were not Indian at all." Culture had a lot to do with it: "That came perhaps from seeing movies and reading books in which the white guys always won, had all the money, nice cars and girls. Indians were always the bad guys, killing innocent settlers who only wanted us dead and our land theirs." It was attended by economic disempowerment and racism: "in most towns on the reservation, the stores and other businesses were owned by whites. In reservation border towns, we often faced discrimination. In short, our futures sometimes didn't look all that promising as Indians." As one might expect, young Indians responded by adopting the culture and identity of the dominant: "we bought into what was being pushed on us anyway—assimilation—and we acted out what was expected of us to . . . fit into the larger society."[2] My father used to play cowboys and Indians in Bena, "and everybody wanted to be the cowboys." So much for tradition. Indian activism of the sixties and seventies changed these attitudes, however, instilling new pride in cultural traditions and leading to the restoration of lodges, languages, and beliefs. One could do a lot worse than date the beginnings of that rather noteworthy shift in attitude around 1961.

We are still experiencing this cultural revival. Indigenous cultures are now being brought back in force, and for once this seems to be something that nearly everyone supports. Our current cultural revival, which is by no means an American Indian phenomenon but a genuinely globalized indigenous movement, is pursued in four basic ways. First, through heritage language revitalization, as seen in the development of new immersion schools, bilingual education, adult education courses, and "language tables" and "language nests" in places like New Zealand, Canada, and the United States. Second, through ceremonial renewal—the return of dormant practices—sometimes through "ethnological feedback" and the (always controversial) translation of ceremonies into English. Third, in everyday life practices, such as the giving of Indian names and seasonal feasts, traditional child rearing, fasting, dream analysis, and the conscious consumption of traditional foods. Fourth, in academic indigenization, as seen in innovative new scholarship on tribal law,[3] Native science,[4] indigenous political theory,[5] "tribally-specific aesthetics,"[6] decolonized research methodologies,[7] as well as the ongoing introduction of Native culture to academic social environments (for instance, campus powwows and Indian clubs). Heritage language revitalization, ceremonial renewal, everyday life practices, and academic indigenization: these are the dominant sites where indigenous culture revivifies today.

This is all, for the most part, an excellent development. Who wouldn't support the revival of Native cultures? They typically promote sustainability, produce happiness and equality, and are usually geared toward inclusion and justice. Traditional knowledge and philosophies, especially those concerned with environmental concerns, and democratic action are immensely valuable. And it is no small matter to detect a growing sense of pride in Native communities that for centuries have been among the most fragile in the world. Through our current cultural revival, imperialism is resisted, development is pursued, independence is growing, and people's lives are improving. For these reasons alone Native cultures are most definitely worth reviving.

That said, as with all cultural revivals around the world and across the ages, ours carries potential problems. For one, history has proven time and again that the revival of cultural traditions can be used to oppress individuals or groups, especially minorities and women. For another, cultural revivals possess a peculiar tendency to head directly for the political sphere of communities, attempting to put into policy ideas and practices that are best left at church, synagogue, temple, mosque, or lodge. Cultural revivals forged in colonial or postcolonial contexts can pursue certain activities at the cost of other worthy initiatives, especially those deemed "secular" or "Western," such as science education or human rights protections. Sometimes revivals can deny the hybridity and interactions inherent in all cultures. Finally, cultural revivals can actually work against the positive self-esteem that one would reasonably expect to result from the proud reclamation of traditions. This can happen when cultural elites emerge and relentlessly "correct" their peers or decry certain cultural forms as "inauthentic." Let's call these folks "culture cops."

Every reservation has its culture cops—at Leech Lake they were also called "Talibanishinaabe"—and they are not the same thing as "elders." Elders are bearers of traditional knowledge who are recognized in the community as preservers of languages, ceremonies, stories, and songs that were endangered during those decades when people were moved away from them. Culture cops are enthusiastic reclaimers of culture, often young, male, and educated, frequently with urban roots, who straddle a fine line between support and condemnation in the name of cultural revival. Like elders, they passionately believe in the power and worth of traditional culture, but they possess a certain inflexibility and zeal that one doesn't often encounter with elders. Culture cops are not the same thing as teachers or critics, although they usually engage in both teaching and criticizing; what distinguishes them are the *judgments* they make upon that hapless lot deemed less than culturally competent, as well as their overarching claims to possess an absolute truth. They are, to cut to the chase, something like religious fundamentalists, defining cultures as timeless, static, pure, and above all else literal. Their understandings of culture differ substantially from the articulations one normally hears espoused by elders—including, I will later argue, the particular articulation of the elders that was recorded in the "Declaration of Indian Purpose."

I want to interrogate the idea of culture in the context of revival and the presence of cops. What is Native culture? Is it a coherent body of specific beliefs and practices owned by a given group of people? Who has the authority to determine what counts as culture, and how are such determinations put to use? What are the potential dangers of cultural revival? Is it ever used to oppress or exclude people? Does it endanger political freedoms or claims to sovereignty? Finally, how can we understand our current cultural revival historically? Are we truly answering the call of the American Indian Chicago Conference, or are we doing something entirely different? To address these questions, let's board the Good Ship Culture and make a few stops along the way. We'll start with the culture that gave us "culture"—and that would be Europe, I'm afraid, because culture is a European idea and word (which is not, of course, to say that only Europeans have culture). From there we will sail back home to examine the language of culture as it appears in certain "culture words" of *Ojibwemowin*, and we'll examine some Indian culture wars featuring cops of various stripes. Our little voyage of exploration will conclude with a brief consideration of culture understood as specific beliefs and practices versus a more general system of *values*, the latter being in my view a more traditional—and politically desirable—understanding of this complex modern concept.

The Nature of Culture

Before there was culture there was nature. Both culture and nature are human ideas, and both started out as verbs before becoming nouns. Nature originated in the Latin *natura*, signifying the processes of birth; it has referred ever since to that which is "innate," the word being one of *natura*'s etymological descendants (along with "natality" and "native"). Nature was that quality or force that existed inside something and revealed its essential character; simultaneously it referred to the material world, with or without people, which was likewise filled with certain qualities or forces. By contrast, "culture" comes from the Latin *colere*, signifying the activities of nurturing, caring for something, tending to it, and subsequently bettering it. *Colere* additionally meant "honor with worship" (which is why culture gave us "cults") and "inhabit" (*colere* also gives us "colonies"). But the dominant meaning of *colere* was to nurture. What was nurtured was nature itself: in fact, the nurture of nature *was* culture. This was the stuff of agriculture, a manipulation of nature to produce a desirable outcome—like a crop—which may explain why nature and culture (not to mention nature and nurture) are typically opposed. It also reveals why we have long thought of culture as an engine of personal "growth." Just as a farmer made agriculture by planting, tending, and improving crops that used to grow on their own "naturally," so too could a person become cultured through educational and civilizing processes.

During the modern era, culture became eminently more complex. For one, culture changed from a verb, to a modifying noun of process, to a more generalized abstraction altogether. Until the eighteenth century, English speakers would normally specify the particular thing that culture cultivated (for instance, "the culture of their minds"), but eventually folks came to speak of culture as an independent noun (e.g., "the advantage of culture"). It had moved, in other words, from signifying something someone did to something someone had. Further, as Raymond Williams explains, during that same eighteenth century understandings of culture elaborated ancient notions of nurturance in three basic ways.[8] First, culture turned on the notion of civility: a concept that captured the important difference between politely chastising someone and punching him or her in the nose. Restraint of one's "natural" impulses was implied in this understanding, as culture indicated a sense of proper decorum; it also contributed to the development of "civil law." Second, culture became synonymous with civilization, a concept imbued with connotations of progress, so culture became a teleological affair. Culture as civilization implied that humanity was leaving something uncivilized and uncultured behind as it progressed toward a more civil state of existence: a new world of which most humans were yet tragically unaware, especially "savages" who lived in the "state of nature."

These eighteenth-century shifts in thinking—from process to product, and from civility to civilization—left little room for a notion of "Native culture." Rather, Indians were thought to lack culture completely. This is not to suggest that eighteenth-century Europeans thought of culture as just one universal thing, however. In Germany, Johann Gottfried von Herder championed what we would now call cultural relativism, arguing that the *Volk* of any nation possessed a *Kultur* of its own that could be accessed through folktales, mythologies, music, dance, craft, art, and social customs, and this was by no means to be denigrated as lesser: "What one nation holds indispensable to the circle of its thoughts has never entered into the mind of a second, and by a third has been deemed injurious."[9]

They're just different! Along with Wilhelm von Humboldt, Herder initiated a line of inquiry that would eventually become the twentieth century's
Sapir-Whorf hypothesis—the idea that language determines thought—
and it was securely fastened to the concept of the nation. The *Kultur* of a
remote Germanic village could be viewed as the foundation of "national
spirit" that differed meaningfully from, say, that of the French.[10] Herder's
work inspired the labors of people like the Brothers Grimm, who traveled
the Black Forest to collect rural folktales and other evidence of a national
Kultur, just as one might expect an indigenous nationalist to collect tribal
tales and songs for similar reasons today.

So there was culture as civility, then culture as civilization, then *Kultur*
as distinct national spirit or civilizations in the plural. We've already
come a long way from *colere,* but culture wouldn't stop there. Williams's
third sense of modern culture was associated with the seismic political
shifts of the nineteenth century, when culture morphed from a synonym
for civilization to its antonym; that is, civilization became a disease and
culture was the cure. The Romantics found in the concept of culture an
antidote to a depressing, dangerous, and dehumanizing bourgeois society
that lacked the nurturance of culture. On this view, industrialization, ur-
banization, and widening class divisions threatened to wipe out human
creativity and individuality through mechanization and exploitation (basically, the logic of the factory), so culture became a weapon to deploy
against those deadening impulses. "The more actual civilization appears
predatory and debased," Terry Eagleton writes in regard to this view, "the
more the idea of culture is forced into a critical attitude. *Kulturkritik* is
at war with civilization rather than at one with it."[11] So the Romantics
romanticized—the poor, the rural, the natural, the way things used to
be, and the cultural imagination—all the while bemoaning the historical
development of industrial capitalism. In this context, savages appeared
"noble" and peasant folk were transformed into unlikely symbols of
freedom. "Civilization was abstract, alienated, fragmented, mechanistic,
utilitarian, in thrall to a crass faith in material progress," Eagleton writes,
while "culture was holistic, organic, sensuous, autotelic, recollective. The
conflict between culture and civilization thus belonged to a full-blown quar-
rel between tradition and modernity."[12]

Yet in many respects it was a bogus battle. While the Romantics promoted the powers of the imagination over the death drives of civilization,
others were theorizing culture as a means of solidifying the status quo. In
the face of increasing social unrest, Matthew Arnold's 1869 treatise *Culture
and Anarchy* attempted to quell emergent class conflict by defining culture

in a way that made it seem more like religion than art (by this time the two spheres were becoming difficult to distinguish). Arnold wanted to establish a class-transcending common culture that would place everyone on the same symbolic terrain that religion used to provide. Arnold's idea of culture was "a *study of perfection*," one that would "do away with classes; to make the best that has been thought and known in the world current everywhere; to make all men live in an atmosphere of sweetness and light."[13] Sweetness and light was certainly preferable to revolutions and guillotines, so in Arnold's view a cultural figure like Shakespeare, who could be provided to the masses by way of public education, wouldn't compel readers to question things like structural social inequalities so much as give people a common symbology to share across classes. In this way, culture would save civilization through the establishment of schools that taught "the best that has been thought and known," while simultaneously providing England with a coherent ideology for social control that would stave off "anarchy."

Meanwhile, on this side of the Atlantic a new breed of American thinker was theorizing the relationship between culture and civilization in yet another way. In the political context of a westward-ho American empire whose frontiers had not yet closed, the concept of "cultural evolution" was offered up by ethnologists like Lewis Henry Morgan, positing the West as the pinnacle of human development and proclaiming that everyone's cultures proceeded through the same evolutionary stages until civilization would finally be attained by all. Morgan proposed a developmental scheme that moved from "savagery" to "barbarism" to "civilization," each with its "lower," "middle," and "upper" stages, using technological signposts like the acquisition of fire and alphabetic literacy to chart the evolution of culture.[14] On this view civilization—or Civilization with a capital C—was the goal, and culture was the thing that had to change in order to realize it. Spiritually related to the project of cultural evolution was the "scientific racism" of Robert Knox, Josiah Clark Nott, Samuel Morton, and others who tried to create elaborate taxonomies of "racial" differences and then ranked the races' capacities for Civilization.[15] Not everybody would become civilized, they believed, because not all races were fully human. Some were actually considered different species.

It wasn't until the twentieth century that Franz Boas and his students found this sort of hierarchical reasoning both scientifically flawed and morally reprehensible.[16] In opposition to this now-obvious ethnocentrism (especially the kind that beat a path to racial theories), the Boasians developed a new cultural anthropology that maintained a basic respect for all peoples, while making a more rigorous science out of anthropology. Boas advanced certain beliefs still embraced by most anthropologists today: empiricism, but not the kind that leaps too hastily to the making of scientific laws; ethnography, the kind requiring one to actually learn the local language and work closely with native collaborators; and a new notion of culture as fluid, dynamic, historical, and lacking well-defined boundaries. For Boas, culture could be described in evolutionary terms, but not in the ways the cultural evolutionists proposed. He understood cultural evolution in the same way that Darwin understood natural evolution, as life adapting to material environmental conditions. After Boas, it became unseemly to disparage other people's culture, much less their race, and one tended to think of culture more historically than before. Civilization lost its capital C, too.

In our own time, multiple definitions of culture abound. Everyone is interested in culture now, and with so many theories of culture around one scarcely knows where to begin criticizing them. Making matters all the more confusing, many of the new cultural theories seem invested in the hunch that there is apparently something deeply political at stake in culture, something having to do with terrorism or global wars. In what appears to be our dominant understanding of culture today—well, not dominant for anthropologists perhaps, but probably for most politicians, pundits, and the general populace—those things we call cultures are somehow responsible for the emergence of a "clash of civilizations." This ubiquitous phrase and the theory of culture that supports it belong to Samuel P. Huntington:

> It is my hypothesis that the fundamental source of conflict in this
> new world will not be primarily ideological or primarily economic.
> The great divisions among humankind and the dominating source of
> conflict will be cultural. Nation states will remain the most powerful
> actors in world affairs, but the principal conflicts of global politics will
> occur between nations and groups of different civilizations. The clash
> of civilizations will dominate global politics. The fault lines between
> civilizations will be the battle lines of the future.[17]

Huntington defines "civilization" as a "cultural entity" comprised of both "objective elements" like language, religion, and institutions (culture) and the "subjective self-identification of people" (identity). Identifying seven or eight civilizations in the world—"Western, Confucian, Japanese, Islamic, Hindu, Slavic-Orthodox, Latin American and possibly African"— Huntington believes that these civilizations are destined to clash because the cultures that comprise them are essentially irreconcilable. No longer will wars be waged between nation-states or rebel purveyors of world-historic ideologies. Tomorrow belongs to the conflict of cultures.

Huntington is mentioned here not because he thinks of himself as a theorist of culture in the way of a Herder or a Morgan—he does not; his interests lie primarily in politics—but because his implicit theory of culture resembles the way that many people think about cultures today: as discrete, coherent, and ultimately conflicting entities that tend to combine with the fiery rhetoric of identity politics to produce political fever pitches that can reliably lead to political violence. On this view it might appear logical to assume, say, that the 9/11 attackers acted out of a culturally driven hatred of "the West" while caught in the throes of "Islamofascism," as opposed to considering other, more overtly political reasons for the attacks (for instance, American support of the Saudi royal family, its militarization of the Middle East, or American–Israeli coalitions against Palestine and Lebanon: the actually stated reasons given by Osama bin Laden for 9/11).[18] Why do they hate us? This time it's cultural.

This particular view of culture has been much interrogated by scholars who object to its habitual reliance on what Seyla Benhabib calls the "reductionist sociology of culture": a simplistic way of thinking about culture that Benhabib thinks is governed by three "faulty epistemic premises":

> (1) that cultures are clearly delineable wholes; (2) that cultures
> are congruent with population groups and that a noncontroversial
> description of the culture of a human group is possible; and (3) that
> even if cultures and groups do not stand in one-to-one correspondence,
> even if there is more than one culture in a human group and more
> than one group that may possess the same cultural traits, this poses no
> important problems for politics and policy.[19]

Benhabib's own approach to culture would recognize "Arab culture" or "Islamic culture" as neither coherent nor discrete, nor even necessarily congruent with a given group. Far too many differences must be elided for the reductionist sociology of culture to make sense; far too many exceptions have to be ignored for it to accurately predict associations between a culture and a civilization. Likewise, Amartya Sen has criticized Huntington's theory for an "illusion of singularity" founded upon "a rather foggy perception of world history which overlooks, first, the extent of *internal* diversities within these civilizational categories, and second, the reach and influence of *interactions*—intellectual as well as material— that go right across the regional borders of so-called civilizations."[20] Who among us has only one cultural identity? Which of our cultures lacks diversity, internal disputes, or interactions? Which of the seven or eight Huntingtonian civilizations definitively describes you?

Both Benhabib and Sen agree that culture matters, but they object to the illusory understandings of culture that govern many discussions today. Benhabib writes: "much contemporary social science, like the advocacy of identity politics itself, has retreated into nineteenth-century banalities that all too quickly create seamless analogies between cultures, nations, territories, value attitudes, worldviews, and institutional patterns." For her part, she holds a narrative view of culture that distinguishes between observers and participants. The observer "is the one who imposes, together with local elites, unity and coherence on cultures as observed entities. Any view of cultures as clearly delineable wholes is a view from the outside that generates coherence for the purposes of understanding and control." Observers can come from within the culture (hence the importance of those local elites), but once they make an observation of a coherent whole they effectively stand outside it:

> Participants in the culture, by contrast, experience their traditions,
> stories, rituals and symbols, tools, and material living conditions
> through shared, albeit contested and contestable, narrative accounts.
> From within, a culture need not appear as a whole; rather it forms
> a horizon that recedes each time one approaches it.[21]

The most important issue for Sen is not ascertaining a better definition of culture per se; "the real question is: '*How* does culture matter?'"[22] Sen's sense of culture privileges heterogeneity, discord, change, hybridity, and interactions with others, and he warns against isolating culture as an explanation for everything: "important as culture is, it is not uniquely significant in determining our lives and identities. Other things, such as class, race, gender, profession, politics, also matter, and can matter powerfully."[23]

That, I believe, is where culture is today: caught in a minor culture war over the meaning of culture itself. Is it any wonder that Raymond Williams famously called culture "one of the two or three most complicated words in the English language"? That particular line of Williams's is often recalled, but less often remembered alongside what he wrote next: "because of its use in several distinct and incompatible systems of thought."[24] For Williams, all of our various definitions and understandings of culture—culture as nurture, culture as national spirit, culture as relativistic, culture as civility and civilization, culture as an antidote to civilization, culture as clash of civilizations, culture as the "best that's been thought and known," culture as evolution, culture as narrative description, culture as permeable and heterogeneous, culture as discrete and coherent—have to be examined in their historical and (for lack of a better word) cultural contexts for proper evaluation. They must also be situated epistemologically with the possibility of encountering differences in the ways we think about culture. "Incompatible systems of thought" means that the logic behind any given use of a concept might not only differ from that of another system; it could actually oppose it. The trick is to interrogate all of these systems and ascertain what a given use of culture might indicate by way of an agenda, for it is in the political uses of culture that incompatibilities most willingly uncloak themselves. Now, this doesn't mean acting like the Nazi character in Hans Johst's 1933 play *Schlageter* who famously exclaimed, "Whenever I hear of the word culture . . . I release the safety catch of my Browning!"[25] It simply means thinking critically about culture and acknowledging that whenever we talk, argue, or fight about this important but shape-shifting idea, we might very well be discussing different things.

To get a better sense of how these differences sometimes play out, let us now turn to the particular system of thought embedded in *Ojibwemowin* and consider some Ojibwe understandings of culture as evoked by fluent speakers.

"More Life"

There is no word for "culture" in the Ojibwe language, or at least there's nothing that's clearly translatable, like *miskwaa* and *makwa* for "red" and "bear," so right off the bat that says something meaningful about the Ojibwe system of thought. But there are words and phrases addressing practices, beliefs, and objects that we can recognize in English as cultural. As we examine these "culture words," keep in mind that Ojibwe, like most indigenous languages, is driven by verbs, thus describing a world of actions more than a world of objects; that is, from the outset we can safely assume that Ojibwe senses of culture will tend to conceive of processes more than things.[26]

We begin with a sense of culture that speaks to ceremonial practice. *Izhitwaa* is an animate intransitive verb signifying "having a certain custom" or "practicing a specific ceremony." In addition to being verb-driven, the Ojibwe language makes grammatical distinctions between animate and inanimate things, the difference being just what those words suggest:

living and not living. *Izhitwaa* is a good example of how this distinction works, as the word describes not just doing a ceremony or having a custom but implicitly characterizing ceremonial or customary objects and actors as living (or at least potentially, spiritually).[27] There is another connotation built into *izhitwaa* as well, the sound of deep respect *(-twaa)*, although in this context the sound might signify something like reverence. But *izhitwaa* speaks more than just a reverent respect for life. There are other Ojibwe words employing the root word *izhi,* all of them expressing the basic idea of doing something meaningful in a certain way to produce a desired or expected outcome. *Izhitoon* is to cause something to happen; *izhiwebizi* is to behave or fare in an expected manner; *izhitigweyaa* is to flow, river-like, to a specific place; and *izhise* denotes one who flies to a certain place. *Izhitwaa* links to these words insofar as customs or religious practices are, like natural processes, designed to produce correct results.

The nurture of nature? At first glance *izhitwaa* does seem to compare to *colere*'s invocation of smart agriculture and honoring with worship. But on closer inspection we find that *izhitwaa* and its cognate words recognize no real separation between nature and culture, or between nature and people, at all, which is quite unlike the one implied in the split between *colere* and *natura.* As with culture, there is no Ojibwe word for "nature" either. Rather, just as *izhitwaa* signifies the right conduct of a ceremony, and *izhitigweyaa* refers to the proper flowing of water, *izhi* describes the actions of both people and rivers, both culture and nature. Their logic is the same; nature cannot be abstracted. Even birds have their *izhise.* It is a testament to the poetic power of the Ojibwe language that it can describe the flowing of rivers, the flight of birds, and the practice of human religion with the same basic sound and idea: *izhi,* the idea of doing things properly in order to attain an expected goal. For Ojibwe speakers, this makes a cultural practice like a ceremony look, sound, and feel like one of the rhythms of the natural world. Nature cannot be abstracted from it, because such a division would be literally unspeakable.

Another Ojibwe word that addresses a "nurturing" sense of culture, in the classical meaning of "tending to growth," is *nitaa.* There is an explicitly pedagogical meaning built into *nitaa,* as the word signifies being good or skilled at something, knowing how to do it, and doing it frequently. One has to learn, that is, how to *nitaa.* But once again the most revealing meanings of *nitaa* are found in its related words. *Nitaawigi'* means raising a child, while *nitaawigitoon* refers to the growing of something in general, for instance, a crop. These words are actually interchangeable, placing on common ground both the raising of kids and the raising of crops, which says something significant about *nitaa* namely, that these are things not left to amateurs. The entire point of raising someone, whether children or corn, is to ensure the healthy proliferation of life, and one does not accomplish that task without the skill acquired in what we would call a culture. Other *nitaa* words include *nitaawe*, signifying speaking or singing well, and *nitaage*, to kill game or to mourn. Yes, the killing of game is just like the raising of crops, both requiring substantial know-how in order to produce food, while proper mourning is considered an important aspect of living well. Similarly, *nitaawe* invokes the power of speech and song, two highly valued practices pertaining to the substance and maintenance of life, since they are the lifeblood of ceremonial discourse. Life, in fact, is what all of these *nitaa-* words have in common (including the one that refers to killing): they all possess the sense of doing things well in order to bring about *more life*.

One Ojibwe word invokes a sense of culture that resembles the anthropological notion of a "whole way of life." *Inaadizi* signifies living with a particular character; its noun form *inaadiziwin* can be translated fairly precisely as "way of life." And again, *inaa* is another root word whose cognates reveal a discernible pattern. *Inaabaji'* means to use someone, *inaabadizi* means to be useful (or employed), while *inaabandam* signifies the act of dreaming. So this way of life possesses connotations of use, to use or be used in a particular manner, even while unconscious and dreaming (when visions are given and spiritual messages delivered). It posits, that is, the suggestion of practical utility. There is also a sense of the visual in *inaa* words. *Inaabam* suggests seeing someone in a dream, *inaabate* refers to watching smoke rise in a particular direction, and *inaabi* means to look, or more precisely to peek, raising the question of who peeks at what when lightning *(inaabiwin)* strikes. Utility is linked to vision, as if one can see a proper course of action and become useful through living this way of life. Finally, there is a judicial connotation here, as *inaakonan* refers to deciding something formally, and *inaakonige* means making a judgment. Our word for law is *inaakonigewin*. Seeing, using, being useful, judging, deciding: all of these acts inform *indaadiziwin*, suggesting that our "way of life" is defined by certain values, namely, things like utility, and clear-sighted judgment, and visionary decision making.

One elder I consulted about these words, George Goggleye of Leech Lake, gave me two additional phrases to consider: *gaaminigoowisieng*, "that which was given to us," and *gaaenakowinid*, "that which was given to *anishinaabeg* to live by."[28] These two expressions are instructive for their explicitly spiritual connotations: the idea of something being given.

Who is doing this giving? None but the Creator. To whom is this culture given? To "the people"—*anishinaabeg*—understood in the same basic way Vine Deloria and Clifford Lytle once described this important concept:

> The idea of the people is primarily a religious conception, and with most American Indian tribes it begins somewhere in the primordial mists. In that time the people were gathered together but did not yet see themselves as a distinct people. A holy man had a dream or a vision; quasi-mythological figures of cosmic importance revealed themselves, or in some other manner the people were instructed. They were given ceremonies and rituals that enabled them to find their place on the continent.[29]

In this sense, that which was given to us to live by, meaning ceremonies and rituals, is concerned with helping the people live well, including the provision of an origin story. This gift of identity, by which the people come to see themselves as distinct from others, explains why George Goggleye, who conducts a wide array of Ojibwe ceremonies, once told me, "When I live my day-to-day life, I'm just George, a person like anyone else. But when I light my pipe, I am *only Ojibwe*." That's identity! But it is out of his bigger desire to live well that George conducts his ceremonies in the first place: "I do this to help the people." So in retrospect we might see these two expressions attesting to a sense of culture characterized as follows: as gifts of the Creator designed to help the people live well, including but not limited to an intersubjective identity.

How do these various words and expressions add up? All of these Ojibwe senses of culture—*izhitwaa, nitaa, inaadizi, gaaminigoowisieng,* and *gaaenakowinid*—indicate a single overarching concern: the desire to produce *more life.* As rivers flow and birds fly, practicing religious ceremonies and other customs *(izhitwaa)* produces an intended result: more life. Behaving skillfully *(nitaa)* leads to more life as well, as evidenced by the proliferation of happy children and healthy crops. Living in a certain way *(inaadizi)* allows a community to see, use, decide, and make clear judgments, all values guiding the making of more life. These ways of living were given to us *(gaaminigoowisieng, gaaenakowinid)* by Someone, or maybe Something, who wanted us to survive, thrive, and thereby produce more life. But perhaps the clearest indication of this general goal is another phrase commonly used to describe Ojibwe culture, *anishinaabe bimaadizi,* or "living as an Indian." *Bimaadizi* is used to describe the general state of someone being alive, and it possesses connotations of movement that can be understood in a physical sense. Consider the cognates:

bimaashi means to be blown along, *bimaadagaa* to swim effortlessly as if carried by the current, *bimaada'e,* to skate, and *bimaawadaaso,* to move along with a group like a school of fish. This flowing sense of living in rhythm with others, of going along with the ebb and flow of nature, never swimming upstream or cutting against the grain, suggests that *anishinaabeg* are to live and move in concert with the rhythms of the natural world. Perhaps it is for this reason that Winona LaDuke translated *anishinaabe bimaadiziwin,* the noun form of this expression, as "continuous rebirth."[30] Her translation reveals the ethic of sustainability that seems built into the Ojibwe ideal of living as an Indian.

Another point must be made regarding the nature of these Ojibwe culture words. Earlier I said that Ojibwe is a language of verbs rather than nouns, describing actions over objects, processes over things. As we see with *bimaadiziwin,* however, verbs can be turned into nouns by adding *–win* as a suffix: *izhitwaa* can become *izhitwaawin, inaadizi* can become *inaadiziwin,* and, as in LaDuke's example, *bimaadizi* can be transformed into *bimaadiziwin.* The difference in meaning made when *–win* is affixed to a verb is major; it is the difference between "living as an Indian" and "Indian life," or the difference between "doing something religious" versus "religion." What happens in this shift from verb to noun, which similarly occurred in Europe somewhere between *colere* and "culture," is the objectification of processes: the creation of concepts where once existed actions. It is out of a concern over these meaningful differences that some Ojibwe speakers today will caution students of the language against using (or making) too many nounified *win*-words, finding their recent proliferation indicative of an increasing English influence and with it the adoption of a new system of thought. I would guess that these same folks would likely agree that in the minds of speakers there is a desire to "do cultural things" as opposed to having a "culture," hence the absence of an easily translatable word. Perhaps it would not be going too far to suggest that Ojibwe speakers do not have a culture at all. Rather, it may be more accurate to say that they spend their time *culturing.*

Culturing would mean producing more life, living in a sustainable manner as part of the flow of nature—and never separate from it, because any claim to live divorced from nature would probably be taken as a sign of mental illness, like someone who has "gone windigo" or become a cannibal. *More life* is the goal of Ojibwe culturing, *anishinaabe bimaadizi,* and it is the goal of nature itself, so how could it be otherwise? This, I submit, is the basic "system of thought" behind these Ojibwe culture words, and clearly there are differences between this system and the European one we discussed earlier. One such difference exists in the space between the noun and the verb, between culture as a thing and "culturing." Another is tightly wedged between different ideas concerning the relationship between culture and nature; for the one there's a split, for the other none possible. Any other differences we might note (and we can certainly speak of similarities as well) will probably come down to these two sites of meaning: noun/verb, culture/nature. Therein lies incompatibility.

These different systems of thought might explain why some meanings of culture are not implied in Ojibwe words, for example, national spirit or civilization(s), or the idea of culture being a "whole." Such ideas would rest upon an untraditional notion of culture as a noun, a concept—a discrete body of meanings abstracted from actions—and the idea of civilization in particular seems born of a culture/nature split. Perhaps these omissions, and the Ojibwe system of thought itself, explain why missionaries weren't immediately destroyed when they first encountered the Ojibwe; they were not seen as a cultural threat, and why would they be? They simply cultured differently, and so did the Ojibwe who joined them in practicing the new religion. Perhaps this also explains why the Ojibwe word for Christmas says nothing about the "mass of Christ" or Jesus' birth but simply describes an activity, a "long night of praying." The praying done on Christmas Eve was how the Christians did their culturing, presumably for the production of more life—yes, in part because the priests had explicitly stated that it was all geared toward the making of "new life." Culture was about the practice, not the thing, the action, not the content, the verb, not the noun. There were no "civilizational" conflicts here, thus no need to "clash."

Obviously, cultures are understood rather differently today, encountered and interpreted in ways that reflect our own historical concerns and systems of thought, and dominant among these is a new Huntingtonian sense of culture as singular, coherent, and oppositional. We shouldn't be surprised that Native people now characterize culture this way as well. For example, it has become somewhat fashionable for critics to read new meanings into the old cultural practices of their people, for example, Craig Womack's claim that traditional Creek stories possess an implicit "sense of Creekness" that has always been "nationalistic" and "told for the purpose of cultivating a political consciousness."[31] One immediately recognizes the political desire built into this sort of interpretation and also a present value. But this claim would conceive of culture as possessing a "national spirit," an idea originally formulated by Herder and now pushed to extremes by Huntington, and it relies on assumptions that we might recognize as fairly recent arrivals: first, a concept of culture (or "oral tradition") as a noun, abstract and discrete; second, a circumscription of its unique content, understood as pure at the root; third, an interpretation of its meaning as a definitional component of a politically distinct civilization. At the end of this road, culture is linked to identity and securely attached to the nation. Given Womack's explicitly nationalist approach to criticism, one can easily appreciate his attraction to this system of thought; on the other hand, it seems a short walk from this point to the "clash of civilizations" thesis. My analysis of Ojibwe culture words convinces me that this kind of reading of Native culture speaks more of an underlying European system of thought than a traditional indigenous one.

Remember, sometimes it really is the case that different "systems of thought" are incompatible, as Raymond Williams said. Sometimes these differences have a great deal at stake—I'll hesitatingly call it a worldview for now—although saying so does not mean that we live in radically different, wholly incommensurable, completely untranslatable worlds. We're talking about culture here and considering how different languages— systems of thought—address it. Doing so, however, inevitably leads us to consider different ways of living on Earth, including different approaches to socialization, child rearing, food production, ceremonial practice, community understandings, and one's own self-concept in relation to other living things. For *anishinaabeg,* what we now call culture was always geared toward the production of *more life,* not political theology, and it was not defined by a discernible content that we can abstract, circumscribe, and interpret as a coherent whole but experienced through a wide and constantly evolving array of practices performed in concert with the rhythms of the natural world. If you think about it, that's quite a difference. Then again, it might be impossible for us to think about such differences at all if we do most of our thinking in English.

Now that we have considered some understandings of culture in European society and contrasted them to the culture words of the Ojibwe, let us return to the culture cops and consider the systems of thought they nurture, as revealed in a recent skirmish from our Indian culture wars.

Drummed Out: The Case of Sweetgrass Road

In November 2001, four decades after the "Declaration of Indian Purpose" called for the protection of indigenous cultures, the Sweetgrass Road drum group, comprised of six Ojibwe women from Winnipeg, was turned away from an annual powwow at the University of St. Thomas in Minnesota. The stated reason for their dismissal was their gender, since it is the custom of many Indians—including some Ojibwe, who because of their proximity and numbers exercised a notable cultural authority over the St. Thomas powwow—to prohibit women from singing at the drum. In response to their dismissal, Sweetgrass Road (Linell Maytwayashing, Shanolyn Maytwayashing, Carrie Okemow, Tammy Campeau, Tara Campeau, and Raven Hart-Bellecourt) filed a discrimination lawsuit against the university claiming that the school had violated their civil rights when they were disallowed from participating in the drum competition. What they sought was the right to compete in future years, a point made moot the following October when the University of St. Thomas canceled not only its upcoming powwow but all future ones as well. "St. Thomas does not want to find itself involved in further litigation relating to the religious traditions of American Indians," said Vice President Judith Dwyer.[32] The object of their litigation no longer in existence, the women dropped their lawsuit, and the annual St. Thomas powwow is now history.

That powwow was a site of indigenous culture, so its demise can be understood as a reduction of the same: one less powwow, a little less Native culture in the world. (We might add, a little less Ojibwe cultural authority too.) The St. Thomas event was also an occasion for economic exchange. One of the Midwest's larger powwows, the St. Thomas event paid dancers and singers more than half a million dollars during its fourteen-year run and drew crowds of five thousand spectators annually. Vendors, artisans, and craftspeople sold their wares at the event, dancers and drummers competed for generous payouts, and the university received publicity and credit for being a good community partner. But the St. Thomas powwow was above all a site of cultural exchange, as both Natives and non-Natives intermingled at the event, the former celebrating their culture, the latter learning about it through observation, conversation, and even participation. When the powwow died, so too did all of this exchange.

Who is to blame? For the Ojibwe cultural expert Larry "Amik" Smallwood, who supported the ban on women drummers and called it "a cultural no-no," the dispute never should have gone to court: "it should have been handled by cultural people."[33] "Cultural people" would be the purview of the powwow committee, a group consisting of Natives and non-Natives from the university and local community who were budgeted and charged with organizing the event. It was the powwow committee who invited the drums, lead dancers, emcee, vendors, and the other participants that one would expect to find at any powwow; who planned all of the events and organized the schedule, arranged for space, security, dressing rooms, and dinner; and who oversaw the judging and the distribution of prize money. And it was the powwow committee who was responsible for setting policy, including the unwritten ban on female drum groups. As with most powwow committees, St. Thomas's drew its authority from Indians, consulting elders and respected powwow veterans like Smallwood on matters of protocol. Smallwood decried Sweetgrass Road's involvement of legal people in a matter best left to cultural people, but in truth the powwow committee always answered to both; that is, a cultural matter became a legal issue when the culture discriminated on the basis of gender, which is a legal no-no. The entire point of antidiscrimination laws is precisely to prevent cultures from producing inequalities on the basis of gender, race, class, and other categories of identity, which is exactly what happened at St. Thomas. Culture fought the law and the law won.

Was the law just? Or was Sweetgrass Road a bunch of sore losers who enlisted the support of the American legal system as a means of taking their ball and going home? Perhaps the cancellation of the powwow was the fault of the women, who inappropriately colluded with the legal people, as Smallwood suggested. Having been turned away from other powwows before for the same exact offense—I once saw it myself at another locale—surely Sweetgrass Road knew of the cultural restrictions but flouted them anyway; and when the predictable result emerged, perhaps they just ran to the courts in a fit of litigiousness and killed the powwow. Further, although the law was clearly on their side in this case, the particular legal system they entered was not an Indian one but that of a colonizing power that many Indians still view as problematic. Perhaps Sweetgrass Road unwittingly collaborated in yet another instance of cultural imperialism promoting the destruction of Native cultures. Is that what happened?

In their own defense, Sweetgrass Road spoke publicly against the idea that a ban on female drum singers ever constituted a cultural norm. "I don't see it having anything to do with tradition," said Raven Hart-Bellecourt. "It's ignorance."[34] For Hart-Bellecourt, it was not at all the case that Sweetgrass Road violated traditional cultural norms. Rather, it was the cultural people themselves who lacked not only an understanding of tradition but an awareness of their own contradictions:

> I think a lot of people are ignorant. What we need today is not what
> was needed then. I think this is a clear case of discrimination, because
> if it was tradition, what is a non-aboriginal doing running the powwow

and . . . wearing eagle feathers? It's okay to dance for money, but it's
not okay for you to sing because you're a woman?[35]

On the legal side of things, this was a "clear case of discrimination"; on
the cultural side, it was a double standard. Hart-Bellecourt pointed to
other questionable cultural practices, from non-Natives wearing feathers and running powwows to competitions for cash prizes, things that
are not only new but apparently lacked controversy. From Sweetgrass
Road's perspective, tradition had been selectively defined and inequitably
applied, reinforcing certain values over others. The cultural people had
targeted Native women but not—as seen through her specific examples—
money, men, or white people.

"What we need today is not what was needed then." This is a statement
implying that culture is not timeless but situated and pragmatic, a way to
meet needs. What are our present needs? Hart-Bellecourt explains:

> We come from a generation of abuse. We're trying to hold on to the
> little bit we have left. A lot of [our] girls cried, they were so hurt.
> There used to be no women fancy dancers, now there are many. Now
> we're lawyers, doctors, performers. We have to welcome change,
> especially if it's positive. [Detractors] were judgmental, they say "that's
> not the Indian way," but *that's* not the Indian way![36]

Two different worlds are invoked here, both constituting Indian reality. On the one hand, we live in a world marked by legacies of abuse
and loss; on the other hand, this world does have some positive changes
afoot. Indian women live under conditions of hardship in that first world,
dealing with pain, recovering from trauma, and raising children, sometimes alone, in urban locales like Winnipeg or Minneapolis. But they also
live in the second world, becoming lawyers, doctors, performers, fancy
dancers—occupations that were once reserved exclusively for men. For
Hart-Bellecourt, Sweetgrass Road's singing should be considered part of
that second world, the positive one that combats the first world of loss,
loneliness, and abuse.

Between these two worlds, who else will teach children how to sing
if not their mothers? Who else will pass on "the little bit we have left"?
Understanding culture not as stable content or rules but rather as pragmatic processes geared toward the production of more life, Ojibwe culture words might cast a different light on the songs of Sweetgrass Road.
By seating themselves at a drum usually reserved for men and singing
traditional songs, Sweetgrass Road engaged in a custom (*izhitwaa*) requiring a tremendous amount of know-how, and they did so to pass this

knowledge on to their young *(nitaa, nitaawigi')*. They knew it would likely be controversial, but they saw, decided, and made a judgment call about it in order to be useful and live a particular way of life *(inaadizi)*. In so doing, they respected the original god-given gifts of the past *(gaaminigoow-isieng, gaaenakowinid)* by keeping them alive. They sang in order to live as Indians *(anishinaabe bimaadizi)* in a complicated world, or actually two worlds: the first being a world of trauma and pain, the second a world of new opportunities and recovery. Moving from one world to the next, the women of Sweetgrass Road sang as men normally would—not to resist nature, but on the contrary because it felt completely natural to do so.

They found themselves thwarted by culture cops who conceived of *inaadiziwin* in different ways: as circumscribed, stable, timeless content defined by rules and regulations and clashing with the values of American civilization. This notion not only froze Ojibwe culture in an imagined past and denied an Indian way of life to Indians; it created a space for the assertion of a stubborn value from the Euro-American system of thought: sexism. But who were the culture cops? Certainly one must look to the powwow committee and "cultural people" who produced the rule that Sweetgrass Road broke. Anyone who says no-no to the practices of Indians must be a culture cop on some level, policing as they do the supposed boundaries of culture and casting judgment on transgressors. But it cannot be argued that Indians were ultimately responsible for the demise of the powwow. That decision belonged to no one but the University of St. Thomas, which apparently became a culture cop itself. "That women cannot play the drums is a long-standing tradition for American Indians," said Vice President Dwyer. "The university supports the right of American Indians to follow their traditions." Thus the annual powwow must end forever "because we are unwilling to sponsor an event that is inconsistent with the traditions and sacred beliefs held by members of . . . the broader American Indian community."[37] For the university, then, this really did come down to legal people versus cultural people, and St. Thomas sided with culture—well, the culture defined by certain traditions and sacred beliefs but not others. St. Thomas officials did not support the traditions and beliefs held by the Indians of Sweetgrass Road. They were eminently clear where they stood on that cultural question—women do not sing at the drum, it being a cultural no-no—so the powwow must be canceled forevermore. Native culture must be destroyed in order to save it.

But was the decision to cancel future powwows really made out of a noble desire to protect the integrity of culture? On closer inspection, we find a more mundane tale of old-fashioned litigation phobia. After

Sweetgrass Road filed their discrimination lawsuit, the University of St. Thomas asked a Ramsey County district court judge for a dismissal of the case on its merits and was denied. It was only after the judge's refusal to dismiss that the university canceled all future powwows, so the decision actually seems to have been made out fear of future lawsuits—which is, of course, perfectly understandable. But was it really necessary? Why couldn't the university simply tell the powwow committee that the law forbade them from discriminating on the basis of gender and let the Chipps fall where they may?

The St. Thomas powwow, remember, was a valued site of indigenous culture in Minnesota and it enabled a great deal of exchange. It was also a boon to the substantive Native population in the Twin Cities. The university benefited from it too, as it put into practice their stated commitment to diversity and community involvement, not to mention learning, so its demise was a loss to many communities. Above all, I see it as a reduction of Native culture—one less powwow, a little less culture in the world—as it sent Indians back to the reservation where, presumably, they can make all the cultural rules they want, thus segregating cultures at a time when exchange possessed real benefits. I'm guessing that university administrators were just confused in the presence of an unfamiliar dispute and, not wanting to be cultural imperialists, decided to get out of the powwow business. But they did it by taking a pretty firm stand on culture, one siding with the culture cops, and that decision not only devalued the culture of Sweetgrass Road but denied a worthy value of their own culture: antidiscrimination laws. Such laws are legal, but the values behind them are entirely cultural, stressing equality and resisting the discriminations of traditions, and they are something to be proud of. Further, these values are in constant need of defense, because just like those values invoked by the American Indian Chicago Conference in 1961, they are under attack today too. Benhabib says, "the greatest challenge for contemporary democracies will be to retain their dearly won civil liberties . . . while defusing the fundamentalists' dream of purity and of a world without moral ambivalence and compromise."[38]

Native Fundamentalism

Are culture cops fundamentalists? Benhabib characterizes fundamentalism as "a deep reaction . . . against the increasing hybridization of cultures, peoples, languages, and religions that inevitably accompanies globalization."[39] The more things change, the more they absolutely have to stay the same. I am reminded now of several arguments I had as an instructor at Leech Lake Tribal College with culture cops who wanted to shut down our science programs because they taught evolution. "Nothing in our oral traditions says that we came down from trees." Science was considered suspect because its origins lay outside an Ojibwe epistemology; because the latter was deemed separate and pure, it had to be protected from contamination. My side eventually won the day, though not (as one might expect) through our claim that we needed to teach science to produce more local doctors and nurses. It was only after we successfully argued that our clan origin story could be read as a kind of proto-evolutionary theory that the culture cops backed off.

If fundamentalism is a reaction to globalization and hybridity, then culture cops are reacting to a process that is not really new but, on the contrary, something that Indians have experienced through a long history of colonialism and assimilation, a history that includes prohibitions on certain ceremonies during the nineteenth and twentieth centuries, the loss of traditional knowledge through assimilative education, and the discomforting sense that legitimate knowledge exists not in one's own community or history but always in someone else's. So the reaction is understandable. Compounding the problem, Native people have had their own forebears' contributions to modern science, medicine, and public culture hidden from them, thus denying them the opportunity to see people like themselves in positions of esteem. (Can you name a single Native scientist or doctor?) Finally, we still live in a world where a young Native person is rarely, if ever, viewed as someone with the potential to make a significant mark in the world. Far too many Indian kids are still seen as problems by schools and the dominant culture, a perception that can compel them to close the door on their own futures. If modernity doesn't make space for the Indian, the Indian may respond by denying the validity of modernity and becoming a culture cop. At least in that role he or she will be valued.

Ironically, culture cops try to resist Western modernity and the "white world" by employing discourses that are themselves rather Western, modern, and "white" in character. For one, the policing of traditional knowledge—typically characterized as oral tradition—exhibits a certain way of thinking about culture that would be highly unlikely without literacy. As Jack Goody has observed, it is not oral traditions that are culturally conservative so much as written ones. Goody characterizes oral cultures as "open to internal change as well as to external imports," whereas in literate cultures the "dogma and services are rigid."[40] Literacy conserves; orality incorporates. When change occurs in a literate society, "it often takes the form of a break-away movement . . . rather than the process of incorporation that tends to mark the oral situation."[41] Texts limit knowledge, limits produce schisms, and schisms become competing orthodoxies (e.g., Catholicism versus Protestantism). Conversion is thus a "function of the boundaries the written word creates."[42] By contrast, oral societies are always hybrid creatures because there is no sacred text to mark knowledge as permanent, no priests to police it, no ninety-five theses to nail to the door when a difference presents itself. Adaptation is a function of orality's elasticity and boundlessness.

It is the bounded logic of literacy that provides the common ground held by both culture cops and theorists like Huntington. It would be impossible to argue that the rise of literacy and print culture in Europe did not contribute to the reification of culture as a thing rather than a process—a noun rather than a verb—and Native people have inherited this idea (along with literacy) as part of our ongoing colonization. The result is ironic: culture cops defending the primacy of oral-traditional Native knowledge while rejecting written "white" knowledge, all the while deploying understandings of culture as a thing that are probably derived from the impact of literacy. It's like reading from an invisible book.

Fundamentalism almost always rests upon Benhabib's faulty epistemic premises, and it tends to produce what Sen calls "reactive self-perception": an identity defined against the dominant so adamantly that people actually come to see themselves as the Other. As Sen elaborates, "They are led to define their identity primarily in terms of being *different from* Western people."[43] Not only different from, I would add, but victimized by. Calling it an indication of a "colonized mind," Sen warns us against reactive self-perception in the realm of identity politics, because thinking this way is irrational: "It cannot make sense to see oneself primarily as someone who (or whose ancestors) have been misrepresented, or treated badly, by colonialists, no matter how true that identification may be."[44] It ultimately works to reinscribe, not resist, the same colonizer/colonized relationship it militates against, and it can also keep one mired in victimhood. Reactive self-perception doesn't negate so much as reinforce the position of the colonizer as the center of reference; the identity it produces therefore cannot claim to be sovereign or independently self-determined, no matter how strenuously one asserts his or her separatism. Even the word *separate* describes a relationship to another position.

Reactive self-perception may be what Gerald Vizenor had in mind when naming "victimry" one of his "eight native theaters" for the performance of identity. The other seven native theaters (in each case beginning with the phrase "native by . . .") are "concession," "creation," "countenance," "genealogies," "documentation," "situations," and "trickster stories."[45] But "victimry" holds a special place in Vizenor's analysis and receives more treatment than the others because it is "one of the most common" (as well as the "most wearisome") tropes of identity, as "natives in this theater are cast as representations . . . the absolute victims of modernity."[46] Vizenor isn't saying that Natives can never claim to be victimized; he is calling into question the typical habit of defining and discussing Native identity through tropes of victimry. (His examples are Jimmie Durham and Ward Churchill.) "The real natives are fugitives" from this theater, as evidenced by the fact that "there is no word in *anishinaabe* that indicates the abstract possession of victimry."[47] In a manner of speaking, victimry is for Vizenor yet another ironic appropriation of a non-Native logic, for in traditional contexts "stories of the soul are sources of survivance, not victimry."[48]

To become Native by victimry is to develop a reactive self-perception, and this is a risk of ethnic fundamentalisms in general and culture cops in particular. Both victimry and reactive self-perception can emerge at the site of what we identified earlier as a "resistance identity" (see chapter 1), but they are no more than possible expressions of a resistance identity and not the same exact thing. It is always entirely possible to promote a resistance identity that rejects the dominant culture and the political status quo without falling prey to the temptation of defining oneself as Other and/or always defined by a history of victimization. It is important (and certainly more historically accurate) to assert an identity and culture that consists of more than grievances or stories about abuses suffered at the hands of the white man. One needs to know about the contributions one's ancestors made to world history, to universal knowledge, and to common culture as well. That these contributions have often been hidden is no excuse for reproducing the myth of their absence. It makes little sense—and plays a potentially deadly game—to show disdain for modern science and medicine in particular. Better to know some Indian scientists and doctors who really have lived and worked and pass that information on to the young.

To the extent that culture cops are fundamentalists, their vocation in life will be to promote conversion to their eternal and bounded Truth defined in opposition to "Europe," as opposed to promoting adaptation and contribution to the modern world, and this distinction provides us with a useful way of distinguishing culture cops from elders. Culture cops express disdain for white or European cultural accomplishments—such as a college degree (often derided as no more than "a piece of paper")—thus producing reactive self-perception in the process. Elders, on the other hand, typically take the more cosmopolitan approach of "taking your roots with you," to paraphrase Kwame Anthony Appiah, producing a sense of what Appiah calls "cosmopolitan patriotism," and what Arnold Krupat has identified as "indigenous cosmopolitanism."[49] Taking your roots with you means opening yourself up to new experiences while never forgetting where you came from, and in my experience elders do encourage young people to go to college, travel the world, and learn new things, while remaining proud of who they are. It's culture cops who are more inclined to characterize other cultures and other forms of knowledge as "not our way," thereby construing the whole world as something of a threat.

Sometimes culture cops and elders come into visible conflict. Years ago I wrote about witnessing this sort of conflict between what I called "new elders" and "young traditionalists" at an Ojibwe language retreat.[50] Basically, the young traditionalists—or culture cops—visibly disrespected the new elders who were presenting, because what they presented were Christian hymns translated into Ojibwe. As Michael McNally shows in his fine study of this group and cultural practice, Ojibwe "hymn-singers" like these are not only fluent speakers of *Ojibwemowin* but also widely recognized for their knowledge of traditional arts and crafts, skills in hunting and gathering practices, and other arcana.[51] (These are the kind of traditional Ojibwe who can brain-tan a deer hide in no time flat.) When it came time for their presentation, which involved singing from their hymnals, the culture cops loudly departed the event and took a good number of the small children with them. The elders looked sad to me, and the organizers of the event—middle-aged Ojibwe women—were visibly angry. Although I originally attempted to provide a nuanced reading of this event in my writing—explaining that no matter how rude they appeared to be, the young traditionalists were ultimately trying to do a good thing by defending traditional (non-Christian) religious practices alongside language—in my own middle age, I am less inclined to give them a pass. Now it just looks to me like they disrespected their elders, not to mention fluent speakers of Ojibwe, and that can't really be called traditionalist, even less language activist. It can, however, be called fundamentalist. Returning to Benhabib, it seems to have been "a deep reaction . . . against the increasing hybridization of cultures, peoples, languages, and religions that inevitably accompanies globalization."

It was not elders but culture cops who disrespected the fluent speakers of Ojibwe because they were Christian; it was not elders but culture cops who proposed eliminating our science programs at the tribal college in the name of cultural preservation; and it was not elders but culture cops who most stridently objected to the songs of Sweetgrass Road at the powwow. This is no argument against elders, much less against traditionalism. It is, rather, a warning about culture cops, many of whom will doubtless assume the mantle of elderhood as generations pass. When they do, they will be recognized by a tendency to think like highly literate people, assuming an outsider's point of view to characterize their cultures as discrete, timeless, bounded things—invisible books—and then placing them in oppositional fashion to the discrete, timeless, bounded cultures of other "civilizations." In so doing, they will resist new and hybrid cultural expressions like Native Christianity and female drum groups, and therefore resist the cultural expressions of the majority of actually existing Indians. However, it might also be the case that old age will moderate the culture cops, making them think more like the elders we have known in the past and still admire today. In that case, they will be recognized by more traditionally oral values: not conversion but adaptation, not separatism but incorporation, not culture as a noun but culture as a verb. Above all, they will be known by their ultimate concern, and if traditionalism is still playing a role, the object of that cultural faith will be the making of *more life*.

Indigenous Intellectuals as Culture Cops

We have to consider another aspect of the culture cop phenomenon: the curious appearance of fundamentalist doctrines in Native critical theories. It's not only "cultural people" on reservations who have lately assumed the role of culture cops; writers and scholars have been moving into this territory as well. I have already mentioned Craig Womack's explicitly nationalist approach to literary criticism; like many nationalisms, his can't resist conceiving of culture as a circumscribed, stable thing. Nationalism functions by describing a group identified by its culture, so it comes as little surprise that nationalists will characteristically adopt the observer's perspective on culture over the participant's. For nationalism to function, a sense of Creekness must always remain distinguishable from a sense of Americanness (or Cherokeeness or Ojibweness); hence all the arguments made by literary nationalists against that poor, beleaguered concept of hybridity, a little theory term that assumes no more than the (fairly oral) hunch that all cultures and peoples interact and influence each other. This aversion to hybridity has reappeared in Womack's essay "The Integrity of American Indian Claims (or, How I Learned to Stop Worrying and Love My Hybridity)," where he writes: "I have yet to meet an Indian who introduced him or herself to me as a 'hybrid.' Maybe someone should wonder why a word that used to reference seed corn and cattle is now the term of choice for critics describing people of color."[52] The short answer to that would be that hybridity is not used to describe people (although it certainly was during the nineteenth century when scientific race theories were popular), but instead to describe the mixing and blending of cultural expressions, much in the same way that Womack himself described it in his "pure versus tainted framework" from *Red on Red*.[53] I've always thought Womack's defense of the "tainted" side of that framework constituted an endorsement of the concept of hybridity; after all, things that aren't hybrid or tainted are usually considered pure.

One might suppose that hybridity is naturally the enemy of nationalism, including literary nationalism, because it calls into question the possibility of discrete cultural boundaries and makes the case for political nationalism a bit more difficult to sustain. Nationalists usually tend to be culture cops, because at first glance hybridity, postmodernism, and other boundary-busting threats to pure separatism might appear to put their political objectives in danger. Presumably, the same would hold for recent reactions to the old "mixed-blood" metaphor that used to be quite popular in Native discourse but has apparently lost its former allure. Once again Womack provides us with a good example of this second aversion. In *Red on Red* he comically expresses little love for "a bunch of mongrelized mixed-bloods who weren't sure if they were Indians as they muddled about in some kind of hybridized culture, serving as the footpath between whites and Indians," and bemoaned the "mixed-blood malaise, where blood and marginalization, rather than the ongoing life of the nation, become the overriding issue."[54] Mixed-bloods, hybridity, postmodernism, *mestiza* consciousness, *métissage,* and other theoretical metaphors for border crossing will probably continue to be held up as antagonists to the nationalist project, even if hybridity is actually a perfectly reasonable idea. A few nationalists will admit as much but draw a different line in the sand. "To acknowledge the truth of hybridity," Jace Weaver writes, "does not mean that we are globally merging into a single McCulture in which we must all consume the same Happy Meal, using the same critical utensils, and then excrete the same McCriticism."[55] Surely there must be someplace between Jihad and McWorld where hybridity can exist in peace. I will return to this topic later in this book.

Although nationalists tend to be culture cops, not all culture cops are nationalists. A good number of them are language activists or religious revivalists, two valuable groups whose stated political objectives—in the former case, language revitalization; in the latter case, ceremonial renewal—seem to require clear and present boundaries. Some combination of these objectives appears to have influenced David Treuer's *Native American Fiction: A User's Manual,* a book released in 2006 that quickly generated some lively debates. In a nutshell, Treuer attacks the idea that Native American fiction can represent Native or tribal culture, by which he seems to mean traditional culture, suggesting that the most literature can do is portray a "longing" or "desire for culture"—not the culture itself—because English is an inherently non-Indian language and fiction an inherently non-Indian form.[56] By contrast, Treuer writes, "Indian culture . . . is lived through language and custom and community and history," and since that culture can never be represented in literary form without becoming non-Indian, Treuer concludes that "Native American fiction does not exist."[57] What does exist are texts written by authors whose personal identities are intended to authorize critics' interpretations of their supposedly authentic Indian cultural expressions; but their works would be better read for "style" than for, or as, signs of authentic tribal culture. In fact, "style IS culture; style creates the convincing semblance of culture on the page."[58] But it is *literary* culture that gets created, not Native or tribal culture, and Treuer wants to keep the two cultural realms distinct: "It is crucial to make a distinction between reading books *as* culture and seeing books as capable of *suggesting* culture."[59] Why so crucial? "It seems that readers and writers of Native American literature have made the mistake of assuming that writing and culture are interchangeable."[60]

The reason writing and culture cannot be interchangeable—why assuming so is a "mistake"—is that Treuer believes that Native cultures are always found in their usual and accustomed places: at ceremony and wherever heritage languages are in use. They cannot be discovered, or even accurately portrayed, in, say, Louise Erdrich's incorrect usage of Ojibwe language, or James Welch's inconsistent "literal renderings" of his Indians' thoughts about culture, and least of all in Sherman Alexie's figurative language ("Indian tears"), because these portraits of culture always carry a "surplus"—the contamination of non-Indian ideas, expressions, and translations—and are therefore always part and parcel of a much larger culture that cannot be accurately characterized as Native or tribal.[61] To do so would be like eating "smartberries," which, according to the Wenabozho story that Treuer tells, amounts to a shitty meal; or worse, becoming a literary critic: "and when Alexander Pope declaimed 'Lo, The poor Indian!' he really meant 'Lo, the poor Native American literary critic!'; 'whose untutor'd mind / Sees God in clouds, or hears Him in the wind . . .'"[62] Well, you get the gist. Writing and culture cannot be interchangeable, because Treuer thinks Native culture cannot exist in written form; it is always by definition oral and never expressed in English, but always and only in heritage languages. In fact, in order for something cultural to count as culture, both the oral and heritage language requirements would apparently have to be fulfilled, as Treuer insists he "is not involved with the new essentialist project of defining only texts in Native American languages as authentic Indian texts and those in English merely fantasies in the conqueror's language."[63] He is involved, rather, with the old essentialist project of protecting traditional culture from the threats of incorporation, exploitation, and change. That makes him a culture cop for sure, but it also makes him something of a language activist and religious revivalist.

Language activists like David's brother, Anton Treuer, depend on authenticity as a motivational force, for without the sense that *Ojibwemowin* is the "real" language of a truly authentic Ojibwe person, there is less motivation for people to enroll in language classes or for tribal governments to fund language programs. The likely result, as Anton writes in *Living Our Language,* would be sadly ironic: "We are not losing our language. Our language is losing us."[64] Religious revivalists rely on a similar argument: *You must come to ceremony because this is our original form of spirituality, gaaminigoowisieng!* When a new hybrid form emerges and lays claim to linguistic and cultural authenticity—say, the Three Fires Midewiwin Lodge, which conducts its ceremonies in English, or the literary-critical idea that Native American literature retains connections to oral traditions, which Treuer ridicules in *Native American Fiction*—language activists and religious revivalists will play the authenticity card in ways that resemble his book's argumentative strategy: by denying the mantle of authenticity to impure expression. Such is the ultimate culture cop tactic because it draws a line around the culture and polices the boundaries.

Now, I am not calling foul on language activists or religious revivalists who do this, nor even on Treuer to the extent that he seems to be supporting their efforts. Rather, I am remarking on the logical resemblances that exist between David the literary guy and his brother Anton the language guy. That said, I cannot side with Treuer's argument in *Native American Fiction* for the same reason I cannot buy into the nationalist attack on hybridity: because it seems true to me that our cultures, like all cultures, are constantly changing, adapting, and evolving as time goes by; that they are doing so largely as a direct result of contact with other cultures; and that they are changing precisely as Franz Boas said they would—through adaptation to the historical and environmental conditions of our lives. From that perspective, we might insist that Louise Erdrich's Ojibwe language mistakes in *Love Medicine* aren't "incorrect" at all, but to the contrary a remarkably accurate portrait of Ojibwe language usage in the late twentieth century, a time when the majority of actually existing Ojibwe in the United States were screwing up their verb conjugations with stunning regularity; that James Welch's "literal renderings" are not reducible to what Treuer calls "Cooperspeak" (even less so to Homer), but should be read precisely as an authentic Blackfoot translation of historical experiences into fictive form; and that Treuer's students' interpretations of Sherman Alexie's "Indian tears" ("Indian tears represent the loss of land, culture and language"; "Indian tears are for pain and suffering at the hands of the white man . . .") do not constitute an "exoticized" "form of knowingness based on nothing" or "a story based on supposition and received ideas it can't ever rise above," but instead indicate a pretty savvy ability to interpret what I now believe was a remarkably effective use of figurative language on Alexie's part.[65]

The unstated assumption in Treuer's argument that Native American fiction lacks any actual connection to oral traditions or heritage languages— that it all ultimately goes back to Cooper, Homer, Hemingway, or whomever—is essentially that translation is never possible, which unfortunately takes us back to the Sapir-Whorf hypothesis. For Treuer, translation might be able to approximate something like an intended meaning, but it always comes with "surplus," the best example of which, for him, is the history of the "Chant to the Fire-Fly," a children's verse first recorded in 1845 by Henry Rowe Schoolcraft in two different forms, one "literal" and the other "literary," and an object of scholarly interest ever since. Treuer writes that Schoolcraft's original source for his translation was an Ojibwe children's song consisting of only six words—*waawaatesi* ("firefly"), *waawaatese'amawishin* ("flicker me, firefly"), *jibwaa* ("before"), *nibaayan* ("when I sleep"), *bi-izhaan* ("come here"), and *waasakonenjigan* ("lantern," "candle")—yet both Schoolcraft's literal and literary translations added the surplus of "at least eight extra words, whose meaning does not appear in the original Ojibwe": *flitting, white, fire, bed, little, dancing, beast, bright,* and *instrument* in the literal; and *bright, little, song, sing, fly, over, head, merrily,* and *bed* in the literary. Treuer concludes from this example that "immediately, surplus meanings and surplus words have crept in and supplanted the original meanings."[66]

This is an uncontroversial statement insofar as it applies to all translation per se, but most linguists today would in all likelihood add that it applies to all language use, not just translation, because meanings reside not only in semantics but also in syntactic structures and pragmatic uses of language (and, of course, poststructuralism would add that meanings are never stable anyway). It is always possible that two speakers of the same language will bring their own individual "surpluses" to bear on a conversation or other linguistic exchange. But what of Treuer's charge that Schoolcraft's surplus words "supplanted the original meanings" of the Ojibwe source text? I think Treuer overstates the differences. "Flitting" and "white," for instance, seems to me a remarkably strong translation of the image conveyed in the word for "firefly," *waawaatesi,* for whenever you encounter the sound-image *"waawaa"* in Ojibwe, it is extremely likely that you are picturing something white and, well, flitting. *Waabishkaa* is the word for "white"; and *waa* appears in words where something white or bright exists, for example, *waabooz* (rabbit) and his white tail. When an animal's tail is known to move quickly—as in the case of *waawaashkeshi* (white-tailed deer)—its name may reflect that characteristic with two consecutive *waa*'s—*waawaa*—in exactly the same fashion as *waawaatesi.* As for the word *bed,* I don't see how that constitutes a surplus unless we're going to charge Treuer with bad translation of English. What Schoolcraft wrote was "go to bed," by which he meant, of course, "go to sleep," not literally walking to a bed and just standing there. "Go to bed" is way of saying "go to sleep" in the English language, and therefore it is a completely acceptable translation of the Ojibwe *nibaa* or *nibaayaan.* I think most of Schoolcraft's alleged surplus words can be explained in similar ways; that is, they can be read as *translations,* not bad ones at that; and even if errors could be shown to exist, it hardly seems fair to charge Schoolcraft with creating a "perversion" or a "wild and willful misinterpretation" of the Ojibwe source material.[67]

To be clear, I am not suggesting that every meaning in any language is completely and easily translatable to another without doing violence to the original. That would be a particularly bad claim to make when considering the difficulties of translating oral songs and oral performances to written or literary forms. As Arnold Krupat writes in his essay "On the

Translation of Native American Song and Story: A Theorized History"
(which is the best essay on this subject that I've found), "it is not possible
to imagine the discovery or invention of any ultimately and absolutely
correct or fully adequate way to translate from oral performance to page
of text"; the best that one can do is acquire a "command" of the language
to be translated, "competence" in the culture in which it gets used, and
a sense of "the strategies of literary expression both oral and textual in
general."[68] What I am saying is, first, Treuer's understanding of surplus
is contingent upon a reading of translations—"Chant to the Fire-Fly,"
Schoolcraft, the work of Dell Hymes, and so on—that isn't quite fair;
and second, that in any case the idea of surplus doesn't illuminate the actual functions of fiction or any other Native cultural expression. To suggest that "Native American fiction doesn't exist" because it is (a) written,
(b) in English, and (c) thereby indebted *only* to ideas received from whites
and (d) *not* oral traditions, heritage languages, or other repositories of
culture tells us nothing about what the literature is actually trying to do.
Instead, as Treuer himself ironically put it in a different context, it seems
"to police the boundaries of our domain . . . to protect our cultural
resources," and this ultimately makes *Native American Fiction* "little
more than the literary equivalent of a badge and a gun: a symbol of
our pledge to protect and serve, and the means to do so."[69] In other
words, the culture cops may have just been presented with their official
user's manual.

Again, I am not saying that all culture cops are always and essentially
bad. To the contrary, as a variant of what we earlier called "professional
Indians," they can make extremely effective arguments in certain contexts
that lead to some good results, for example, the funding and filling of heritage language programs and the revival of traditional ceremonial lodges
that had previously gone dormant. All I'm saying is that culture cops don't
always make the best literary critics because their definitions of culture,
explicit or implicit, are going to be dependably flawed—"nineteenth-
century banalities," as Seyla Benhabib characterizes them—and the typical
(written) ethos of a culture cop nurtures a reactive self-perception. Instead
of policing culture, critics and scholars actually need to be the ones who
will, following Edward Said, "question patriotic nationalism" and keep
"nations and traditions at bay."[70] For Native intellectuals, this sort of
independence can pose a real challenge, for it is a worthwhile question to
ask how we might be able to produce intellectual work that protects our
heritage languages and traditional cultures from further assault and decay.
Whatever answer exists will have to wait for another time; for now, suf-

fice it to say that I fail to see how attacks on hybridity or the existence of Native American literature gets us any closer to one.

Beyond Culture

I opened this chapter by recalling the 1961 "Declaration of Indian Purpose" and its stated desire to protect our cultures. I then examined how culture was defined in two different "systems of thought"—the first originating in Europe, the second located in the culture words of *Ojibwemowin*— and suggested that any incompatible differences between them likely came down to noun/verb and culture/nature. Following that discussion, I considered the example of Sweetgrass Road as illustrative of how culture cops, Native and/or otherwise, can diminish indigenous culture—and exclude women—by policing cultural boundaries in a manner that reflects a narrative view from the outside and, ironically, a system of thought derived from (Western) literacy. Finally, I warned against the temptation to import culture cop modes of thought into academic or critical writing. By now my own view on culture is probably painfully clear: I privilege the insider's view that would resist any stabilizing or coherent description of culture as a noun but that deals instead with the scraps, patches, and rags of everyday life; the Ojibwe view preoccupied with the renewal of *more life;* and the democratic view that would comprehend culture as a conversation marked by diversity and contest, yet ultimately seeking to protect women or minority groups from subordination and marginalization. That means I'll tend to side with the cultural groups that typically get a bad rap from culture cops for their impurities: Native Christians, female drum groups, speakers of "rez English" who can't speak more Ojibwe than *boozhoo* and *miigwech,* teens into indigenized versions of hip-hop, English-language ceremonial lodges like Three Fires, people who engage in pan-Indian practices like sweat lodges and powwows, Native American fiction writers, atheists, secularists, postmodernists, skeptics, cosmopolitans, and all those Indians who wrote themselves into the universal human story but have been lost (or discarded) to history: doctors, scientists, ethnologists, journalists, artists, professors, architects, curators, filmmakers, teachers, and others who refused to stay on the reservation where they were supposed to belong, and who refused to silence their Indian voices in a world that they sought to join and even improve.

Having said all that, I also support Native nationalism, language revitalization, and ceremonial renewal, and I have recognized and affirmed the roles that culture cops play in those important projects. Aside from the appearance of culture cop discourse in written intellectual and academic work, and cases where culture leads to discrimination on the basis of gender, race, class, and so on, I am not attempting to disable anyone's projects (well, at least not the worthwhile ones). There should be more, not less, room for diverse cultural expression in Native America, as diversity not only characterizes the spirit of our age but also brings in the new and sometimes the good. Claiming our own cultural diversity is the making of an x-mark that could contribute to an eventual ceasefire in the Indian culture wars, and it would also expand the scope and meaning of our cultural revival.

Let's conclude this chapter by returning to the "Declaration of Indian Purpose" and considering its curious characterization of culture as "values" rather than as a stable set of practices and beliefs. What exactly did they mean by that? Perhaps we should begin by asking, what are values? Values are beliefs held by a community that are assessed not for their correctness versus incorrectness but for what they hold to be good versus bad. They tend to be more general and enduring than specific orthodoxies or practices, because they possess a universality in the sense of being recognizable across lines of significant cultural difference. Compare Aristotle's "moral virtues" in Book II of *Nicomachean Ethics*—courage, temperance, generosity, magnificence, magnanimity, gentleness, agreeableness, truthfulness, and wit—to the values embodied in the "Seven Grandfathers" of Ojibwe tradition: love *(zaagi'idiwin)*, respect *(minaadendamowin)*, courage *(aakode'ewin)*, honesty *(gwayakwaadiziwin)*, wisdom *(nibwaakaawin)*, humility (deb*aadendiziwin*), and truth *(debwewin)*.[71] Both Aristotle's moral virtues and the Seven Grandfathers exemplify what I mean by values— worthy characteristics and ideals that clearly benefit the community—and we can see meaningful differences between these two sets. Different kinds of people would be produced through these two different value systems and respected for different things, but all of these virtues would be universally recognized as more or less valuable, and that's what makes them values and not specific orthodoxies. Values are universally understood, whereas cultures are often not. I may not understand the bar mitzvah but I can easily recognize the value of initiating children into adulthood; likewise a Baptist might find sweat lodges incomprehensible but fully appreciate the value of prayer and purification by water. Cultural practices are how we pursue our values; they are vehicles in which our values are formed, taught, and carried forth. All communities today have a diversity of cultures within. What truly distinguishes communities from each other is not culture but the dominant values they hold, and that difference is one of priority and not of kind. Different communities will prioritize different values, and in every case these can be rearranged.

Why were values invoked in the "Declaration of Indian Purpose"? Were the authors claiming a right to live in societies defined by different value systems than what they had witnessed in the dominant society, one that had placed them in boarding schools for the explicit purpose of changing their values? Were they insisting on the legitimacy of indigenous arrangements of value that would privilege, say, loving, respectful, honest, wise, humble, and truth-seeking personalities over the kinds of people most highly valued in a militarized, imperialist, consumer culture? A society prioritizing indigenous values would be a very different world than the one we all know today. This other world probably wouldn't value people like Donald Trump and Donald Rumsfeld so much as those kind, gentle elders that many of us have been fortunate to know during our lifetimes, and saying so is not to invoke a culture war or clash of civilizations. It is only to posit the small suggestion that perhaps the American Indian Chicago Conference had something quite ambitious in mind when they heralded the importance of Native values and called it a sign of complexity and an inherent human right. Perhaps what they meant was no more than a desire to live according to a value system of one's own, but perhaps they held the more ambitious hope that others might come to value Native values as well.

CHAPTER THREE

Nations and Nationalism since 1492

In his classic 1950 *Discourse on Colonialism,* the great Martinican poet Aimé Césaire outlined the important task that lay before anticolonial activists and intellectuals:

> For us, the problem is not to make a utopian and sterile attempt to repeat the past, but to go beyond. It is not a dead society that we want to revive. We leave that to those who go in for exoticism. Nor is it the present colonial society that we wish to prolong, the most putrid carrion that ever rotted under the sun. It is a new society that we must create, with the help of all our brother slaves, a society rich with all the productive power of modern times, warm with the fraternity of olden days.[1]

This was the voice of decolonization at the dawn of the postcolonial era, and it was uncompromising and pragmatic. Césaire's "new society" wouldn't be exotic, nostalgic, or utopian; rather, it would blend the best of old and new—yesterday's "fraternity" with today's "productive power"—and with no contradiction therein. This vision entailed a rejection of racism and illegitimate rule, the destruction of empires, and the making of revolution—but not the revolutions of nations, not nationalism. No, Césaire wanted to see the revolution of "the only *class* that still has a universal mission, because it suffers in its flesh from all the wrongs of history, from all the universal wrongs: the proletariat."[2]

Forty-nine years later, the Kenien'kehaka' nationalist and political philosopher Taiaiake Alfred wrote this in *Peace, Power, Righteousness: An Indigenous Manifesto:*

It is incumbent on this generation of Native people to heal the colonial sickness through the re-creation of sound communities, individual empowerment, and the re-establishment of relationships based on traditional values. This is a burden placed on young shoulders by the elders and ancestors who carried the torch through many years of darkness. It is not enough to survive and heal; there is also a responsibility to rebuild the foundations of nationhood by recovering a holistic and traditional philosophy, reconnecting with our spirituality and culture, and infusing our politics and relationships with traditional values.[3]

This vision was advanced further in Alfred's *Wasáse: Indigenous Pathways of Action and Freedom* (2005), which states: "rather than setting out to destroy or replace the state or eject the colonizer, the end goal should be formulated as the achievement in positive terms of the creation of a *new society*."[4] Yes, another call for a "new society," only this time the emphasis is placed on nationhood, not the proletariat, on culture, not class, and on the local, not the universal. Like Césaire, Alfred sees no reason to reject the technological benefits that accompany modern society, but he does argue more directly for a revitalized cultural traditionalism to guide the decolonization process, not because he goes in for exoticism but because "the real reason most Onkwehonwe endure unhappy and unhealthy lives . . . is that we are living through a spiritual crisis, a time of darkness that descended on our people when we became disconnected from our lands and from our traditional ways of life."[5]

So, between the mid-twentieth century and the new millennium we can note both continuity and change in radical anticolonial discourse. Perhaps the greatest continuity is the problem both thinkers exhibit toward cultural workers whose labors seem to prevent the making of their "new societies." Césaire was excruciatingly clear who he thought deserved the greatest blame for preventing social change, and it wasn't "sadistic governors," "greedy bankers," "subservient judges," and other obvious colonizers, but the producers of culture and ideology: all those "venomous journalists," "goitrous academics," "chattering intellectuals born stinking out of the thigh of Nietzsche," "hoodwinkers," "hoaxers," "hot-air artists," "humbugs," and others whose writings supplied the justifications for the status quo.[6] Likewise, Alfred excoriates "left-wing intellectuals" who produce an ostensibly progressive discourse but "hold a strong attachment to the colonial state and to their own privileges within Settler society"; why, they're nearly as bad as the gung-ho "colonizer who accepts his or her role."[7] Intellectuals, critics, artists, journalists, and the makers of public discourse—and not just Indian agents or the imperial police—have been charged with preventing decolonization and the creation of "new societies" by both Césaire and Alfred. But here too lies a change, as Alfred's tirade against left-wing intellectuals would have struck Césaire as odd; after all, he was a left-wing intellectual himself.

In keeping with these continuities and changes, and in pursuit of a dream that has not disappeared, indigenous thinkers today are generating new theories of decolonization and new nationalisms. Following Anthony Cohen's distinction between *nationality*, "an argument about legal status," and *nationhood*, "a claim about the character and integrity of one's cultural identity," we can see that these nationalisms are addressing both nationality and nationhood.[8] Nationalisms are now articulated in political theory and law, film studies and literary criticism, as well as in activist communities like Caledonia, Ontario, and Chiapas, Mexico, and this has been producing a paradigm shift in Native studies: from "mosaic multiculturalism" and anthropological senses of culture, to visions of nationality and nationhood that are, well, more nationalistic than ever before.

They are increasingly separatist too, despite claims to the obverse, such as Ronald Neizen's assertion that we are now witnessing a world-historic formation of a new political subject called "indigenist" that is defined by a general lack of separatist or secessionist impulses. "Indigenism . . . is commonly placed in the same category as . . . ethnonationalism," Neizen writes, adding that indigenous people "do not as a rule aspire toward independent statehood."[9] What they do is address global governance bodies like the United Nations and prominent NGOs in an effort to gain recognition for the purpose of maintaining cultural integrity and at least a "measured" degree of political sovereignty in the states that still contain them, thus redefining the meanings of "self-determination" while not threatening the cohesion of the state. Although this is doubtless true, we must admit that indigenous intellectuals and activists are nonetheless using the *language* of nationalism in this age of indigenism, and to the extent that it is always best to deal with the discourses actually in use, we should take them at face value.[10]

Hence this chapter is about indigenous *nations* and the *nationalisms* that produce them, and it starts with the most basic of questions: What exactly do we mean by nationalism, and how does that apply to indigenous peoples? What are the historical, epistemological, and moral foundations of nationalism? What are nationalists, what do they do, and why?

Because I take seriously (some might say hopelessly literally) the "nation" in nationalism, I want to begin by asking what nations are and where they come from. There hasn't been much discussion of these basic questions in Native nationalist discourse, yet, as we shall see, they come with their own extremely contentious debates. After reviewing some of these general issues, I will consider the work of one Native nationalist writing today, Taiaiake Alfred himself, and compare his nationalism to "literary nationalism": a critical movement that dominates Native literary studies and constitutes a new call for cultural workers. This chapter will conclude with a consideration of those "new societies," asking how Native nationalisms might (or might not) contribute to a dream as visionary as that. At the end of it all, I suppose another goal here is simply to articulate for myself an answer to the "nationalism question"—because, you see, it is always highly problematic.

The Idea of an Indian Nation

In 1491 there were some ten million people living north of the Rio Grande and speaking at least 300 languages representing more than 50 different language families. (By contrast, Europe at the time had only 3 active language families: Indo-European, Finno-Urgic, and Basque.) Linguists have counted more than 40 languages in the Athabaskan-Eyak-Tlingit family, 30 in the Algonquian-Ritwan family, 30 in the Uto-Aztecan, and 23 in the Salishan. Other language families had fewer tongues but more speakers and covered vast geographic territory: Iroquoian in the Northeast and Southeast, Eskimo-Aleut in the Arctic, Muskogean in the Southeast. Many of these languages are still spoken. There are roughly 362,000 fluent speakers of the 154 Native languages that still survive in the United States, with Navajo spoken by more than 100,000 people. The speakers of these languages had different explanations for their origins. Some, like the Iroquois, believed that their ancestors had fallen from the sky, others, like the Pueblo and Navajo, thought they emerged from underground, and others said that they came into the world through a hollow log. They lived in different ways too, some groups following seasonal patterns of hunting and gathering, while others were engaging in systematic agriculture. Finally, they had different systems for making decisions in their communities, some granting limited powers to chiefs, others forming democratically oriented councils, and all of them exercising to various extents theocratic modes of governing. All of this is to state that pre-Columbian Native America was constituted by a great diversity of peoples, cultures, languages, lifestyles, beliefs, and forms of political organization. Were they "nations"?

"Nation" comes from the Latin word *natio* and shares an etymological link with *natura* insofar as both words have something to say about the processes of birth (e.g., *natus, nasci*), the general idea being that one is born into his or her nation. The English word *nation* has been in use since at least the thirteenth century, and for much of its history it referred to "race," "stock," or "breed." But the concept became more political and cultural—and less racial—by the sixteenth century, and it was understood that way by nearly everyone in the seventeenth.[11]

There is no obvious word for "nation" in *Ojibwemowin*, although there are terms that describe some connected ideas: for instance, "territory" (*aki*, which can also be used for "earth," "land," "ground," or "country"), "people" (you will remember *anishinaabe*; if you don't, see chapter 1), and "governance" (*odaake*, meaning "to direct affairs" or "steer" in the mechanical sense of driving a car). *Odaa-* in particular is a sound that makes speakers think in terms of cause and effect in a mechanistic sense; for example, *odaabii'aagan* is the word for a draft animal such as an ox, and *odaabii'iwe* is how you say "drive"; one recently invented word, *odaabii'iwe-mazina'igaans*, means "driver's license." Is it so great a leap to *odaakewigimaa*, "director" or "governor"? Although I haven't come across a word for "constitution," one could do worse than say *gichi-inaakonigewin*, or "Great Law." But no word for "nation" as such. So, what of all those different groups who were here in 1491? Were they "nations"?

To answer that question we must take a detour and examine a theoretical debate that has been argued for some time. Scholars who study the nation have long disagreed about its origins and character, but most now say that nations as we recognize them today are an essentially modern development whose logic cannot be discovered prior to the modern era. This was famously the view of Ernest Gellner, who thought the notion of nationhood was a distinctly modern idea indelibly associated with industrialization, mass literacy, public education, and other such modern developments. Further, Gellner thought that nations were always produced by nationalism and not the other way around; this too was a distinctive product of modernity, as "agrarian [or tribal] civilizations do not engender nationalism but industrial societies do."[12]

It had to do with the profound historical developments that accompanied industrialization and had the unintended effect of creating anxieties for elites who responded by transforming "low" cultures into "high" national cultures:

the role of culture in human life was totally transformed by that
cluster of economic and scientific changes which have transformed
the world since the seventeenth century. The prime role of culture
in agrarian society was to underwrite people's status and people's
identity. Its role was really to embed their position in a complex,
usually hierarchical and relatively stable social structure. The world as
it is now is one in which people have no stable position or structure.
They are members of professional ephemeral bureaucracies which are
not deeply internalized and which are temporary. They are members
of increasingly loose family associations. What really matters is their
incorporation and mastery of high culture; I mean a literate codified
culture which permits context-free communication. Their membership
in such a community and their acceptability in it, that is a nation. It
is the consequence of the mobility and anonymity of modern society
and of the semantic non-physical nature of work that mastery of
such culture and acceptability in it is the most valuable possession a
man has. It is a precondition of all other privileges and participation.
This automatically makes him into a nationalist because if there is
non-congruence between the culture in which he is operating and
the culture of the surrounding economic, political and educational
bureaucracies, then he is in trouble.[13]

In other words (and bringing this discussion closer to home), when a
modern Ojibwe becomes educated in modern institutions (like "universities") and begins his career in, oh, let's say Syracuse, New York, he
enters a "professional ephemeral bureaucracy," engages in "context-free
communication" (say, publishing or doing e-mail all the time), realizes
his "increasingly loose family associations" and lack of a "stable position or structure" in the cultural realm in which he now operates, and
subsequently begins to experience anxieties that have everything to do
with what the modernists called "alienation." When combined with a
nagging sense that his people have been on the receiving end of raw deals
in the past and perhaps still in the present, these anxieties can produce a
sentiment holding forth that "the political and the national unit should
be congruent": in other words, nationalism.[14] This new nationalist might
then start describing his people in terms that are decidedly national in
tone (perhaps he begins scouring *Ojibwemowin* for nationalistic language like *odaake* and *aki*), and if enough people join him in this project,
if their arguments seem reasonable, and especially if they are backed by
some compelling force, we will soon have a bona fide Ojibwe nationalism
on our hands.

But how will we recognize the nation that this nationalist is producing through his efforts to transform his people's "low" culture into a "high" national culture? In Gellner's view, all nations are defined by a combination of culture and recognition:

1. Two men are of the same nation if and only if they share the same culture, where culture in turn means a system of ideas and signs and associations and ways of behaving and communicating.

2. Two men are of the same nation if and only if they *recognize* each other as belonging to the same nation. In other words, *nations maketh man;* nations are the artifacts of men's convictions and loyalties and solidarities. A mere category of persons (say, occupants of a given territory, or speakers of a given language, for example) becomes a nation if and when the members of the category firmly recognize certain mutual rights and duties to each other in virtue of their shared membership of it. It is their recognition of each other as fellows of this kind which turns them into a nation, and not the other shared attributes, whatever they might be, which separate that category from non-members. (7)

(We assume Gellner would now include women in this discussion too.) A nation is not defined only by a distinctive culture or language or some territory; nor is it reducible to the intersubjective recognition of citizens with "mutual rights and duties to each other." In fact, both culture and recognition have to be present for the nation to be a nation as such. Nationalists must claim both nationality, "an argument about legal status," and nationhood, "a claim about the character and integrity of one's cultural identity," in one fell swoop.

Modernity produces elites who experience alienation and anxiety and respond by transforming "low" cultures into "high" national cultures, thereby producing the nation, itself defined by a modernized combination of culture and intersubjective recognition, rights, and duties. But we also have to recognize the important role played by the *state,* which Gellner defines as "that institution or set of institutions specifically concerned with the enforcement of order . . . such as police forces and courts"; the state is that which holds the "monopoly of legitimate violence" (3). There have been many different kinds of states over time, but all have in common the idea of a ruler, or, in other words, sovereignty. Because not all societies are state-endowed, Gellner says, "the problem of nationalism does not rise for stateless societies" (4). Lacking the general idea of governance by a sovereign ruler, or institutions producing the same effect, there is no need to make a nationalist claim, for without it "one obviously cannot ask whether or not its boundaries are congruent with the limits of nations" (ibid.).

It is important to recognize that Gellner's theory is partly an answer to Marxism's "national question" as to why the universal proletariat revolution never happened (as had long been predicted according to supposedly ironclad laws of historical materialism). "Contrary to what Marxism has led people to expect, it is pre-industrial society which is addicted to horizontal differentiation within societies," Gellner writes, "whereas industrial society strengthens the boundaries between nations rather than those between classes" (12). In other words, and whether we like it or not, history has produced more nationalism than class-consciousness.

Coming back to our 1491 Indians, Gellner would probably insist that they weren't nations in the modern sense because of the unmodern ways they lived:

> Mankind has passed through three fundamental stages in its history: the pre-agrarian, the agrarian, and the industrial. Hunting and gathering bands were and are too small to allow the kind of political division of labour which constitutes the state; and so, for them, the question of a state, of a stable specialized order-enforcing institution, does not really arise. By contrast, most, but by no means all, agrarian societies have been state-endowed. Some of these states have been strong and some weak, some have been despotic and others law-abiding. They differ a very great deal in their form. The agrarian phase of human history is the period in which the very existence of the state is an option. Moreover, the form of the state is highly variable. During the hunting-gathering stage, the option was not available. (5)

By the same token, moreover, the Europeans who encountered the Natives and began treating with them weren't really nations either, at least not according to Gellner. They were subjects of a sovereign, or the church, or the Hudson's Bay Company, or some other kind of corporation, until modernity finally encouraged the modern nation and state to emerge. And, incidentally, Indian treaties played a very significant role in *that* social process. In its infancy, the United States held up treaties as evidence of its legitimacy as a nation at a time when the idea was anything but certain, because, after all, those Indians who used to treat with the European powers had been treating with them.

If our old-time Indians weren't nations in the ways we think of nations today (which is, remember, always a very modern thing to do), what were they? Or, more to the point, what were they doing? I would submit that they engaged not in nationalism but in *cultural resistance,* and further, this resistance was often connected to military resistance. In 1680, Popé led the great Pueblo Revolt, which involved the unenviable task of organizing some seventeen thousand Pueblos across more than two dozen independent communities who spoke six different languages into a united front; according to one account, after the revolt Indians dove into the rivers and scrubbed themselves clean "of the character of the holy sacraments."[15] In another example, from 1736, water played a very different role than it did for the Pueblos:

> ostensibly Christianized Natives left Spanish hegemony, both
> ideologically and geographically, when a viable alternative presented
> itself. They transferred their allegiance to the British, because the
> British had offered them arms and more trade goods and did not
> require them to commit cultural suicide in order to get those things.
> Baptized Natives simply struck themselves on the forehead saying,
> "Go away water! I am no Christian!"[16]

After the birth of America in the eighteenth century, Indian cultural resistance continued to be pursued via military means. In 1805, Tenskwatawa, the Shawnee Prophet, advanced a powerful message of cultural resistance across tribal lines, emphasizing sobriety, rejection of Christianity and intermarriage, abandonment of European technology and clothing, reclamation of traditional diets, and tribal land rights, while his brother Tecumseh organized a pan-tribal military alliance against the whites. Their cultural resistance came pretty close to what we would call nationalism today, advancing as it did a compelling vision of a great Indian Territory from Canada to Mexico, but their project was unsuccessful.

Indian cultural resistance movements shared two things in common—protection of a way of life, and protection of tribal land and resources—and thus they underscored the first of the nation's two definitional requirements: specifically, nationhood, or the idea of a shared culture requiring protection. The other, more legalistic, component—nationality—and the relationships between them has been addressed by Anthony D. Smith, who thinks Gellner tells only half the story.

Smith believes nations are modern too, but not made out of thin air: "nations . . . are the products of preexisting traditions and heritages that have coalesced over the generations."[17] Smith calls these preexisting things *"ethnie,"* and they constitute the raw materials for the making of nations. *Ethnie* was a term invented in the nineteenth century by the

French anthropologist Georges Vacher de Lapouge to describe human groups that formed coherent entities and achieved solidarity, and the word is derived from the Greek *ethnos,* which is sometimes translated as "people" in that specifically cultural sense that suggests the need for an article (e.g., "a people," "the people," perhaps "those people" or "my people"; the point being to remark upon a certain kind of difference or Otherness).[18] The Greek term *ethnie* invoked ideas that are broader than what is usually meant by "ethnic" today. *Ethnos* could refer to animals just as much as people, to women in contradistinction to men, to castes, occupations, swarms of bees, and religious groups, and not just to "a people" in the biological sense of a tribe (although the Greeks had a word for tribe too, *genos,* which was considered a subdivision of *ethnos*).[19] "In all these usages," Smith writes, "the common denominator appears to be the sense of a number of people or animals living together and acting together, though not necessarily belonging to the same clan or tribe."[20]

The French *ethnie* was picked up by intellectuals to describe "primitive" or "archaic" peoples, and it played a significant role in the eventual popularization of *ethnicity,* a word that first appeared in the Oxford English Dictionary in 1933. Smith's reclamation of *ethnie* is a challenge to the modernist theory of the nation by its emphasis on the organic roots of many (but by no means all) nations today. Smith's own definition of *ethnie* is "a named human population with a myth of common ancestry, shared historical memories, elements of a shared culture, and association with a specific homeland." As for the nation, Smith defines it as "a named human population inhabiting an historic territory and sharing common myths and historical memories, a mass public culture, a common economy and common legal rights and duties." Finally, as to their historical relationship,

> the nation is a sub-variety and development of the *ethnie,* though we are not dealing with some evolutionary law of progression, nor with some necessary or irreversible sequence. While the *ethnie* is an historical culture community, the nation is a community [with a] mass, public culture, historic territory and legal rights. In other terms, *the nation shifts the emphasis of community away from kinship and cultural dimensions to territorial, educational and legal aspects,* while retaining links with older cultural myths and memories of the *ethnie.*[21]

Hence, while the *ethnie* is primarily culturally defined, the *nation* emphasizes intersubjective recognition of membership, duties, rights, and responsibilities against the backdrop of a mass public culture and common economy; in fact, the grand historical transformation from *ethnie* to nation is the conscious decision to move away from kinship and culture toward "territorial, educational, and legal aspects" of community. But the former was "always there," at least in one sense, and it is effectively carried forth in time. In other words, Smith finds continuity where Gellner sees only invention.

The implications of Smith's work for indigenous nationhood are enticing. Whenever an indigenous community claims to have been a nation "since time immemorial," it is not waved off by the argument that nations didn't exist prior to the industrial era, even though that claim may be true to a certain extent. The *ethnie* is what we mean, and it connects to our present nation. Nor, on the other hand, should we be quick to dismiss the modernist theories of nationalism like Gellner's as little more than exhibiting "inherent bias toward the particularly Western form of the nation-building process," as Gerald Alfred charges.[22] The nation isn't "Western," it's "modern," and to assume otherwise would be to locate its development spatially rather than temporally: a bad idea unless one is prepared to deny the existence of nations in "non-Western" locales all over the world. It's better to simply claim your nation's right to existence based on an "unbroken" descent from an ancient *ethnie*. The idea of an Indian nation may be as modern as anyone else's nation, but that doesn't mean its origins aren't as old as the hills.

Not all nations in the world today have ethnic origins, of course, and not all nations that do will retain visible markers of the *ethnie* in politico-legal realms of nationality. Nor is it necessary to do so. All that is required for an ethnic nation to be a nation as such is the combination of nationhood and nationality described by Gellner, the historical transformation of which has been described by Smith. Nationalism is the political movement that makes the transformation happen.

Modernize Your *Ethnie*

So, how does one transform an *ethnie* into a nation? This is what distinguishes cultural resistance from nationalism proper: the former says No, the latter says Yes. Tecumseh and Tenskwatawa (to mention only two of a long and esteemed line of cultural resisters) said No to the imposition of cultural and political dominance, but they didn't say Yes to modernity. Much to the contrary, they and others like them rejected modernity precisely to keep their existing ways of life intact. This was certainly the tactic of Red Jacket, Petalesharo, and others who advanced "separatist" proposals regarding culture and politics, but they would be better considered cultural resisters than actual nationalists. Nationalists do not reject the modern; they modernize their *ethnie*. Let's consider these differences.

On February 4, 1822, Petalesharo presented a speech before President James Monroe, arguing that the same "Great Spirit made us all" but "intended that we should live differently from each other." How differently?

> He made the whites to cultivate the earth, and feed on domestic animals; but he made us, red skins, to rove through the uncultivated woods and plains; to feed on wild animals; and to dress with their skins. He also intended that we should go to war—to take scalps— *steal horses from* and triumph over our enemies—cultivate peace at home, and promote the happiness of each other. . . . We differ from you in appearance and manners as well as in our customs; and we differ from you in our religion; we have no large houses as you have to worship the Great Spirit in; if we had them today, we should want others tomorrow, for we have not, like you, a fixed habitation—we have no settled homes except our villages, where we remain but two moons in twelve.

Given these notable differences in culture and ways of living, the most rational thing to do is divide the lands and distribute them fairly, thus allowing different cultures to thrive on both sides:

> Some of your good chiefs, as they are called (missionaries), have proposed to send some of their good people among us to change our habits, to make us work and live like the white people. . . . I love the manner in which we live, and think myself and warriors brave. Spare me then, my Father; let me enjoy my country, and pursue the buffalo, and the beaver, and the other wild animals of our country, and I will trade their skins with your people. I have grown up, and lived thus long without work—I am in hopes you will suffer me to die without it. We have plenty of buffalo, beaver, deer, and other wild animals—we also have an abundance of horses—we have every thing we want—we have plenty of land, if you will keep your people off it.[23]

This is cultural resistance insofar as Petalesharo articulates the differences that exist between Pawnees and whites and resists the latter. In remarkably concise fashion he covers the gamut of culture—religious belief, food production, clothes, occupations, "appearances," and methods of worship—and he understands how cultural changes are bound to produce new desires among his people ("if we had them today, we should want others tomorrow"). The thing is, he does not want them. Modernity is not his bag.

Because of his separatism, Petalesharo is the sort of historical figure who is sometimes held up by writers today as a nationalist in his own time. But we do so only if we are willing to commit a bad kind of historical revisionism—reading our present desires into the past—because Petalesharo was no nationalist. He was an antimodernist who reasonably wanted his people to be left alone, and he was a cultural resister in the way of many of his contemporaries: one who resisted the imposition of new and foreign ways. To be a nationalist, remember, is not only to assert one's separatism; it is to argue for the right of one's group to be recognized as a nation. Because the nation is always a modern construct, it depends on at least some willingness to modernize. Petalesharo was uninterested in that project. Yet, if not someone like him, which of our nineteenth-century Indian ancestors were the nationalists?

Writers. I have in mind not only figures like Elias Boudinot and William Apess but also everyone who ever signed a treaty (and not everyone did; those who refused were not nationalists but cultural resisters). For what else is a treaty if not a legal contract between nations? When Indians made their x-marks on treaties during the nineteenth century, they entered into a social process that has no meaning at all outside a modern national paradigm; therefore, treaty signers committed themselves to nation status at the moment they made their x-marks. That mark, whether by implication or conscious intent, makes one a nationalist, at least of a sort. (Call them "weak nationalists," if you absolutely must.) The scene of writing was where indigenous ethnic groups began transforming themselves into actual nations, and treaty signings were the original and most ubiquitous occasion for that remarkable historical shift.

Never was this more the case than after the establishment of the United States, the great historical significance of which Indians understood all too well. Beginning in 1778, Indians entered into 367 ratified treaties with the United States, another six whose status is "questionable," according to Francis Paul Prucha, and approximately as many illegitimate or nonratified treaties and "agreements" (the term that replaced "treaty" in 1871 with passage of the End of Treaty Making Act).[24] In other words, even if we leave aside the long history of treaty making with Europeans prior to the establishment of the United States, Natives entered into more than six hundred treaties at the apex of the age of nationalism. While there was a tremendous amount of diversity across specific treaties, there were some common themes that inhere to the treaty-making process in general: the establishment of peace and diplomatic relations, the articulation of "friendship," the drawing of territorial boundaries, and commitments on both sides to the "civilization" process, including certain provisions for schools and churches; the construction of mills and mechanical shops; agricultural implements, seeds, and livestock; blacksmiths, farmers, doctors, teachers, missionaries; Euro-American clothing, cooking utensils, tools, "treaty cloth," and more chickens than you can shake a stick at. Schooling in particular was deemed to be especially important, as education was considered the most powerful method of civilizing there was. In 1819 the United States created a "Civilization Fund" supporting missionaries in their educational efforts, and in 1867–68 the Indian Peace Commission made certain to include this article in all of its treaties:

> In order to insure the civilization of the Indians entering into this treaty, the necessity of education is admitted, especially of such of them as are or may be settled on said agricultural reservations, and they therefore pledge themselves to compel their children, male and female, between the ages of six and sixteen years, to attend school; and it is hereby made the duty of the agent for said Indians to see that this stipulation is strictly complied with; and the United States agrees that for every thirty children between said ages who can be induced or compelled to attend school, a house shall be provided and a teacher competent to teach the elementary branches of an English education shall be furnished, who will reside among said Indians, and faithfully discharge his or her duties as a teacher.[25]

This sort of language is usually characterized (not at all without justification) as "paternalism," "assimilation," and thus part and parcel of colonialist domination: a program designed to "civilize" people who were characterized as "savages" and little else. From such a view one could conclude that the treaty era was actually a setback for Indians; a killing blow against the possibility of resistance.

However, looking at the treaty experience from the Indian side of things—a point of view that is still often overlooked—the embracement of new tools and ways of living, and especially the commitment to send one's children to school, can just as easily be interpreted as a commitment to modernization. The treaty signers said Yes, not No to the schools and other technologies of modernity, and they did it in the context of a contract between nations that assumed legitimate nationhood on both sides. Their reasons for doing so should be obvious: they wanted a better life for their children, and they were resigned to the imposition of a new order, so they made a rational decision to get what they could from it.

It wasn't only about resignation, however. Sometimes modernity was viewed as a good thing in its own right. This was certainly the case with Jacob Eastman, father to the great Dakota writer Charles Alexander Eastman, who, after spending more than a decade in exile as a result of the 1862 Dakota War, returned to his teenage son and preached a compelling case for embracing modernity. As Eastman tells it in *From the Deep Woods to Civilization,* even though his father's attempts to modernize his life were thwarted (his initial crops were destroyed by grasshoppers and drought), he never lost sight of his dream that one day his son would walk the "white man's trail." For Jacob, that road was paved with useful technologies:

> "Here is a race which has learned to weigh and measure everything, time and labor and the results of labor, and has learned to accumulate and preserve both wealth and the records of experience for future generations. You yourselves know and use some of the wonderful inventions of the white man, such as guns and gunpowder, knives and hatchets, garments of every description, and there are thousands of other things both beautiful and useful."[26]

What enabled these "wonderful inventions" was writing: "'he is able to preserve on paper the things he does not want to forget. He records everything—the sayings of his wise men, the laws enacted by his counselors.'"[27] Most important in the eyes of the father, the embracement of modernity would allow the son to improve his quality of life: "'if you are able to think strongly and well, that will be a quiver full of arrows for you, my son. All of the white man's children must go to school, but those who study best and longest need not work with their hands after that, for they can work with their minds.'"[28] Meritocracy, the father believed, would accompany modernity.

Jacob Eastman was portrayed in his son's prose in much the same way that Sarah Winnemucca Hopkins portrayed her grandfather Captain Truckee: as a well-intentioned if naive Indian who took the whites at their word, when in fact whites proved to be unworthy of that trust and didn't realize their own lofty words and ideals. That these damning critiques of white hypocrisy called into question the "civilizing" mission should not be taken as indictments of Indians who took the promises of modernity to heart. That this happened in the coercive contexts of colonialism does not diminish the fact of agency on the Indian side of the treaty. Those treaties had to be signed to be legitimate, and they were signed, but the subsequent political effect wasn't the "continuation" of the Indian nation so much as its *birth*. By entering into treaties, the people shifted the emphasis of their communities "away from kinship and cultural dimensions to territorial, educational and legal aspects." The moment of treaty was literally the invention of the modern Indian nation.

On the American side of the divide, we have a historical commentator on this transformation in John Marshall, the Supreme Court Chief Justice who in the 1830s wrote the decisions of three major Indian law cases—the Cherokee Trilogy—which still reverberate as legal doctrine. In *Cherokee Nation v. State of Georgia* (1831), Marshall characterized the Cherokees as "a State, as a distinct political society, separated from others," owing to treaties they had signed with the Americans:

> They have been uniformly treated as a State from the settlement of our country. The numerous treaties made with them by the United States recognize them as a people capable of maintaining the relations of peace and war, of being responsible in their political character for any violation of their engagements, or for any aggression committed on the citizens of the United States by any individual of their community. Laws have been enacted in the spirit of these treaties. The acts of our government plainly recognize the Cherokee Nation as a State, and the courts are bound by these acts.

The following year in *Worcester v. Georgia* (1832) Marshall reaffirmed this view by reminding Americans of the history and meanings of national concepts:

> The very term "nation," so generally applied to [Indians], means "a people distinct from others." The Constitution, by declaring treaties already made, as well as those to be made, to be the supreme law of the land, has adopted and sanctioned the previous treaties with the Indian nations, and consequently admits their rank among those powers who are capable of making treaties. The words "treaty" and "nation" are words of our own language, selected in our diplomatic and legislative proceedings, by ourselves, having each a definite and well-understood meaning. We have applied them to Indians, as we have applied them to the other nations of the earth. They are applied to all in the same sense.

Marshall was refreshingly clear that Indian nations were nations "in the same sense" and the reason for it was treaty making. Marshall, you see, understood and valued the political significance of the x-mark.

To be perfectly clear, I am not idealizing the moment of treaty; nor am I suggesting that there was no coercion, deception, misunderstanding, or fatalism involved at this key historical site. Obviously, the hundreds of treaties made between Indians and Americans during the nineteenth century were a mixed bag on every level. What I am saying is that Natives understood what was at stake in their treaties and argued passionately, not only with commissioners but with each other, about their implications; that not all chose to sign treaties (and often made speeches explaining why), but most did; and that doing so signified agency and consent— yes, limited on both counts. But it was not something that was simply "thrust" upon the Indians, as is implied by the stereotype of Natives as childlike innocents whose Edens were tragically lost forever when the Americans "forced" them to sign treaties "they didn't understand" and were "broken" anyway. I am arguing that at least on some level Indians who signed treaties were making a choice to modernize and nationalize. Perhaps, as Robert Warrior has written on the subject of sovereignty, Indians were making "a decision . . . in our minds, in our hearts, and in our bodies—to be sovereign and to find out what that means in the process."[29]

That decision was recorded in writing, especially by "strong nationalists" who, unlike the cultural resisters, said yes and not no to modernity (typically characterized as "civilization" in nineteenth-century parlance); I mean Indian intellectuals who published their x-marks in essays, speeches, books, pamphlets, tracts, sermons, tribal histories, autobiographies, poems, short stories, novels, and op-eds in the scores of Indian newspapers that were published during the nineteenth century. Native writers were nationalists in the classical sense: elites experiencing anxieties that accompanied modernity (which, remember, rode in on the back of colonization) and responded by transforming "low" cultures into "high" national ones. The emergence of Native writers coincides with the birth of the Indian nation.

The most obviously nationalistic writers worked during the 1820s: the era of removal. Elias Boudinot began publishing the first tribal newspaper, the bilingual *Cherokee Phoenix,* in October 1827, with a "Prospectus" that promised the following:

1. The laws and public documents of the Nation.
2. Account of the manners and customs of the Cherokees, and their progress in Education, Religion and the arts of civilized life; with such notices of other Indian tribes as our limited means of information will allow.

3. The principal interesting news of the day.
4. Miscellaneous articles, calculated to promote Literature,
   Civilization, and Religion among the Cherokees.[30]

It doesn't get any more modern than that. The *Phoenix* was established by the Cherokee General Council precisely to promote nationalization and defend the nation from the prospect of removal, and there were no perceived conflicts between political nationalism and cultural assimilation. Boudinot, a fervent Christian, spent much of his time attacking efforts by the state of Georgia and the United States to impugn Cherokee sovereignty in violation of treaties, but he also devoted much energy to chronicling Cherokee "progress." Boudinot was no cultural resister, but he was a dedicated nationalist who viewed assimilation in the same way that some see "economic development" today: as a modernization program.

Again, the word for it then was "civilization," and in retrospect Boudinot's endorsements of civilization and assaults on Cherokee traditionalism can seem condescending and smug. In their own time, however, they put the lie to popular notions regarding Indian destiny—the widespread idea that vanishment was inevitable and just; "Fate"—that undergirded the policy of removal. Boudinot's consistent argumentative strategy was to suggest that savagism and vanishment would be ensured, not combated, by removal. In a January 18, 1829, editorial he warned: "While he possesses a national character, there is hope for the Indian. But take his rights away, divest him of the last spark of national pride, and introduce him to a new order of things, invest him with oppressive laws, grievous to be borne, he droops like the fading flower before the noon day sun."[31] As for the Indian's cultural character, Boudinot never failed to remind his readers that the times were a-changing. In an editorial on "Indian Clans" (February 18, 1829), he assumed a proto-ethnological discourse that sought to discredit the traditional clan system, not only because it was inherently bad, but because "it was the mutual law of clans as connected with murder, which rendered this custom savage and barbarous."[32] He was speaking of the practice of blood revenge, which the Council had outlawed twenty years earlier, and he characterized it as an obstacle to the goal of nationalization. "The Cherokees as a nation, had nothing to do with murder" before the Council's ban, there being no government to prohibit it, therefore "the Cherokees were then to be pitied." Yet "we can now say with pleasure" that those older laws "are all repealed and are remembered only as vestiges of ignorance."[33] The nation had acquired a monopoly on legitimate violence, making it, and not tradition, sovereign at last. But not everything that was traditional had to go. Cherokee language, for instance, was privileged in the pages of the *Phoenix*; Boudinot never condemned it, and that's more than can be said of most tribal newspapers today. Heritage language is one of the clearest manifestations there is of an *ethnie,* and Boudinot kept it around.

Nationalists must take a careful account of the past. At roughly the same time Boudinot was working, in 1827, David Cusick published *Sketches of the Ancient History of the Six Nations,* a collection of Haudenosaunee legends and myths that (as my Haudenosaunee students never fail to remind me) took some liberties with their contents (I'm dependably told that his versions are "wrong"). But he named "History" what other writers had consigned to "myth," told an *Iroquois* story instead of an *Indian* one, and depicted a territory where the "Real People" (Iroquois) fought with "monsters" who metaphorically stood in for other Native peoples. At a time when removal had been proposed for the Six Nations, and savagism was increasingly being located in "race," Cusick produced an Iroquois "History" for readers who more or less believed that having a History was a mandate for Being Human. Cusick was so effective at delineating his people's national boundaries, textually speaking, that as recently as 2002 the critic Susan Kalter could characterize his writing as "literature from a foreign nation."[34] Cusick provides another example of how a nationalist turns a "low" local culture into a "high" national culture: give it a boundary, point to its History, then proudly hold it up for all the world to see.

Likewise, the Indian authors of what Maureen Konkle (following Samuel Gardner Drake) calls "traditionary histories" were never chroniclers of the past in an empiricist's sense. Writers such as William Whipple Warren, Peter Jones, and George Copway resisted "idealized, romanticized stories that described Native people as inhabitants of the distant past" and instead wrote histories that made sense in the context of the contemporaneous present:

> Native writers did exactly the opposite of what white writers did when they wrote about their traditions, and histories, in the period. They not only explained traditions but also explained their experience of whites and that of their tribes generally; they wrote about treaties and broken agreements; they wrote about the progress of Indian nations as they understood it—usually all in the same book.[35]

Traditionary histories discussed myths, legends, songs, ceremonies, and religious beliefs as a kind of cultural patrimony akin to that of the Greeks—perhaps in the same way that Cusick presented Haudenosaunee stories as if they were biblical; thus they circumscribed cultural, hence national, boundaries around the people. Although they typically advanced the argument that "for Indians to move forward in time as Indians, they must be brought up to speed morally and intellectually," as Konkle says, their "rejection of the political insubordination of Indians makes 'assimilationist' an inaccurate characterization" of their positions.[36] It would be more accurate to say "modernist" and most accurate to say "nationalist."

Traditionary histories presented portraits of Indian people that clearly resonated as nationalistic in their own day, not only in their content but through their rhetorical tactics. George Copway's *Traditional History and Characteristic Sketches of the Ojibway Nation* (1850), for example, begins with a description of "the country of the Ojibways," covers much cultural and historical experience, and ends with policy proposals for removal to the Northwest Territory between Nebraska and Minnesota on the Missouri River. This work and other writing by Copway is often denigrated as overwrought, sentimentalized, and misguided, and certainly those cases can be made. What often goes unobserved, however, is Copway's canny use of a particular rhetorical strategy that was often employed in the nineteenth century by literary nationalists of many origins: namely, his description of Indian bodies as metaphors for nationhood. Generally speaking, this strategy held that bodies could stand in for nations; they were either healthy or sick, strong or feeble, clean or dirty, and, in the age of colonialism, "fair" or "darker." In his chapter on games Copway proclaims "what every one probably knows, that the plays and exercises of the Indians have contributed much to the formation of that noble, erect, and manly figure for which they are so remarkable," adding that "the law of the nation, like that of ancient Greece, has been enacted with a view to the health of its subjects."[37] This sort of language metaphorically characterizes the Ojibwe nation as "noble, erect, and manly"— "like that of ancient Greece"—in keeping with synecdochic portrayals of bodies common to much nineteenth-century nationalist rhetoric.

As another example, consider Copway's artful description of a young lacrosse player, Mah-koonce, which in a way evokes Michelangelo's *David* much more than, say, Horatio Greenough's "vanishing Indian" sculpture, *The Rescue:*

> His body was a model for sculpture; well proportioned. His hands and feet tapered with all the grace and delicacy of a lady's. His long black hair flowed carelessly upon his shoulders. On the top of his raven locks waved in profusion seventeen signals (with their pointed fingers) of the

feathers of that rare bird, the western eagle, being the number of the
enemy he has taken with his own hand. A Roman nose with a classic
lip, which wore at all times a pleasing smile.[38]

This body not only stood in for Ojibwe nationhood; its essential quality
was comparable to that of the esteemed cultural forebears of the whites.
David, it seems, exists over here too. Of course, not all Indians were as
strong, manly, and erect as the Ojibwe. The poor Mohawks, once "the
Turks of the American forest," had become "a weak and puny race" thanks
to "strong drink."[39]

Nineteenth-century Native nationalism said yes to modernity, no to
the domination of outsiders, and addressed the cultural past in three important ways: by (1) characterizing it as "History," (2) circumscribing it
as unique, but also (3) making it seem comparable to the cultural pasts
of other nations. Nationalists were rarely culture cops, because they were
not engaged in cultural revitalization but political evolution; thus they
can be distinguished from cultural resisters like Petalesharo and Popé
too. I want to suggest that despite their different strategies, all of these
nationalists had one thing in common: they modernized their *ethnie*.

Modernizing the *ethnie* involves a great deal more than simply agitat-
ing for a state or seeking rights on the level of nationality, and it tran-
scends acts of cultural resistance or focusing purely on the level of nationhood. An effective nationalism must function on political and cultural
levels simultaneously. It will reveal to both the interior population and
the exterior world an unbroken line of descent connecting an *ethnie* to a
modern community distinguishable from others and hence deserving recognition, respect, and rights. An *ethnie* that has been modernized won't
resemble its cultural ancestors down to the smallest details, as culture
cops like to believe. Sometimes it will function more like a tribal flag: a
national symbol whose images evoke the past without reproducing it. It
is the memory of the *ethnie* that gets modernized by a nationalist, and
it can happen in different locales and in different ways. This becomes
rather difficult to do, however, if a culture is sequestered or quarantined.
For an *ethnie* to become a nation, its old cultural memories have to be
publicized: depicted, displayed, and shared, so nationalists must always
wear their cultures on their sleeves.

What we now call an Indian nation was a modern invention born at
the moment of treaty, and it was addressed by a host of Native writers
who used literacy and the English language to modernize and nationalize
their political communities. This is another reason why David Treuer's

statement, "Native American literature doesn't exist," cannot stand (see chapter 2). To the contrary, it must exist for the simple reason that it walks hand in hand with the idea of the "Indian nation." Indeed, both Native American literature and the Indian nation were born under the same moon.

One more social force needs to be mentioned before we move on. The treaty era and the removal era came to a close at roughly the same time—the end of the nineteenth century—when the Indian wars had ended, the treaties had stopped being made, and the United States assumed legal jurisdiction over major crimes on reservations. This period also saw the rise of off-reservation boarding schools, land allotment, and loss of religious freedom in Indian country. All told, the difference amounted to this: Indian nations had their promise of fulfillment taken away and placed squarely in the hands of the Americans. Clearly, this was a stunning blow to nationalism. Remember, it is one's aspiration for a state that produces nationalism, and it is nationalism that produces the nation. From the assimilation era until the civil rights movement, Native nationalism was basically dormant. It has now revived.

New Traditionalism

Today indigenous nationalisms can be found across the planet: in Canada and the United States, Latin America and Mexico, Australia and New Zealand, the South Pacific, Africa, Scandinavia, and elsewhere. Some nationalisms are entirely grassroots in nature and take the form of land occupations and standoffs with the state, others can be found in statehouses where Natives seek recognition by their colonizing governments, still others are engaged in the international project of petitioning global institutions like the United Nations for rights. As we noted earlier, some call this global development by a singular name—"indigenism"—but as Kay Warren and Jean Jackson warn, "the *indigenous movement*—a classic example of a new social movement at one level of abstraction—dissolves into widely diverse and divergent sets of goals, discourses, and strategies."[40] We have to recognize the diversity of Native nationalisms; at the same time, indigenous nationalisms do seem to hold something in common. As Warrior puts it, "Something similar is happening in indigenous communities all over the world."[41]

"Indigenous peoples are not engaged in a liberation struggle that aspires primarily or exclusively toward nationalist or racial equality," writes Ronald Neizen in *The Origins of Indigenism.* "'Assimilation' and 'cultural genocide' are the terms commonly used by indigenous leaders to describe the kind of censorious 'equality' that was often (and in many cases continues to be) imposed on them."[42] If not a secessionist movement seeking a new state, or a civil rights movement demanding more inclusion, then that something would appear to be resistance against incorporation into the dominant culture. *Equality-as-sameness* and *cultural genocide* play the villain in today's nationalisms, while *equality-of-differences* and *cultural survival* are the objectives. True enough. On the other hand, it would be a mistake to suggest (as Neizen slightly does) that there isn't a politically separatist dimension to these otherwise cultural claims. More often than not, indigenous nationalism links the goals of equality-of-differences and cultural survival to the more conventional political goals that one would expect from any nationalist movement, from land rights to legal jurisdiction. Native nationalisms seek both cultural survival and political power, that is, both nationhood and nationality, and not just resistance to the dominant culture.

All of these issues are addressed in the work of Taiaiake Alfred, a prominent and often inspiring theorist of Native nationalism working in the Canadian-American context. Alfred's first three treatises, *Heeding the Voices of Our Ancestors: Kahnawake Mohawk Politics and the Rise of Native Nationalism* (1995), *Peace, Power, Righteousness: An Indigenous Manifesto* (1999), and *Wasáse: Indigenous Pathways of Action and Freedom* (2005), all written over the span of a decade, provide both nationalists and scholars with a useful political vocabulary and some interesting models. They also exhibit noteworthy shifts in thought. As Alfred himself has described their progression, the first book was addressed to a general audience and justified the right of indigenous nations to exist, the second was addressed to Native leaders and argued for a stronger embracement of traditionalism, and the third went deeper still into the Native community and sought to "work on ourselves in an effort to improve our lives."[43] The movement, then, has been from exterior to interior, from an intended general readership to a specifically Native one (although obviously all books address all readers), and from justification to reflection. Alfred is a brilliant thinker who has already inspired young people to organize a Wasáse Movement in Canada, and his ideas should be taken seriously by anyone who professes a nationalist political orientation.[44] I want to examine the trajectory of Alfred's thought as an example of how one variant of nationalist argumentation is now taking shape and address what I think are some of its problems—"conceptual separatism," the "problematic peoplehood paradigm," and a habit of privileging "being" over "doing"—that seem counterproductive. This critique should not be taken as a dismissal of Alfred's ideas but simply as an interrogation of his unstated assumptions.

Published just five years after the Oka Crisis, Alfred's first book was a case study of nationalism in his own Mohawk nation, Kahnawake (near Montreal), and it argued for the legitimacy of Indian nationhood in the face of ongoing colonization practices. Alfred wrote that nationalism's goal was "cultural sovereignty and a political relationship based on group autonomy reflected in formal self-government arrangements in cooperation with existing state governments,"[45] and he situated these objectives historically and socially:

> The majority of communities in North America are no longer
> threatened with immediate extinction. Cultural survival and revival
> and the achievement of a basic level of material well-being have
> become only the prerequisites for a movement seeking a more
> consciously political set of objectives. The Mohawks of Kahnawake
> are one of those communities who have advanced beyond the survival
> mode to an explicit assertion of nationalist goals.[46]

Alfred has since rethought the likelihood of cultural survival and "immediate extinction," as we shall see, but in 1995 his emphasis was directed more toward nationality than to nationhood, the latter understood as an already achieved "prerequisite" for political goals. In a vein that continues across all three of his books, Alfred also attacked the conceptual language used to characterize political relationships between Natives and non-Natives:

> Observers of the political process from within and from outside
> Native societies have tended thus far to characterize the [nationalist]
> revitalization as a movement toward enhanced "self-government"
> powers or an expanded concept of "aboriginal rights." But these
> are narrow views which assume that Native politics functions in an
> environment created exclusively by non-Natives. Those who see the
> defining feature of modern Native politics as an attempt to synchronize
> Native values and institutions with those of the dominant society are
> trapped within a paradigm created to subdue Native peoples.[47]

Self-government and *aboriginal rights* are terms developed in the context of a colonizing relationship, so, despite their connotations of independence, they amount to no more than window dressing. The paradigm is colonization, and it is governed by power, but not a militarized power so much as a rhetorical or ideological power. Subsequently, language isn't just problematic in a theoretical sense; rather, it becomes essential to deconstruct political terms constantly. Because conceptual language can function like the proverbial master's tools, autonomy is impossible without new ascriptions.

The intensification of this basic argument between Alfred's first and second books, the latter now called a "manifesto," leads to his abandonment of more "Western" concepts that he thinks are too imbricated in the colonization paradigm to be of any value. Among them is our old friend *sovereignty*, which Alfred calls "inappropriate" for its irredeemable European theological and feudal roots:

> sovereignty is an exclusionary concept rooted in an adversarial and coercive Western notion of power. Indigenous peoples can never match the awesome coercive force of the state; so long as sovereignty remains the goal of indigenous politics, therefore, Native communities will occupy a dependent and reactionary position relative to the state.[48]

Pursuing sovereignty guarantees that you won't be sovereign, as the concept possesses a logic that is foreign to the consensus-based political traditions of Native peoples, and the settler state never means it in a literal sense anyway. Down, therefore, with sovereignty! But if concepts like *self-government, aboriginal rights,* and *sovereignty* won't save Indians, what will? Alfred concludes his manifesto with four basic objectives that he thinks are worth pursuing. First, traditional governments (for example, the Longhouse) must be restored. Second, heritage languages should be made the official languages of Indian nations. Third, economic self-sufficiency is required, but since that cannot be achieved without an expanded land base, fourth, that too is required. "Native communities must reject the claimed authority of the state," Alfred declares, "assert their right to self-govern their own territories and people, and act on that right as much as their capacity to do so allows."[49] This project seems to begin when leaders reject the conceptual language they inherited from the colonizers.

Therein lies a conundrum. How can nations make specific claims to anything at all without using the universal language, terminology, and conceptual apparatus of nations in general? The idea of the nation is universal and modern; there are not radically different kinds of nations in the world, only nations that do things differently or have different degrees of sovereignty. And speaking of sovereignty, that too is a modern and universal political concept indissolubly associated with the idea of the nation. To reject this conceptual language out of hand risks getting out of the national game altogether and ending up with something that might be "ethnic," or "racial," or even a "community," but it won't be a "nation" unless it is willing to speak the language of nations. That language is by definition a modern, universal lingua franca. Having said all that, Alfred is correct (or playing the nation game fairly) when he identifies "problems with" legal terminology such as *aboriginal rights* or *self-government,* but that places us in the realm of argument and not rejection of the language that all nations must use to argue about things. Vine Deloria Jr. had a problem with self-government too, but for the way it abstracted political life from cultural and community life, not because it was alien, incomprehensible, or expressed in English.[50] Similarly, Joanne Barker has convincingly argued that "sovereignty must be situated within the historical and cultural relationships in which it is articulated," that it has "no fixed meaning," "nothing inherent about its significance"; thus it can be asserted, contested, revised, or rearticulated in myriad different forms, and often is.[51] The point is, these kinds of concepts have to be claimed in order to contest or revise them. I would go so far as to suggest that claiming your right to engage in these debates is precisely what makes you a nationalist. Playing the rejection game is more the work of a cultural resister.

That is what I mean by *conceptual separatism:* the assertion of radical conceptual differences that are deemed incommensurable with other concepts and systems. It is usually asserted in the context of different cultures, as we see here—and also in some variants of cultural anthropology (e.g., Peter Gordon)[52]—and while it amounts to cultural separatism, it will not be effective nationalism. Nationalism is the sentiment holding that the national and the political ought to be congruent, and Native nationalism is a claim to nationhood and nationality based on an indigenous group's historical descent from an *ethnie.* How any claim to conceptual separatism in the realm of politics could be used to advance a nationalist argument is a mystery to me. We must be careful not to accentuate our differences to the point of incommensurability lest we drop out of political conversations altogether.

I think this general rule holds true for descriptions of culture as well. Alfred's third book, *Wasáse,* is his most deeply "cultural." Whereas his first studied Native nationalism as it functioned through tribal governments, and his second book assessed the limitations of those governments and exhorted a swift return to traditional leadership, his most recent is a subjective analysis of Natives on the interior and spiritual levels of life.

"*Wasáse*" is an ancient warrior's dance, the Thunder Dance, and a metaphor for the self-examination and lifestyle changes that Alfred thinks are necessary for Indian people to undertake in order to prepare for a decolonization movement that really matters. Alfred suggests that most Natives just aren't ready to pursue nationalism: "How can we regenerate ourselves culturally and achieve freedom and political independence when the legacies of disconnection, dependency, and dispossession have such a strong hold on us?"[53] These grim legacies are all too apparent in a variety of ways, from addictions and violence to suicide and selling out, but freedom is possible in the reclamation of a strong traditionalism: "I am searching for . . . not the surface aspects of the lifestyle and manners of our peoples in past times but the *quality* of an indigenous existence, the connective material that bound Onkwehonwe together when 'interests' and 'rights' were not a part of our people's vocabularies" (254). In other words, Indians must return to thinking, acting, and being like our ancestors again, not on a superficial level but *deeply*. Anything less would be like living as modern-day Tontos.

First those negative legacies must be transcended: "People must be made whole and strong and real again before they can embark on a larger struggle" (279). This is not really an individual pursuit so much as a community project of "warriors" empowering each other. Alfred wants to witness "one-to-one mentoring, face-to-face interaction, and small-group dialogue to effect the regeneration of our minds, bodies, and spirits. This is the ancient way of the warrior" (ibid.). Of course, this was also the ancient way of second-wave feminists, who called it "consciousness raising," but there are traditional Indian equivalents to what he describes: talking circles, sweat lodges, vision quests, and other such occasions for dialogue and introspection (and which were proudly reclaimed during the Red Power era). Alfred sees mentoring, interaction, and dialogue as the necessary first step toward regeneration, with the ultimate goal being yet another rejection of a supposedly "Western" concept:

> "aboriginalism," the ideology and identity of assimilation, in which Onkwehonwe are manipulated by colonial myths into a submissive position and are told that by emulating white people they can gain acceptance and possibly even fulfillment within mainstream society. Many Onkwehonwe today embrace the label of "aboriginal," but this identity is a legal and social construction of the state, and it is disciplined by racialized violence and economic oppression to serve an agenda of silent surrender. The acceptance of being aboriginal

is as powerful an assault on Onkwehonwe existences as any force of
arms brought upon us by Settler society. (23)

"Aboriginalism" is justly comparable to the "indian" critiqued by Vizenor,
as we said in chapter 1, but for Alfred it's not just a simulacrum or a legal
concept. It reaches most deeply into the innermost recesses of a person's
being. *Wasáse* is the adamant rejection of all that, "not to live without
white government, culture, and society, but to *live against them*" (282).

Living against another group (in this case, whites) is what we called
in chapter 2 "reactive self-perception": defining one's identity in opposition to another, usually more powerful and dominating group. Alfred's
dismissal of aboriginalism, which undergirds everything else in this book,
falls into a trap of binary oppositions. One is either Onkwehonwe or
aboriginal, either a warrior or assimilated, either doing the *wasáse* or
"emulating white people." This way of thinking represents something of
a notable shift for Alfred. In 1995, remember, he assured us that most indigenous nations "are no longer threatened with immediate extinction,"
but now "it must be recognized that the cultural basis of our existence
as Onkwehonwe has been nearly destroyed and that the cultural foundations of our nations must be restored or reimagined if there is going to be
a successful assertion of political or economic rights" (29). Onkwehonwe
have to be cultural resisters before they can be nationalists. The People
must learn to walk before they can run. All of which is to say: the People
are presently a Problem.

The problem with this line of thinking is not only its chicken-or-egg
dilemma (that is, we could just as well argue that strong sovereign nations
would produce cultural revitalization), but mainly its reliance on what
we might call the "problematic peoplehood paradigm." "Peoplehood" is
an increasingly popular idea in Native studies, and it has anthropological
roots. Edward Spicer was the first to advance the idea in his work on "enduring peoples" in *Cycles of Conquest: The Impact of Spain, Mexico, and
the United States on the Indians of the Southwest, 1533–1960,* a book
published in 1962.[54] For Spicer, land, spiritual life, and language use constituted a cultural foundation for identity that distinguished Native peoples
from other ethnic groups. The Cherokee anthropologist Robert Thomas
further developed the idea in a popular 1990 essay, "The Tap-Roots of
Peoplehood," that added "sacred history" to Spicer's tripartite structure.[55]
In 2003, Tom Holm, Diane Pearson, and Ben Chavis published an essay,
"Peoplehood: A Model for American Indian Sovereignty in Education,"
presenting "sacred history, ceremonial cycles, language, and homelands"

as a definition of peoplehood.[56] Alfred invokes peoplehood in a 2005 article (coauthored with Jeff Corntassel) that comes straight to the point when quoting the Apache scholar Bernadette Adley-Santa Maria, whose grandmother told her, "If you do not sing the songs—if you do not tell the stories and if you do not speak the language—you will cease to exist as 'Ndee.'"[57] That is precisely the "problematic" part of the peoplehood paradigm. If you do not conform to the model—land, religion, language, sacred history, ceremonial cycle, and so on—if you happen to live away from your homeland, speak English, practice Christianity, or know more songs by the Dave Matthews Band than by the ancestors, you effectively "cease to exist" as one of the People.

One can hardly build a nation on so rigidly defined a People as that. It's all too wrapped up in the *ethnie,* and it comes very close to reproducing the logic of culture cops (or perhaps anthropologists). Now, I am not saying that the general idea of the People is illegitimate. To the contrary, most of the names we use to identify ourselves (e.g., *anishinaabe*) translate to just that, and, as Deloria and others have observed many times over, the concept has great power in Native communities.[58] Plus, it was a major battle at the level of the United Nations just to move from a discourse on indigenous "issues" to "populations" to "peoples," and the last thing I'm trying to do here is move backwards. But elsewhere I have advanced the concept of "nation-people" to recognize and honor traditional reverence for the People while simultaneously trying to move beyond it toward a political identity that more closely resembles a "nation-state."[59] By nation-people I meant a modern community of people that receives its identity from the myths and memories of an *ethnie,* the cultural integrity of which may still be apparent in some communities today, but sometimes not, and never necessarily so. The *ethnie* (as we imagine it today) may well be static, timeless, or defined by four-part models, but the nation is always shifting "away from kinship and cultural dimensions to territorial, educational and legal aspects" of community. When a community's actually existing diversity is unacknowledged or unrecognized, then what we are seeing is cultural resistance and not actual nationalism. Or, if put into practice, then it becomes the worst sort of nationalism there is: the kind that can be accompanied by cultural purification programs or ethnic cleansing. I know Alfred isn't calling for that sort of thing, but some people might.

Rather than rely on problematic peoplehood paradigms, I would suggest developing the notion of a nation-people further to envision a nationalism that starts from, not denies, the actually existing diversity of Native communities. Let us give it a paradoxical name: "realist nationalism" (for what gets described as pure idealism more than nationalism?). Realist nationalism works in the same basic way as any ethnonationalism: turning "low" cultures into "high" national cultures while based on the historical fact and memory of an *ethnie,* but it recognizes that the nation-people that came into existence at the moment of treaty are more culturally diverse than the ancestors as we imagine them today. I also have in mind a different metaphor for culture than the one that is usually implied in most nationalistic discourse: that all-too-common characterization of culture as if it resembled a *tree,* with its characteristic references to "tap-roots," "branches," "hybridity," and other such horticultural fare. In opposition to the persistent metaphoric logic of the tree, realist nationalism could theorize culture through the use of a different natural metaphor: the *rhizome.* As Gilles Deleuze and Félix Guattari explain,

> A rhizome as a subterranean stem is absolutely different from roots
> and radicles. Bulbs and tubers are rhizomes. Plants with roots or
> radicles may be rhizomorphic in other respects altogether. Burrows
> are too, in all their functions of shelter, supply, movement, evasion,
> and breakout. The rhizome itself assumes very diverse forms, from
> ramified surface extension in all directions to concretion into bulbs
> and tubers. . . . The rhizome includes the best and the worst: potato
> and couchgrass, or the weed.[60]

As a metaphoric description of nonhierarchical networks, the rhizome is not like a tree. Rhizomes exist underground and are composed of very complex and extremely diverse systems and networks of roots, bulbs, tubers, and burrows that are indescribable in any totalizing manner from above. They exist because nature always abhors a vacuum, and they are necessarily impure because nature needs biodiversity to survive. Further, rhizomes are never isolationist but connect some points to other points, interlocking different sign systems into a natural network. However, while it lacks a stable core, a rhizome is never without its "middle." It "has neither beginning nor end, but always a middle *(milieu)* from which it grows and which it overspills."[61] That middle for us is the memory of an *ethnie.* Conceiving of culture as rhizomatic, a realist nationalism constructs the nation-people without denying its inherent diversity; at the same time, it recognizes the *milieu* that makes a people the People.

Indigenous nationalism can pursue the goals of equality-of-differences and cultural survival without denying the cultural diversity that always exists within any community. The trick is never to lose sight of what Smith calls the *mythomoteur* or "constitutive myth of the ethnic polity" that explains in some way, through "mythicized" language, the origins of the People. For the Ojibwe, that would include stories about the Creation, the Flood, the Great Migration, probably Wenabozho too, but it need not close off other stories or cultural forms as fundamentalism would prefer. Rather, it just acknowledges constitutive myths and stories as the privileged *milieu* of the "myth–symbol complex": "the corpus of beliefs and sentiments which the guardians of ethnicity preserve, diffuse and transmit to future generations," not as religious dogma but as explanations of ethnic origin.[62]

There are numerous locales where Native cultural expressions honor constitutive myths while changing, incorporating, or blending other cultural beliefs and practices. As revealed by several contributors to *Native and Christian: Indigenous Voices on Religious Identity* (1996), Native Christianity is certainly one example of this (although not universally, as many Indian churches continue to attack the *ethnie* as an example of savage heathenism). The Choctaw theologian Steve Charleston's contribution to that collection characterizes oral traditions as the "Old Testament of Native America," while the New Testament would be the universalist message of brotherhood brought to humanity by Jesus Christ.[63] One tribe's ancient prophet is just like another's, but the Jews have a different story than the Choctaws, and *that* is what we mean by a "constitutive myth." In a different spiritual vein, Native people who have lately been attracted to a fairly new (nineteenth century) religion called Bahá'i—including the famous Lakota hoop dancer and lecturer Kevin Locke—provide another example of how new cultural expressions can honor a constitutive myth. As Locke explains on his Web site:

> I believe that the Covenant or relationship between God and humankind is and has been binding over all peoples; and that all peoples have been informed of its existence and parameters either through major prophets and messengers of God such as Krishna, Abraham, Moses, Zoroaster, Buddha, Jesus, Muhammad, the Báb, Bahá'u'lláh, or through other holy souls who established spiritual pathways within unique cultures worldwide, such as among my people, the Lakota.
>
> The Lakota tradition is a gift from God, and our way is based upon the manifestation of the maiden, White Buffalo Calf Woman, whose teachings, spiritual and social and prophetic, uplifted the people and prepared us to recognize the time of fulfillment, the time of renewal, the time when aspirations and hope would

be fulfilled. This is a process by which the people can be connected with God, the Oneness.[64]

Like Charleston's characterization of tribal oral tradition as an Indian "Old Testament," Locke's Bahá'i interpretation of White Buffalo Calf Woman as a "manifestation" of God fulfilled by the arrival of a later prophet acknowledges the divinity of the past while at the same time embracing a new Oneness of the present. No either-or decision must be made. The realist nationalist adopts a similar strategy in an effort to bring his or her people into a different kind of Oneness—the modern community of nations—while acknowledging the manifestation of the *mythomoteur*. That would involve seeing Native culture for what it always is—rhizome, not tree—and connecting that untidy system of signs to the *ethnie*. Few have done this better than the key writers of Native American literature.

Alfred does it well too, for instance, in the Iroquois myths, stories, and songs that he uses to preface his books, and also in his adaptation of ceremonies—such as the Thunder Dance—to modern conditions of life. One must also admire Alfred's obvious concern for Indians that his work never fails to reveal, including his unflinching assessments of an anomie in Indian country that really exists today. Further, I completely agree with Robert Warrior, who writes: "Alfred's work is valuable because he does more than argue for the efficacy of Native philosophies in the development of contemporary politics. More than that, he lays out some of the important steps that would go into actualizing such developments."[65] My problems with Alfred's work are less concerned with his assessments and goals and more with his unstated assumptions: conceptual separatism, the problematic peoplehood paradigm, and a lack of attention to (for lack of a better phrase) the "real world."

Like Warrior, I'd like to see more work that "defines people not on what they *are*, but on what they *do* in relation to what our communities need."[66] Warrior's concern has to do with acknowledging the actually existing diversity of tribal communities and giving some credit to nontraditional Indians who play a role in making the community better or helping individuals improve their lives. It is a reasonable question to ask if Alfred would value or even recognize "one-to-one mentoring, face-to-face interaction, and small-group dialogue to effect the regeneration of our minds, bodies, and spirits" if it were conducted in the context of an Indian church or a Boys and Girls Club and not in a "warrior" sort of way. If Alfred's answer is no, then we are once again in the realm of cultural resistance, not nationalism, and probably in the presence of a culture cop. Another way that Alfred defines people by "what they are" rather than by "what they do" is evident in his curious defense of Kahnawake's stringent requirements for citizenship. In his first book, Alfred defended his nation's 50 percent blood quantum mandate and its moratorium on marriages to non-Natives—that is, if you married a non-Indian, you would be stripped of citizenship—while admitting that Kahnawake's desired goal was apparently no more than phenotype: "physical characteristics were ideal because they helped an individual identify himself as Indian, and represented the difference between Indians and non-Indians."[67] By that logic the comedian George Lopez could become a stellar Mohawk. Alfred's second book was somewhat critical of blood quantum but still ultimately justified it, and Alfred even invented a convenient historical narrative for it: "membership was determined by beliefs and behavior, together with blood relationship to the group. Both blood relations and cultural integration were and are essential to being Indian."[68] That claim is historically false and biologically unwise, as mandated "blood relations" would soon enough produce unsightly genetic issues in any small group of people. Well, just take a look at those old European royal families.

Now, I am not saying that Indian identity definitions cannot be based on "blood" or phenotype, and I am definitely not suggesting that Indian nations shouldn't be allowed to determine their own citizenship requirements (in my next chapter I argue forcefully to the contrary). Although I do believe blood quantum is a dangerous game to play—and I am more than happy to go on record saying that I find moratoriums on marriage to be repugnant—my point is not definitions in general but my sense that these in particular militate against Alfred's own project, which is to escape the prison house of colonization and regenerate traditional values and identities. Citizenship requirements are a crucial issue from any nationalist standpoint because they produce the meanings of a nation's character, and blood quantum has obviously been of major concern for years. But if Alfred's goal is to regenerate traditional values, identities, and political communities, why defend it? There may be no better example anywhere of a retrograde colonialist inheritance than blood quantum, and as I showed in chapter 1, it really was the case that tradition defined people by what they do, not by what they are.

This raises a final issue that deserves mention: Alfred's interest in Native physical health, especially obesity. *Wasáse* addresses obesity on at least three separate occasions, which is fine to the extent that it is a serious health concern in many (but not only Indian) communities today. But the issue became a political slogan ("Decolonize Your Diet") in his 2005 article with Jeff Corntassel, "Being Indigenous: Resurgences against Contemporary Colonialism."[69] That is, dieting became a "resurgence." The implication here is, first, Indians are fat, and second, not dieting can be equated with—no joke intended here—internalized colonialism. I think this issue is better handled by nutritionists and health-care professionals in Native communities who have been dealing with it for years. To the extent that well-compensated professors with access to free university exercise facilities are intent on discussing it, it would clearly benefit from a stronger class analysis. It might also benefit from a stronger nationalist analysis, considering that descriptions of Indian bodies as sick and obese are the exact opposite of what the nationalist George Copway wrote.[70]

Alfred and Corntassel's call to decolonize Native diets resurrects a bad idea that became popular on many reservations during the 1990s: the notion that Natives have a "genetic predisposition" toward certain traditional foods (for us, wild rice, fish, berries, and wild game) and that many of our health issues today, such as diabetes and obesity, can be traced to a moment when we lost our daily connection to those foods and hence had our diets "colonized." Eating "white" is never right, according to this view, because we're just not made for non-Native foods. This is another racialist argument that was also employed by Southern slaveholders to justify their near starvation of slaves ("this is how they used to eat in Africa"), and I think it's answered best by a Leech Lake elder named Wally Humphrey who I remember chastising people who advanced this idea by reminding them that our fish—"probably our wild rice too"—was contaminated by mercury and dioxins and thus should *not* be overprivileged as a traditional food at this point in time. Unhealthy diets have nothing to do with "race" and everything do with available dietary choices and nutritional education. Realist nationalism wouldn't exhort people to improve their health and diet by evoking racialist arguments; rather, it would look to treaties and laws for ways to claim environmental sovereignty over lakes and lands that have been polluted for years, and it would demand greater access to healthy food (food being a key promise made to Indians in many a treaty). But of course this would all be rather difficult to do if "sovereignty" and "aboriginal rights" have been purged from your vocabulary.

Alfred's nationalist theory clears a path for better discussions regarding identity and politics, but while his work is a lot more than cultural resistance, it risks ossifying Indianness through use of conceptual separatism, the problematic peoplehood paradigm, and definitions of people based on Being, not Doing. Such tendencies are not unusual as far as nationalisms go, and Warrior believes they are increasingly common to Native intellectual discourse.[71] Nationalism has this bad habit of letting all of the nuances of life drop out of our discussions, which is one reason why so many thinkers distrust nationalist discourse. Eric Hobsbawm thought no nationalism would ever be well understood unless it was "analyzed from below, that is, in terms of the assumptions, hopes, needs, longings and interests of ordinary people," which he figured were in most cases "not necessarily national and still less nationalist."[72] What does someone like Wally Humphrey really want? Realists would answer that query first, then engage the universal discourse and logic of nations to help him get it. Nationalism should always get Wally what he wants and not the other way around.

Earlier I made the point that there are many different nationalisms in the Fourth World, all of them using different strategies to achieve different particular goals. To the extent that we can see Alfred's thought as emblematic of one particular strain—"new traditionalism" is what I would call it—then we have a sense of the unstated assumptions that challenge it. What unites these unstated assumptions is the "outsider's perspective" (discussed in chapter 2) by which cultures and peoples are seen as coherent wholes rather than the diverse, multiple, and sometimes contradictory scraps, patches, and rags that characterize an insider's perspective. My hopes are pinned on Native nationalists who can modernize their traditional values without succumbing to the easy temptations of an outsider's point of view; that is, my hopes are pinned on the realists.

To be completely honest, however, I am not convinced that traditionalism should be the end of politics. Returning to Alfred's four nationalist objectives, I sense widespread agreement in Indian country about only two of them: economic self-sufficiency and an expanded land base; plus a general sympathy regarding another: heritage languages as official national languages (but only if their daily use is not legally mandated); and I don't sense much support for what seems to be Alfred's personal favorite: the restoration of traditional governments. I am not at all clear how the last would be realized outside of a dramatic eruption of cultural revolution (which may be precisely what Alfred wants, and if so, I wish him well during what is probably going to be a long and frustrating wait). I think the other three objectives are well worth pursuing, however, and nationalism is an appropriate way to go about it. If Indian happiness is the goal of politics, then new traditionalism has a role to play. The danger is that happiness can always be sacrificed on the altar of good intentions and tradition can become a sacrament.

Literary Nationalism

One of the great unstated assumptions of our age—by that I mean approaching the realm of myth—is the idea that Native people are obsessed with spirituality and traditions to the exclusion of nearly everything else in our lives. We're not real Indians these days unless we "resist" the dominant culture at all costs; if we don't, then we can be written off as assimilated, acculturated, incorporated, and so on. Tragically, we go back to the Matrix. Closely linked to this unkind idea is another unstated assumption that our cultures are ultimately what indigenous politics and activism are intended to serve. I don't believe it. If someone was to ask me, what do Indians want?—and, incidentally, no one ever does—my answer would be: same things that all humans want. These would include a decent standard of living, access to good health care and education, economic opportunity, assisted care for children and the elderly, responsible law enforcement and public safety, a strong sense of security regarding one's home and body, reproductive rights, accessibility for the disabled, the right to organize in one's workplace, sexual freedom, racial justice, and the same dreams that all people have: a better future for our children and grandchildren, a sense of improvement over time, an ability to live in a clean and sustainable environment, and the feeling of having the respect of other people. Indians want these at least as much as language revitalization, cultural revival, or traditionalist governments, and I daresay a great deal more. I am not saying that most Indians wish to live as middle-class whites. I am suggesting that, while culture is important, Abraham Maslow would remind us that culture is the exact sort of thing that one obsesses about *after* basic human needs have already been met. Basic human needs are still not being met in much of the indigenous world today.

That said, culture matters because it provides the building materials for nationalism, and nationalism can produce a nation that can help Indians get the things they want and need. It begins with culture, because nations are made when nationalists turn "low" local cultures into "high" national cultures and other nations recognize them as such. The nation doesn't need to have absolute sovereignty or a fully independent state to exist, but it should have enough "statehood" to move away from culture toward more discourse on rights, duties, and responsibilities—what we discuss as "citizenship" in my next chapter—in order to care for the citizens who make up the nation. And, of course, another job of the nation is to defend itself as a nation; for instance, when others challenge the right of the nation to exist, or when sportsmen tell Indians that our hunting and fishing rights are no longer valid because we no longer live in wigwams or travel by birch-bark canoes. Culture matters, and not only because it provides the foundation for nationhood, but crucially because it can be modernized and retain its values and connections to an *ethnie*.

It is the task of the nationalist to do the difficult work of articulation and modernization of culture, but there are some general rules to follow lest one's nationalism end up on another scrap heap of good Indian ideas that never saw fruition. First and foremost, nationalists must investigate the cultural past and bring its "meanings" into the present in a way that makes their modernization appear entirely possible. Second, this archaeology of culture must not only produce a clear sense of cultural difference but the prospect of likely community renewal. Third, it has to be believable. As Smith observes, nationalist interpretations of the political and cultural past "must be consonant not only with the ideological demands of nationalism, but also with the scientific evidence, popular resonance and patterning of particular ethnohistories."[73] This isn't positivism— nationalists are always selective; they must forget as well as remember the past—but neither is it utopianism. As John Mohawk never tired of reminding us, utopian thought characterizes the mind-set of imperialism, not indigeneity.[74] Historically, Natives have been realists; nationalists should be too.

It is the idea of a modernized national indigenous culture that drives the dominant critical movement in Native American literary studies these days: "literary nationalism." I want to end my discussion of nations and nationalism with some consideration of this particular strain because I think it offers a promising model for intellectual work that doesn't require checking one's realism at the door, and because nationalists like Alfred often find problems with cultural workers. Personally, I think it's an x-mark. Literary nationalism is the making of a "high" national culture in the literary sphere, one that is clearly distinguished in certain ways from other "national literatures." It is not really a new idea—in fact, literary nationalism is as old as the idea of the modern nation itself—but it has recently motivated the work of Native literary critics who see it as the best way to organize, interpret, and teach Native literature and culture.

In a landmark collection of critical essays, *American Indian Literary Nationalism* (2006), Jace Weaver writes of the "two prongs" that comprise this most recent literary nationalism:

The first relates to the consideration of Native American literary output as separate and distinct from other national literatures. The second deals with a criticism of that literature that supports not only its distinct identity but also sees itself as attempting to serve the interests of indigenes and their communities, in particular the support of Native nations and their own separate sovereignties.[75]

In other words, these two prongs are *culture* and *politics, nationhood* and *nationality;* thus it is entirely consistent with the general goals of indigenous nationalism worldwide. This nationalism is not the new traditionalism, although "tradition" is an important keyword in this discourse; nor is it simply cultural resistance, although "resistance" has likewise been an important term. I want to characterize it as nationalism in the old-fashioned sense, the modernization of an *ethnie,* and thereby distinguishable from the new traditionalism. But before we get to that, let us situate this discourse in the larger historical context of literary nationalism per se by remembering two intellectual precursors with which it connects: American literary nationalism, and Black Aesthetics.

The birth of literary nationalism as a general aesthetic principle happened in the years following the American Revolution when patriotic writers consciously attempted to produce great epics that would, as Charles Brockden Brown expressed it in 1799, "differ essentially from those which exist in Europe."[76] As their titles indicate, works like *The Conquest of Canaan* (1785) by Timothy Dwight and *The Columbiad* (1807) by Joel Barlow were equal parts nationalism and imperialism. What they wanted to do was draw a clear line between America's intellectual culture (just as mature and enlightened as any other) and that of Europe. For at least two decades, this ambitious nationalist project was pursued against a backdrop of political insecurity, as the Reign of Terror, the restoration of the French monarchy, and the Napoleonic Wars served as cold (and brutal) reminders that the American democratic experiment was hardly assured. However, after the War of 1812, Andrew Jackson's unlikely victory at the Battle of New Orleans (1815), and the rise of a new mythology surrounding the Republican Hero, modeled after Jackson—the man from humble origins who rises to greatness and combats the evils of monarchy and aristocracy—democratic enthusiasm and American patriotism were reignited and led to the birth of what F. O. Matthiessen called the "American Renaissance."[77]

The literary nationalists of that era are well remembered—Irving, Bryant, Cooper, Sigourney, Sedgwick, Child—but its critical discourse is less easily recalled. In fact the critics of that period openly called for American literary nationalism in publications like *North American Review,* for instance, in Wallace Channing's 1815 exhortations for a new "literature of our own."[78] Solyman Brown's *An Essay on American Poetry* (1818) made the questionable argument that "The proudest freedom to which a nation can aspire, not excepting even political independence, is found in complete emancipation from literary thralldom."[79] Tough times required tough talk, and when considering who they were up against—for example, the English critic Sydney Smith, who snobbishly sneered in an 1820 issue of *Edinburg Review,* "In the four quarters of the globe, who reads an American book?"—the nationalists had their work cut out for them.[80] Their task was to show the literary world that they too had a literature that was enlightened, modern, and above all distinctly *American.* Although they immediately gave up on the project of seeking firm formalistic distinctions—they were not conceptual separatists—they sought to write and criticize their way into the English-language pantheon of great literary accomplishment.

It is worth noting the essential role played by Indians in American literary nationalism, especially during its heights in the 1820s. This was, of course, the dawning of the removal era, and it was that prototype of the Republican Hero, Andrew Jackson, who symbolized to Indians all that went wrong during those years: the Removal Act, the Trail of Tears, the nobility ascribed to "Indian fighters," not to mention the increasingly egregious lies and appeals to white fears made by leaders like Jackson in his State of the Union addresses and public talks. "Indian hating" developed its metaphysics long before the foundation of the republic, but it received a shot of enthusiasm during the heyday of American literary nationalism. That said, most of the actual writers were strident critics of the policies that harmed Native people—and women, slaves, the poor, as well as other disenfranchised groups—although we wouldn't call them indigenous nationalists (unlike their Native contemporaries like Boudinot and Apess who were precisely that). We can, however, call them *indigenizing* nationalists. Literary nationalists used the idea and the image of the Indian to create a sense of an "American" cultural past that transferred its energies and meanings to the present and "nativized" the Republican Hero. This strategy is seen in major works such as James Fenimore Cooper's "Leatherstocking" novels (1823–41)—which earned him (much to his chagrin) the distinction of "the American Scott"—as well as in Lydia Maria Child's *Hobomok* (1824) and Catherine Maria Sedgwick's *Hope Leslie* (1827), among others. Literary nationalists portrayed a noble but vanishing Indian who was more or less willing to recede into the hazy mists of time after giving a gift (a pendant, a name, etc.) to the whites who would soon replace "the original American."

The actual gift was not only the land but a remembered trace of the Native cultural past, the same past memorialized in Lydia Howard Huntley Sigourney's poem "Indian Names" (1834), which opens with a rhetorical question: "How can the red men be forgotten, while so many of our states and territories, bays, lakes and rivers, are indelibly stamped by names of their giving?"[81] The answer was: they cannot be forgotten, nor should they be, for Indian cultural legacies—and in a sense Indian identities—would continue to live on in civilized American form. Like the indigenized Republican Hero, America would embody the best of old worlds and new—a romanticized trace of the noble savagery combined with the advances of civilization—and it would have its own national literature, one that was distinctive and deserving of a place in the Western literary canon.

American literary nationalism didn't modernize the *mythomoteur* of an *ethnie*—there being no white *ethnie* to modernize in America—it simply stole its cultural meaning from someone else. The Indians whose images and symbolism were always appropriated (and still are appropriated, whether by sports teams needing mascots, cars needing names, or New Agers needing ceremonies) were supposed to disappear in keeping with the laws of Progress, so the theft was considered no great loss, much less a crime. It was literary nationalism, that's all, and for the most part it worked out pretty well. Most everyone in the world now accepts the idea of "American literature" as something that really exists, and no one ever charges it with "essentialism" or "separatism" for doing so. What makes American literature "American" is not some kind of rhetorical or formal uniqueness; it is simply defined by the American authors who have produced it and, to a lesser extent, its subject matter. The essential differences between one national literature and another are always these—author and subject matter—and nothing more.

American *Indian* literary nationalism both resembles and responds to this history of American literary nationalism in certain ways; at the same time, it departs from it. Its primary resemblance is the basic idea that a "national literature" is necessary for a nation to have for political purposes, and on that score we should note the similarities that exist between Weaver's first "prong" and the emphatic calls by Channing and Brown for "literature of our own" that would "differ essentially" from other national literatures. Yet American Indian literary nationalism is equally defined by its *response* to the imperialism that was always part and parcel of American literary nationalism, in particular the latter's uninvited and often inaccurate appropriations of Native people and cultures (as ideas and images) as part of the American "indigenization" process. "Such an ongoing fascination with Native cultures perceived as exotic remains an impediment to critics who advocate Native national literatures," Weaver writes.[82] It is the necessary task of the Native literary nationalist to begin with the dominant simulacra of the Indian in an effort to undo them and ultimately reclaim the meanings of the *ethnie*. Finally, this new literary nationalism departs from its American predecessor by virtue of its attempted separatism—a desire not to join the American or Western literary canons, but rather to invent, in Craig Womack's terms, "two separate canons"—as well as its aversions to dominant aesthetics and theories.[83] This devotion to aesthetic separatism as an idea links Native literary nationalism to another historical precursor, the Black Aesthetics movement, which is a literary nationalism worth another brief digression.

Black nationalism has more in common with indigenous struggles for sovereignty than most thinkers have acknowledged (including Vine Deloria Jr., whose "The Red and the Black" essay in *Custer Died for Your Sins* presented a rather limited understanding of Black nationalism as it has existed since long before the Revolutionary War).[84] Prior to the Civil War some black leaders like Martin R. Delaney advanced nationalist agendas—for instance, migration to Haiti and the founding of Liberia, both of which happened in the nineteenth century—while other leaders like Frederick Douglass promoted social reform and integration in America. Later nationalists like Marcus Garvey promoted full political independence in Africa, while integrationists like Booker T. Washington argued for more gradualist approaches to U.S. citizenship, stressing vocational education, hard work, and "moral improvement." W. E. B. Du Bois took a more militant view, demanding immediate redress and political enfranchisement from America and, as with Garvey, promoted pan-Africanism (he eventually moved to Ghana). The themes that were generated during the nineteenth century—nationalism and integration, militancy and conciliation, revolution and reform—reemerged during the black liberation movements in the United States and around the world starting in the mid-twentieth century. Generally speaking, there were two phases of black activism in the United States after World War II: the civil rights era from 1954 to 1964, and the Black Power movement from 1964 through the conclusion of the Vietnam War; and it was the latter phase, coming on the heels of the assassination of Martin Luther

King Jr. and the crumbling of his Poor People's Campaign coalition, that sparked a resurgence of nationalist themes: separatism, militancy, racial pride, negritude, and Africanism, as opposed to integration, gradualism, and multiracial coalition building. It was the latter phase that gave rise to black literary nationalism.

Black Aesthetics was devoted to realizing the goal stated by Malcolm X in 1964: "We must launch a cultural revolution to unbrainwash an entire people."[85] In his essay "Towards a Black Aesthetic" (1968), Hoyt W. Fuller sought to found a new movement of arts and culture explicitly linked to Black Power, for "the road to solidarity and strength leads inevitably through reclamation and indoctrination of black art and culture."[86] For Larry Neal, author of the popular essay "The Black Arts Movement" (1968), this entailed a clean break from white aesthetic norms, modes of expression, and standards of taste, as his objective was to rediscover lost traditions and make a distinctive new culture that would allow blacks to escape the burden of constantly having to react to their oppressors. Neal thought that the renowned Harlem Renaissance typified such a reaction because it failed to "address itself to the mythology and the life-styles of the Black community. It failed to take roots, to link itself concretely to the struggles of that community, to become its voice and spirit." It was too integrationist. Implicit in the Black Arts Movement, however, "is the idea that Black people, however dispersed, constitute a *nation* within the belly of white America."[87] This nation had, in Stokely Carmichael's words, "dependent colonial status," one that could be cast off if blacks kept their culture intact: "the community must win its freedom while preserving its cultural integrity."[88] Neal believed that this implied a privileging of oral and musical forms of expression (these being more "traditional") and a rejection of elite, white written modes. "The text could be destroyed," Neal, um, *wrote*, "and no one would be hurt in the least by it."[89]

The public face of the Black Aesthetics movement belonged to LeRoi Jones, who eventually changed his "slave name" to Amiri Baraka. His seminal essay "The Legacy of Malcolm X and the Coming of the Black Nation" (1965) called for a constant disordering of white images and ideas to promote black consciousness, culture, and nationhood. "By the time this book appears," he wrote, "I will be even blacker."[90] This book was *Home: Social Essays* (1965), a collection of twenty-six short essays chronicling his transition to black nationalism and Black Aesthetics from his earlier antiformalist phenomenological poetics. One implication of the new aesthetic was a shift away from the privileging of an individual mind toward a focus on the group, as Black Aesthetics not only emanated from the community but engaged it. Another implication was revolution: "The Black Artist's role in America is to aid in the destruction of America as he knows it. His role is to report and reflect so precisely the nature of society, and of himself in that society, that other men will be moved by the exactness of his rendering."[91] When Baraka abandoned the project of black nationalism for the more internationalist Marxism-Leninism in 1974, the Black Aesthetic lost one of its most talented and popular leaders and soon declined in power, but leaving in its wake a completely changed social, cultural, and political scene: new black theaters and black publications, new Afro-American and Pan-African studies programs and departments, plus a preponderance of up-and-coming black writers, poets, critics, theorists, and public intellectuals, the sheer number of which had never been seen before. In other words, the Black Aesthetic had become institutionalized; it became part of the mainstream. Whether or not it lost its original desire to "unbrainwash" the black community remains an open question.

American Indian literary nationalism connects to the Black Aesthetic in several respects, most clearly in its historical-political roots. Black Power and Red Power were never far apart—in fact, the American Indian Movement's foundation in 1968 was based on the idea and organizational structure of the Black Panther Party—although the groups had different issues and political objectives. What they shared in common was the brutal experience of racism, the erasure of their histories, the denial of their participation, and a general sense of betrayal and rage against white America. And, of course, poverty. Both groups connected, if not always consciously, activism with new creative resurgence. The Red Power movement coincided with (actually it seems more accurate to say *produced*) what is now called the "Native American Renaissance." Every literary nationalism seeks a "renaissance," and while young Indian activists were busy occupying Alcatraz, the BIA headquarters in Washington, and Wounded Knee, South Dakota, Native American writers were busy crafting great works of fiction and poetry for Natives and non-Natives alike, the latter, it seems fair to suggest, suddenly interested in Indian issues and people largely as a result of seeing AIM leaders make speeches on the nightly news. N. Scott Momaday released the Pulitzer Prize–winning *House Made of Dawn* in 1968 and *The Way to Rainy Mountain* in 1969, James Welch published *Riding the Earthboy 40* in 1971 and *Winter in the Blood* in 1974, Leslie Marmon Silko issued *Laguna Woman* in 1974 and *Ceremony* in 1977, Gerald Vizenor worked as a journalist covering AIM for the *Minneapolis Tribune*, publishing *The Everlasting Sky* in 1972 and *Darkness in Saint Louis Bearheart* in 1977, and of course we have to mention the prolific production of the essayist Vine Deloria Jr., whose 1969 *Custer Died for Your Sins: An Indian Manifesto* became something of a bible for many young Natives seeking political and historical answers during those years. This is barely a scratch on the surface of the tremendous literary and intellectual revitalization that happened during the Native American Renaissance and its aftermath.

Unlike the Black Aestheticians, Natives in those days didn't produce a great deal of criticism and theory (although, to be sure, there was some). Most intellectual energies were put into fiction, poetry, political writing, and creating a new academic field called Native American studies. The theoretical statements that now comprise what we consider to be American Indian literary nationalism today didn't emerge until the 1990s, when scholars like Elizabeth Cook-Lynn, Robert Warrior, and Craig Womack started demanding more attention to what Cook-Lynn called "the meaningfulness of indigenous or tribal sovereignty."[92] In contradistinction to previous critical work privileging cross-cultural education, hybridity, mixed-bloodedness, feminism-indigenism, cosmopolitanism, ethnocriticism, postmodern politics, and multiculturalism—all of which literary nationalists have since characterized as far too "mixed" to be of much political value—the new nationalist criticism called for more politicized discussions of Native sovereignty and cultural integrity. Warrior advanced the notion of "intellectual sovereignty" in *Tribal Secrets: Recovering American Indian Intellectual Traditions* (1995) to characterize the history of Native intellectualism that he thought provided a useful model for Native intellectual discourse and criticism today, the latter being somewhat limited in his view by "an avoidance of internal criticism," a "lack of historical engagement" with earlier thinkers, and a dogged preoccupation with "parochial questions of identity and authenticity" at the expense of other important questions that confront Native communities.[93] As its title indicates, Craig Womack's *Red on Red: Native American Literary Separatism* (1999) advocated "separatism" in the realm of Native literary studies, starting with the idea that Native literatures should not be seen as an extension of the American literary canon (and using a slightly modified "logic of the tree" to do it): "tribal literatures are not some branch waiting to be grafted onto the main trunk. Tribal literatures are the *tree,* the oldest literatures in the Americas, the most American of American literatures. We *are* the canon."[94] Womack's "tribally specific aesthetics" would situate indigenous texts in their specific tribal-national contexts, and he advocated a "Red Stick" criticism emphasizing cultural integrity and political resistance.

The Native literary nationalism that emerged in the 1990s connects to the Black Aesthetic in its separatist's desire to create aesthetic norms and principles that wouldn't react to white representations and standards of value (much less join them as an Indian version of American art), but create new ones that could stand on their own two Indian feet. There had to be something beyond always "writing back" to the imperial center, a new tribally specific aesthetic that both emanated from the community and addressed it too, producing what Womack called "a Native consciousness."[95] For Black Aestheticians like Larry Neal, such organic cultural power could be found in black vernacular orality and music. For Native American literary nationalists, it came from traditional cultures that have retained their integrity despite centuries of contact and change.

Weaver, Womack, and Warrior's book, *American Indian Literary Nationalism,* credits Simon J. Ortiz with making a "foundational contribution" to the development of literary nationalism in his 1981 essay (which their book reprints) "Towards a National Indian Literature: Cultural Authenticity in Nationalism."[96] This classic essay by Ortiz argues that despite the adoption of non-Indian languages, names, and cultural practices like Pueblo celebrations of Catholic saints' days, Indians "make these forms meaningful on their own terms." "They are now Indian, because of the creative development that the native people applied to them." The same can be said for indigenous literatures, which Ortiz finds evidencing an indigenization of European languages and cultural forms "in the very same way." Despite its written form, Native literature connects to *oral tradition,* and since oral tradition is known by its "resistance—political, armed, spiritual," Native literature can likewise ascribe "a particular nationalistic character to the Native American voice."[97] Ortiz insists that today's "Indians are still Indians" despite the transformation of languages, cultures, and communication technologies.[98] "This is the crucial item that has to be understood," Ortiz concludes, "that it is entirely possible for a people to retain and maintain their lives through the use of any language. There is not a question of authenticity here; rather, it is the way that Indian people have responded to forced colonization."[99] Remarkably, Ortiz flips the logic of 1820s American literary nationalism on its head. Whereas the Coopers and Childs of that era appropriated the idea and image of the Indian in order to indigenize the Republican Hero and make American identity appear "native," Ortiz effectively does the same thing in reverse: all those alien languages and cultural forms you imposed on us are now ours, and now we're all the more Indian for it!

To the extent that Ortiz's essay can be seen as representative of American

Indian literary nationalism (and that is exactly how Weaver, Womack, and Warrior represent it), we can distinguish this insurgent critical movement from both cultural resistance and new traditionalism and call it a realist nationalism: the modernization of an indigenous *ethnie*. "Indians are still Indians," not because we speak our traditional languages or observe the same ceremonies as before, but because we can trace our cultural practices and self-understandings back to an *ethnie*, the legitimacy of which need not be questioned, even though it may appear less than intact to observers adopting an outsider's perspective (traditional anthropologists, for instance, or culture cops). "It is also because of the acknowledgment by Indian writers of a responsibility to advocate for their people's self-government, sovereignty, and control of land and natural resources," Ortiz adds, pointing to a shift away from kinship and cultural concerns toward a discourse on territories, duties, rights, and responsibilities. Writing is the modernization of oral traditions, nationalization is the modernization of an *ethnie*, and literary nationalism is the transformation of "low" local (oral) cultures into "high" national (written) cultures to push the historical process forward. Ortiz's essay is thus a realist nationalism to the root. Or actually not the root (there's that logic of the tree again); I mean the milieu.

Of course, as a critical movement that has been developing for some time, literary nationalism is many different things, not all of them coherent or lacking contradiction. It is, like culture itself, more rhizomatic than treelike. Its milieu, however, seems constituted by three ideas that have produced much agreement. First, it is justifiable and necessary to organize Native literatures according to their tribal-national contexts, for instance, as "Creek literature." There is no mandate to *always* or *only* organize texts in this fashion (nor is it always desirable to do so), but literary nationalism does call for it to a certain extent, and it is a new call. For my money, this has been the most exciting and productive aspect of Native literary nationalism, because it potentially disalienates Native communities from their own histories. I will confess that even in my somewhat educated Indian household I had little idea that there were any Ojibwe writers before Vizenor and Erdrich until I was well into my twenties. When I finally discovered Copway, Warren, and other writers from the nineteenth century, they embarrassed me because they seemed so *assimilated,* unlike, say, Dennis Banks, whose speeches I remembered from my childhood. Had such literary figures been taught to me as a constitutive part of an Ojibwe national literature, and had they been situated historically, I would have had a very different understanding of them and the Ojibwe Nation at a young age. For this reason, I think every English classroom in every reservation should have portraits of their nation's key writers hanging on the wall. But this does not mean that one must be an Indian to understand or interpret that literature; and on that score one must appreciate Weaver's "coruscatingly clear" statement: "We *want* non-Natives to read, engage, and study Native literature . . . with respect and a sense of responsibility to Native community."[100] Ojibwe in Iroquois country who teach Iroquois texts to Iroquois students should live under the same rule.

Second, too many "mixed" metaphors is a bad thing. "Mixed-bloods," hybridity, and other postmodern metaphors for border crossing and boundary busting are perceived as a threat to the cultural and political integrity that nations and national literatures need. This is literary nationalism's most problematic precept for the simple fact that all cultures are extremely porous, blended, multiple, hybrid, and "mixed," and claims to the contrary necessarily adopt the outsider's point of view. The hybridity haters should reread Ortiz and note not only a complete absence of an attack on hybridity—much to the contrary, his entire argument about the continuation of Indianness rests on it—but also his appreciation of the mixed-blood. *Ceremony*'s Tayo, Ortiz points out, "is not 'pure blood' Indian; rather he is of mixed blood, a mestizo. He, like many Indian people *of whom he is a reflection,* is faced with circumstances which seemingly are beyond his ability to control."[101] Surely, one of those circumstances beyond our control is culture. Hybridity is in fact a decent metaphor to describe the ways all cultures change, and the same can be said for "mixed" identities. The thing to do is not protest the claim that a Native writer or culture evidences hybridity, but simply to point out the continuity that carries forth nonetheless.

Someone who has made the argument about cultural continuity better than anyone is Gerald Vizenor, perhaps the most ill-represented Native writer in literary nationalist discourse, whose concept of "survivance" (to name only one idea from his ample arsenal) gives a good name to the cultural carryover process Ortiz describes. As with all of Vizenor's concepts, "survivance" seems open to different meanings, but one conceptual forefather is probate law, which uses the term to refer to *inheritance*.[102] Vizenor isn't much of a nationalist, but his work hardly seems antithetical to nationalist projects, and it is not at all illuminated when scholars dismiss it as "post-Indian gobbledygook," as Womack does in his latest opus.[103] Womack spends nine pages supposedly summarizing Vizenor's contribution to a history of book-length Native literary criticism, but he

doesn't quote Vizenor once; and his mistaken use of "post-Indian"—
which should read *"postindian"* for reasons that don't need explaining
to anyone who has done his homework—suggests that Womack either
doesn't understand Vizenor's ideas or cares so little about Native theories
that are not his own that typos are of little consequence.[104] It's hard to
say what explains the relentless assault on Vizenor these days—it might
be his intentionally elusive prose style as much as anything else—but the
official reasons are his postmodernist ideas. This sort of aversion to postmodernism is endemic to many nationalisms—the nation, after all, being
modern—so I'm guessing this is going to be a prime site of contestation
in Native discourse for years to come.

The point I am making here is that there is no real contradiction between impurity and nationalization. An Indian nation is an *ethnie* modernized. Realist nationalism must account for all of the diversity and
hybridity that necessarily accompanies contact with others. Like Ortiz, it
should find that "Indians are still Indians" after hybridity and modernity
have appeared on the scene; like Vizenor, it needs to recognize that the
"survivances" of indigenous culture are "more than endurance or mere
response," certainly "more than survival," but an *"active presence."*[105]
Nationalism is the assertion of active presence; denials of hybridity are
the terminal creeds of culture cops. Remember, nationalism is not the
same as cultural resistance. I think our confusion between these two
things is producing needless contradiction and conflict.

The third idea in literary nationalism that has received widespread
agreement has to do with language. As Womack sums it up in *American
Indian Literary Nationalism*, "English is an Indian language."[106] Weaver
makes the point two times: "English is a Native language" and "Claiming
English as an Indian language is one of the most important, if not *the*
most important step toward ensuring Indian survival for future generations."[107] Embedded in these statements is the Ortizian (or Vizenoresque)
idea that cultural continuity can be discovered even on the other side of
a different language; or, as Ortiz stated it in 1981, "it is entirely possible
for a people to retain and maintain their lives through the use of any
language." This is certainly a valuable thesis to advance if one hopes to
justify the cultural integrity and continuity of indigenous culture, or if we
want to "unbrainwash" people in Native communities who may feel a
little less Native for having their languages taken away (hence a little less
national). Indeed, one could argue that literary nationalism would become
a completely lost project without this idea. And yet I can't help but note
that Ortiz's 2006 Foreword to *American Indian Literary Nationalism*

evidences less enthusiasm about "claiming English as an Indian language" than do Womack and Weaver. Ortiz, who is multilingual, characterizes English as both "a knotty problem" and the "enemy's language"; and while he does endorse its use (being the realist that he is), "we recognize they are colonial languages that have been used against us and too often we have been victimized and oppressed by them."[108] English is a *colonial* language, one that can be and often is put to good use by Natives, but that's not quite the same thing as saying "English is an Indian language." There's an ambivalence there, however quiet, that I think nationalists should not be too quick to surrender.

One problem with advancing the notion of English as an Indian language is that it risks disabling the arguments that are often made by heritage language activists who need to keep the opposite view intact in order to get their language programs funded and filled. I remember working with one such group at Leech Lake a few years back, and its leaders would often speak about having to "go shame the tribal council into coughing up some money." (They did it by making a long presentation in *Ojibwemowin*, then translating it.) There's no "shaming" possible if the tribal council buys into the idea that English is now an Ojibwe language. Now, I am not arguing for language activists to turn up the volume on shame in their communities; there's quite enough of that among our people already. I am suggesting that we now live during a historical moment when most indigenous languages are in serious trouble. Marianne Mithun warns us that at current rates of decline "all are likely to be gone by the end of the twenty-first century,"[109] and Norbert Francis and Jon Reyhner concur: "in the Americas, not a single exception exists to the overall tendency toward language displacement by either Spanish or English."[110] Even *USA Today* reports, "Of the estimated 7,000 languages spoken today, one vanishes every 14 days"; the most endangered ones are located in northern Australia, central South America, the Northwest Pacific plateau of the United States and Canada, eastern Siberia, and Oklahoma.[111] In a state of decline like this, we should do all we can to support the language activists who are trying to reverse it. Claiming English as an Indian language doesn't seem like support.

Another problem, however, is more directly political. Claims to nationhood and nationality will always be more quickly accepted when made by folks who really do seem "different" in a national sort of way. Nationalism has two audiences: potential citizens and citizens of other nations who recognize your nation. It is above all an argument for a people's right to be, and be recognized as, a nation, and differences are an essential part of that argument. Ultimately, nationalism comes down to culture, but in these globalized, culture-obsessed times, cultural difference alone may not be enough. There is no more powerful an indicator of nationhood than a spoken national language, so it is important that nationalists promote language revitalization for political goals.

Literary nationalism has the potential to combat language loss and "unbrainwash" a great many people who read, study, interpret, and criticize our literatures. As a critical movement it has connections to both American literary nationalism and Black Aesthetics; the former consciously crafted a distinctive national literature that could assume a respected place in the Western canon, the latter sought a new consciousness for a colonized nation within and challenged dominant aesthetics with radical new ideas. To the extent that it remains realist in orientation, I have high hopes for literary nationalism. Arnold Krupat is certainly correct that Native nationalism is one discourse among others (his others are "indigenism" and "cosmopolitanism"), and he is right to see these different discourses working together more often than not.[112] My own hope is that literary nationalism doesn't become too parochial, and Ortiz's 1981 essay seems to warn against that as well. While looking after "their people's self-government, sovereignty, and control of land and natural resources," indigenous writers should, according to Ortiz, "look also at racism, political and economic oppression, sexism, supremacism, and the needless and wasteful exploitation of land and people, especially in the U.S."[113] That is, they must always remember that they belong not only to Indian nations but to a larger society as well. They belong to a world.

"New Societies" and the Nationalism Question

This chapter was written seven weeks after the death of Aimé Césaire, with whom we started. It was written eighteen years after Amiri Baraka was denied tenure at Rutgers University and six years after the troubles that emerged in the wake of Baraka's post-9/11 poem "Somebody Blew Up America." This was written a year after Ward Churchill was fired by the University of Colorado-Boulder for his own post-9/11 writings, and eighteen months after I heard through the moccasin telegraph that Taiaiake Alfred was questioned by the Canadian authorities about *Wasáse* and its reflections on legitimate violence. This was written seven weeks after the Dalai Lama tried to explain to the Chinese government that Tibet wasn't seeking independence but "autonomy," thereby granting the monopoly on legitimate violence to the Chinese state (which had already used it against the Tibetans); and four weeks after the sixtieth anniversary of the founding of the state of Israel (hence the sixtieth anniversary of the dispossession of the Palestinians, who are a colonized people). This was written five months before the 2008 U.S. presidential election and one day after the Democratic Party selected its first-ever nonwhite candidate, Barack Obama. Just two weeks ago, as I write, Obama visited Crow Nation in Montana and was given a name that translates to "One Who Helps People Throughout the Land." This was written during the War in Iraq. The first female soldier killed in that war was Lori Ann Piestewa, a Hopi.

This chapter was written during a time when the very idea of a nation was called into question. Books such as Peter Singer's *One World: The Ethics of Globalization* and Thomas Friedman's *The World Is Flat: A Brief History of the Twenty-first Century* asked if the community of "nations," even if separate and equal, wasn't problematic for the way it kept the world all too fragmented and disconnected to forge solutions to the common problems we share. Other globalization advocates, for instance, Michael Hardt and Antonio Negri, write that "in step with the processes of globalization, the sovereignty of nation-states, while still effective, has progressively declined," which is not to say that national sovereignty is dead. Rather, "sovereignty has taken a new form, composed of a series of national and supranational organisms united under a single logic of rule. This new global form of sovereignty is what we call Empire."[114]

This chapter was written at a time when Native people were doing nationalism in spite of the nation's heralded decline. Twenty-seven months ago, as I write, Indians from the Six Nations of the Grand River occupied a disputed land parcel in Caledonia, Ontario, to raise awareness of unresolved Native land claims in Canada generally and their Caledonia tract in particular (it was targeted for development into a residential subdivision). The Ontario Provincial Police (OPP) still monitors the site with twenty-four-hour video surveillance. Yes, as I write, this is all still playing out. In fact, this chapter was written forty days after a group of Six Nations protesters blocked a highway bypass and railroad tracks in response to the OPP's arrest of four Mohawks at the Tyendinaga Reserve the day before. The Mohawks had been protesting in support of the Six Nations occupation for well over a year. It's not a stretch to connect these occupations and protests with other nationalist initiatives in Canada, for example, the Oka Crisis in Quebec that ran from August 11 to September 26, 1990, centering on Mohawk lands that had been illegally appropriated to create a golf course. Three people died as a result of that conflict.

This chapter was written fourteen months after an Amnesty International report revealed that one out of three Native women are sexually assaulted during their lifetimes, and two years after Cecelia Fire Thunder, the first elected female leader of the Oglala Sioux Nation, was impeached for proposing a new abortion clinic at Oglala after South Dakota attempted to ban abortions statewide.[115] The Amnesty International report bemoaned the lack of protection that Indian women receive under a "maze of injustice" that perennially results from confused jurisdictional struggles between federal and tribal authorities. Fire Thunder was simply ousted by an antichoice council. This was written three years after the Navajo Nation banned same-sex marriages in the Dine Marriage Act of 2005. It was soon vetoed by President Joe Shirley Jr., but his tribal council overrode it. That same year, the Cherokee Nation similarly banned same-sex marriage.[116] Finally, this was written in the midst of two significant major struggles between indigenous nations and the federal government over race and labor rights: on the one hand, Cherokee Nation's attempted ethnic cleansing of its black citizens (the Freedmen); on the other hand, Native disputes with the National Labor Relations Board regarding the rights of workers to organize in tribal businesses.[117] These are all sovereignty issues that nationalist intellectuals must honestly confront.

I have been situating this chapter in my own historical moment for three reasons. First, I want to suggest that the era of nationalism is far from over, and that our nationalisms should be interpreted in the context of others—for instance, in occupied Palestine and Tibet—rather than granting exceptionalism to Native political struggles. Our use of the word *nation* is not radically unlike other uses, the same rules and implications apply, and if we don't really wish to be nations of some sort, we really shouldn't be using nationalism as a heuristic. Be careful what you wish for. But if you do wish to be a stronger nation, then situate your desire in coalition with other oppressed peoples who are seeking the same. Second, although nations and nationalisms still exist, I think Hardt and Negri are correct with their assessment that sovereignty is shifting away from nation-states and toward a globalized sense of Empire. This is the realm of the world's richest 2 percent who control half of humanity's assets, as the bottom half—more than three billion people—struggles over a scant 1 percent in order to survive. Nationalist accusations against "whites," "settlers," or even "non-Native critics" (as literary nationalists often say) miss an opportunity to identify this real enemy today: the globalized elite power exercised largely through corporations and increasingly using state military power to do it. Indians have long spoken of the "White Man," and that expression has served its purpose, but black nationalists who made accusations against, simply, "The Man" may have been a bit more accurate in describing the actual enemy: "The Man" is the one with all the power. When employed in our critical discourse as a subject of critique, language like "non-Natives" can cast too large a net and end up describing virtually no one. We need a more precise language for characterizing people who are not us (and also people who are us); it should be a language that, like Ojibwe, differentiates between groups based on how they live. *Class* will always be the most meaningful way of distinguishing between ways of living. It's not culture.

Finally, my third point concerns the potential dangers of nations and nationalism. For one, as the examples of Baraka, Churchill, and Alfred indicate, radical ideas can still get you into trouble, but it's not dishing on white people that does it (as discussed earlier in this book, the "protestant ethnic" often gets tenure). It is always *prophetic* discourse that touches the nerve: calling for one's overthrow, predicting retribution, and above all else saying something about the legitimacy of violence. This is no dismissal of prophetic discourse, just a warning to the wise during the "War on Terrorism." A more pressing danger in my view is the use of Native nations and indigenous sovereignty for purposes that can be just as harmful and retrograde as anyone else's oppression. When women, gays and lesbians, workers, black people—or anyone—are harmed in the name of tribal sovereignty, then discourses other than nationalism are called for in the name of justice. I really couldn't disagree more with Alfred's suggestion (quoted at the beginning of this chapter) that left-wing intellectuals are indistinguishable from colonizers who accept their role as such. This sort of position is often held by nationalists to discredit liberal human rights groups that charge their nations with some violation or another (usually rightly so), but for my money it is always the job of intellectuals to "look also at racism, political and economic oppression, sexism, supremacism, and the needless and wasteful exploitation of land and people," *no matter who perpetuates the injustice.* Such social critiques usually come from left-wing intellectuals, and they are essential for the creation of "new societies" that most of us would actually want to live in.

That's why I end this chapter on a skeptical note regarding the prospects of nationalism in intellectual discourse. Here's my own contradiction: while I support the Indian nation, I am leery of nationalism. Sometimes when I am in the presence of nationalists I experience the same ambivalence that Mary McCarthy felt toward the communists of her own age: "it was based on their lack of humor, their fanaticism, and the slow drip of cant that thickened their utterance like a nasal catarrh. *And yet* I was tremendously impressed by them."[118] Yes, I am impressed during those moments when Indians in Ontario, Quebec, or Chiapas, Mexico, use nationalism to fight against Empire in an effort to protect old values, while calling for a new society based on justice not greed, happiness not dogma, and *more life,* not death. And I find myself impressed when I read critical texts in my field that have the power to produce a necessary paradigm shift, as all the works I have discussed here have more or less already done. To the extent that these actions and works represent a realist nationalism that is by definition the making of an x-mark, my answer to the nationalism question, however hesitant, has got to be Yes.

CHAPTER FOUR

Resignations

Long before the new traditionalism appeared on the scene, the cantankerous Ojibwe polemicist Wub-e-ke-niew (Francis Blake Jr.) did something remarkable: he disenrolled himself from the Red Lake Band of Chippewa Indians. I repeat: he disenrolled *himself*. Wub-e-ke-niew was a fluent speaker of *Ojibwemowin*, a member of the Midewiwin (Grand Medicine Lodge), a regular columnist for the *Native American Press/Ojibwe News*, and the author of *We Have the Right to Exist: A Translation of Aboriginal Indigenous Thought*, which he advertised as "the first book ever published from an *Ahnishinahbæóⁿjibway* perspective."[1] In 1991, just before the Columbian quintcentennial, Wub-e-ke-niew ceremoniously sliced up his tribal ID and mailed it to U.S. Supreme Court Justice Thurgood Marshall and Secretary of the Interior Manuel Lujan Jr., accompanied by an open letter that he also published in his column. "This is to inform you that I want my name removed from your basic membership, identification and enrollment lists of your 'Red Lake Band of Chippewa Indians,'" the letter stated. "I will no longer be identified by your racist term of 'Indian.' I am *not* an 'Indian,' I am *not* a 'Chippewa,' and I am *not* a 'Native American.' These words are all European terms . . . I am *Ahnishinahbæóⁿjibway*."[2] It was a letter of resignation. Wub-e-ke-niew was through.

His dramatic assertion of *Ahnishinahbæóⁿjibway* identity and resignation of tribal membership was premised on two ideas. First, any "American Indian" or even "Chippewa" identity represented by enrollment, your standard tribal ID card, or for that matter the English language, was colonialism pure and simple and thereby illegitimate. Second, *Ahnishinahbæóⁿjibway* identity was legitimate because it was based on traditions, definitions, language, and people reaching far back in time:

"My father was *Ahnishinahbæótjibway,* and all of his patrilineal ancestors were *Ahnishinahbæótjibway,* going back for hundreds of millennia." His reference to patrilineal ancestry invoked the Ojibwe clan system, which Wub-e-ke-niew clearly considered to be the sole authentic determinant of *Ahnishinahbæótjibway* identity, and he insisted that clans had political rights. "The land is held *jointly* by the Clans of the *Midewiwin,* and every Aboriginal Indigenous person of the Clans is Sovereign," Wub-e-ke-niew explained. "The land is not, and never has been, held 'in common,' nor has it ever belonged to 'Indians.'"[3] Putting the lie to the *Indian* identity and asserting a new (that is, old) Aboriginal Indigenous identity in its place, Wub-e-ke-niew did more than talk the usual talk about the importance of traditions and sovereignty. He forcefully asserted them in the face of state power.

What was at stake in this display? For Wub-e-ke-niew, most everything important: language, land, culture, religion, identity, the future of the people. The title of his book said it best: *We Have the Right to Exist.* "Indian" identity was bogus, "fabricated," and "artificial," an "abstraction" designed to subjugate us by colonizing our hearts and minds along with our lands.[4] Liberation was possible, but only if one bravely said No to the entire colonizing system outright, a process that Wub-e-ke-niew described autobiographically: "When I turned my back on the Indian identity . . . I became free—again, because I was born free. I could feel the weight lift from my shoulders, and my hands become untied, as I left the shackles of Western European civilization behind me."[5] Wub-e-ke-niew saw identity crisis and political crisis as one and the same. As a writer and a nationalist he embraced modernity and all of its technologies, but as an activist his prescription for the Ojibwe nation was cultural resistance of a common and often problematic sort: a theocracy.

Wub-e-ke-niew took the meaning of decolonization literally, and he was apparently punished for that transgression. After his death in October 1997, he was posthumously reenrolled in the Red Lake Band of Chippewa Indians, and his nonenrolled (but Indian) widow, Clara NiiSka, was served with a Red Lake order of removal evicting her from the home she shared with Wub-e-ke-niew for more than thirteen years. "I am not an Indian— kick me off my land," Wub-e-ke-niew would sometimes taunt during his wranglings with the council.[6] It happened after his death, and it happened to Clara. Although the order of removal was published on Red Lake stationery and signed by the tribal chairman, Wub-e-ke-niew would doubtless insist it came straight from the heart of colonialism.

Red Lake is near Leech Lake, and it is one of the places Leech Lakers

go for ceremonies and fellowship with friends, relatives, and traditionalists (of whom there are many in cultural strongholds like Ponemah). Red
Lake is not like most other reservations, being one of only two in the
United States that never ceded their lands or had them placed in trust. It
is "indigenous land," and as such it possesses different rights: a bit more
sovereignty and the distinction of being a "closed" reservation. Red Lake
never had its lands allotted, so there is no "private property" or "checkerboard" there. The feeling one gets when leaving Bemidji, Minnesota, and
driving north to Red Lake is not unlike the sensation of visiting a completely different country. One immediately notes a sudden decline in road
quality but a drastic improvement in natural beauty. Trees are large and
abundant. There are no billboards, no advertisements of any kind, in
fact nothing resembling what we would recognize as a modern economy.
Poverty is evident, but so too are attempts at community renewal. This is
Indian space for sure.

The reservation is comprised of 880 square miles of wetland, low-
land, peat bog, prairie, and the Upper and Lower Red Lakes; its 564,426
acres makes Red Lake roughly the size of Rhode Island. In *Ojibwemowin*
Red Lake is called *Miskwaagamiiwi-zaaga'iganiing,* the name deriving
from a 1765 battle between the Ojibwe and the Dakota during which
the Ojibwe hid themselves in the gullies of a river outlet and fired upon
a flotilla of Dakota canoes that entered from the tributary. None of the
Dakotas survived the attack. Rather, their bodies fell into the water and
created a thick sludge of red that stayed visible for an entire day: a red
lake. As David Treuer has written, "bloodshed is what put Red Lake on
the map."[7]

Wub-e-ke-niew's homeland has experienced more than its share of violence. In 1979, armed dissidents staged an insurrection after a council member was removed from office, breaking into the law enforcement center,
taking hostages, and eventually burning it down. They also burned down
the house of the tribal chairman and several government buildings. Two
teenagers were killed, several people were wounded, and there was more
than four million dollars in property damage. A few years later, charges
of civil rights violations were made against a tribal judge, and the judge
was killed. Perhaps the most shocking violence at Red Lake happened
on March 21, 2005, when the community became the site of the second-
deadliest school shooting in history. Sixteen-year-old Jeff Weise, a boy who
wore black and assumed the pose of a goth, used a .40 caliber handgun and
a .12 gauge shotgun to kill five students, a teacher, and a security guard,
before ending his own short, tragic life in the hallways of his high school.

Seven other students were wounded, two of them suffering serious head wounds. Earlier that day Weise had slain his grandfather and his grandfather's female companion; he reportedly shot the man ten times.

Weise was obviously a deeply disturbed young man, and it is well known that he was taking Prozac at the time of his shooting. Native teenagers are being increasingly diagnosed with, and drugged for, mental and emotional illnesses, and their suicide rate is more than three times the American average. "Suicide pacts"—pledges made by kids to kill themselves in successive order—have been of recent concern at Cheyenne River and elsewhere in Indian country. Although it is difficult to say what compels a child to pursue violence and death, the psychiatrist Peter Breggin has observed that "the loss or absence of beneficial relationships with significant adults is the single most important source of suffering in a child's life."[8] All other causes—stress, violence, abuse, poverty, stigmatization, racism, fear, guilt, chemicals, and "lack of meaning"—are secondary to that, according to Breggin. One assumes that culture and ethnic identity would be as well.

Wub-e-ke-niew lived in the midst of recurring violence, and he probably knew of young people who resembled Weise: disaffected, disconnected, brown-skinned, betrayed, and angry. Wub-e-ke-niew had been a member of AIM during the Red Power years, so he knew about angry young Indians. One wonders how he might compare them then and now. Perhaps he would think that angry young people in his day weren't so very different from Weise, that perhaps the only real question was whether the anger of young people was directed *externally* versus *internally*. Perhaps anger's expression comes down to the presence or absence of a political movement that can see it, shape it, give it meaning, and steer it away from one's self-perception and self-esteem. Or perhaps anger is not the problem at all in this unhappy age. Perhaps the absence or presence of hope is the key.

Wub-e-ke-niew attended ceremonies conducted by Tommy Jay Stillday, a respected elder from Ponemah who could be seen in the background, praying with the bereaved, in some of the television news stories on the Red Lake school shooting. Until his death in 2008, Tommy Jay was the headman of a Midewiwin lodge and a popular public speaker on Ojibwe culture, and he had tricksterish qualities. In the 1990s, Bemidji State University invited Tommy Jay to deliver the keynote at its annual Native American graduation dinner, and he spoke for more than an hour in *Ojibwemowin*. The only English he used came at the end of his long address: "You study Indians. Study *that*." If Weise is the face of violence at

Red Lake, perhaps Tommy Jay envisaged its enduring survivance—even while shaming his English-only audience.

Wub-e-ke-niew witnessed anger, violence, and social breakdown during his life, but he also saw traditional language and culture reveal power. I think his radical and theological prescriptions for an Ojibwe future should be understood in that complicated social context. Perhaps Wub-e-ke-niew believed that the people's next movement should be primarily cultural in character, that cultural revival could become the next great phase of community renewal, and that the reclamation of traditional religion, language, and the *Ahnishinahbæóⁿjibway* identity would make Red Lake a happier, more peaceful place for its children. This is not to suggest that happiness and peace don't exist at Red Lake already; no homeland is always miserable, and Red Lake's natural beauty and cultural distinctiveness make it the envy of many. All I'm suggesting is that Wub-e-ke-niew may have resigned from the "Red Lake Band of Chippewa Indians," but he wasn't resigned to any fate. There is resignation, and then there is resignation; the one quits, and the other gives up. Wub-e-ke-niew quit, but did he give up?

Wub-e-ke-niew's life and work evidence the great complexities of our age, and its contradictions too. His dramatic and idealistic calls for new cultural, linguistic, and religious revitalization—so understandable in social and historical contexts marred by recurrent violence—ran up against the worst of modernity's excesses and never made much headway in the public. English is still the most common language used at Red Lake, and the U.S.-backed tribal council is still in power. Clara NiiSka is living in the Twin Cities, and those clans aren't sovereign. But those weren't irrational desires; to the contrary, I suspect that Wub-e-ke-niew was simply trying to improve the lot of his people, and that's about as rational as anything gets in this world. The question is: would his ideas work? And I think the answer is: apparently not.

This book opened with migrations and removals, and now it ends with resignations. There is a third possible meaning of resignation—"to sign again," to *re-sign*—to affirm an x-mark that was already made in one's name long ago. An x-mark is a commitment to living in new and perhaps unfamiliar ways, yet without promising to give up one's people, values, or sense of community. It's a leap of faith into the unknown: an irreducibly contaminated place where dreams of disconnection are impossible to realize, but having a place at the world's table is increasingly the stuff of reality. We have already examined some of the most important x-marks of our time—identity, culture, nationalization—and found no pristine purities there, no possibilities for real separatism. But neither have we discovered a reason for quitting or giving up. Our identities are in crisis, and our cultures at war, but we have the idea of the Indian nation at our disposal, and we can use it to get things we want. That this entails an embracement of modernity is no cause for alarm. To the contrary, it may be a reason to celebrate. We are the recipients of a gift, after all, one that was promised to *and by* our ancestors when they put their x-marks on treaties. That gift was a *future,* and the future, as they say, is now.

There's one more thing to be said about Wub-e-ke-niew's theory: it paid a great deal of attention to what people can or should do. You could learn the Ojibwe language, and you could become a member of the Midewiwin. True, there was also a great deal of Being in his thought (you have to have a clan, for example), but everything he wrote about identity and political action was, for the most part, concerned with action. And that brings us to our another x-mark that should be seen as tangential to our last one (the nation).

From "Indian" to "Citizen"

This book has banked on the hunch that most everything is socially constructed and Doing is generally preferable to Being. Our final x-mark to consider is the political identity configured by the technology of the modern nation: the *citizen.* I am not the first to consider it. Native writers are increasingly calling themselves "citizens" (as opposed to "enrolled members") of their Indian nations these days, scholars have been theorizing the meanings of indigenous citizenship, and the United Nations Declaration on the Rights of Indigenous Peoples addresses the idea in Article 32. Sean Teuton has called on Native scholars to "exchange the mixed-blood for the tribal citizen" as the best way to privilege Native identity, even when that identity is conflicted or "mixed."[9] Of course, as always, this idea is not universally embraced. Alfred calls citizenship another "European concept" that "must be eradicated from politics in Native communities," and one assumes that Wub-e-ke-niew would be right there with him.[10] It's also the case that the concept has yet to appear on a few indigenous radars. Neither Weaver, Womack, and Warrior's *American Indian Literary Nationalism* (2006) nor Womack, Justice, and Teuton's *Reasoning Together: The Native Critics Collective* (2008) has index citations for "citizen" or "citizenship," although both books profess nationalist orientations.

Citizenship is an important concept to address in the context of the Indian nation for the simple reason that nations and citizens always go hand in hand, but so far most of us have adopted the former without paying much attention to the latter. David Wilkins finds that a majority of tribal constitutions continue to speak in terms of "membership," with a small handful using the language of "citizenship," and an extremely scant few working with traditional concepts like "clanship."[11] Wilkins would reclaim "member" as a workable concept, locating its etymological roots in discourses on the body (whereby the loss of a "member" is an "injury"), and suggesting that "disenrollment" might be more accurately called "dismemberment."[12] Although one has to appreciate his reinterpretation of "member," I personally don't think it can be recuperated in a nationally useful way. *Nation,* after all, has its own vocabulary. Nations do not have "members"; they have "citizens." Clubs have members, and in fact they often "enroll" them, but clubs never "naturalize" them; that is a right reserved to nations. Clubs can offer "honorary" memberships, but nations do only rarely (just six times in the whole history of the United States). Rarer still are nations that strip people of their citizenship; this is considered a violation of human rights. "Memberships," however, are revoked each and every day. Membership has its "privileges," but citizenship has its "duties" and "rights." No one is ever called an "enrolled member of France." I say not enough Indians are "citizens."

Language matters, but it is not the only thing that matters when contemplating the logic of citizenship. We need to ask a lot of questions in this nationalist age. For instance, what is a citizen? What might that mean in Native contexts? What criteria are best for granting citizenship? Finally, what exactly is citizenship supposed to do? The idea of the citizen has everything to do with Doing, because it is citizens who make the nation and not the other way around. Citizenship is a universal (not Western) concept, operating in Red Lake no less than in Russia, and while it can be resigned just as easily as Wub-e-ke-niew's tribal enrollment, it is much less revocable. As a form of Indian political identity, citizenship brings my text full circle, for I think it has the potential to resolve an identity crisis. Like the *nation,* citizenship is good x-mark to make; but like *sovereignty,* one must claim it in order to have it. As for the criteria used to grant it, I offer a simple maxim: *require what you want to produce.*

Citizenship's Dual Character

A citizen is a member of a political community. There's your definition. There are, of course, many different kinds of communities to which people belong—ethnic groups and neighborhoods, church congregations and ceremonial societies, labor unions and activist organizations, fraternities and sororities, book clubs and basketball leagues—and granted, all communities can be said to have their "politics." But not all are political in the same sense as those that call their members "citizens." Citizenship has been associated with different kinds of political communities throughout world history, from villages to city-states to liberal democracies, but today the concept is universally linked to the modern idea of the nation. Citizenship is not the same thing as identity, although the two concepts often overlap. As we established in chapter 1, identity is "the construction of meaning on the basis of a cultural attribute, or related set of cultural attributes, that is/are given priority over other sources of meaning."[13] Always more nurture than nature, identity is the assemblage of *meanings* that a group holds as important signifiers of identity, and they say something about what that group values. Van Morrison's brown-eyed girl, for example, is heralded for two meaningful attributes—"brown-eyed" and "girl"—but despite the apparently alluring charms of the former, it is only the latter that provides her with identity. She is a "Girl" and not a "Brown-Eyed," because the meaning of gender is given priority over eye color, or at least where identity is concerned. Once meanings are prioritized—say, once gender is deemed more important than eye color—identities become primary and "self sustaining across time and space."[14] Meanings settle to the point of appearing natural, although in truth nature has precious little to say about identity. Everybody thinks they know what a girl is. That's identity. Having brown eyes? Just good luck.

But what about a "girlfriend"? Is that an identity too? Not really, says Castells, that would be a "role."[15] A role is another source of meaning, still culturally constructed and socially prioritized, and vital. In fact, the roles we play in our lives are often much more important to us than our identities. But roles don't describe who we are so much as what we do. I can spend the majority of my time being a worker, a father, a smoker, and a Van Morrison fan, and find communities of like-minded people everywhere who do the same, but we would be in the realm of role and not identity because roles lack the primacy and sustainability of identities. Their meanings are less evolved, less settled, and more geared toward fulfilling tasks (because there is work to be done, children to be raised, cigarettes to be smoked, and Van Morrison songs to be enjoyed). Roles are defined by action in ways that our identities are not; or, to put it another way, "identities organize the *meanings* while roles organize the *functions*."[16]

The really interesting thing about citizenship is the peculiar way it is constituted by *both* identity and role. This dual character is precisely what sets citizenship apart from other kinds of community membership, as suggested by ethicist Herman Van Gunsteren: "Citizenship is an answer to the question, 'Who am I?' and 'What should I do?'"[17] The first question is about identity, the second addresses role, and citizenship answers both. Who are you? A citizen of your nation. What should you do? Whatever it is that your nation requires or expects from its citizens. The first question is easier to discuss than the second because the latter depends on the particular ways that different nations imagine their projects, but in every case both questions have to be asked and answered when we talk about citizenship. Because if they are not—if only the first or the second question is asked—then we may be talking about identities or roles but not quite citizenship per se.

Even in cases where the second question is answered with a resounding No—for example, when the nation asks its citizens to do something immoral or unjust—we're still in the same basic paradigm. Civil disobedience is when the citizen tries to improve the nation by ridding it of some evil, and it should be distinguished from resigning one's citizenship, or for that matter just being a do-nothing sort of citizen. Saying No to an immoral national request or mandate is not necessarily an act of anti-citizenship (although it can be that) but, quite to the contrary, one way that nations are improved. We can see that, say, draft resisters who say No to a nation's unjust war are not noncitizens but actually patriots in the sense of Gandhi, Rosa Parks, or Henry Thoreau. Civil disobedience can be an act of citizenship for the way it redefines the roles and, in so doing, redefines the meaning of national identity.

Citizenship's dual character—its dual emphasis on identity and role, meaning and function—explains why citizenship connotes certain kinds of action, like *rights* (which are to be exercised), *responsibilities* (which are to be met), and *duties* (which are to be performed). Such actions are oriented toward promoting the nation's good health; and despite all nagging sense to the contrary, it really doesn't work the other way around. Oh, to be sure, leaders of nations are always quick to explain how their nations have surmounted incredibly daunting odds to benefit the citizens (especially under their leadership, especially during election season), and certainly we can all think of instances when our nations have indeed provided some benefit to us. If nations didn't benefit their citizens, why would they exist? But those benefits are the results of actions taken by citizens who play their roles through the apparatus of the nation. The calculus of national benefit looks like this: *the actions of citizens benefit the nation, which benefits citizens.* Nations, remember, are no more than abstract concepts, and they do not possess agency. Only citizens have agency.

The point of these theoretical distinctions—between nations and other kinds of communities, between citizenship and identity and role—is to say that there is something rather powerful about the nature of citizenship: namely, it produces other things. By my count, at least three. First, *political identity:* your national identity, like "American" or "Haudenosaunee," which may or may not connect to an *ethnie* but either way is modern and new. It is through political identity that citizenship tells you who you are. Second, *roles:* social functions that legitimize the nation through the actions taken by active citizens, like "voter," "clan mother," "patriot," or for that matter "traitor," and let's go ahead and say "civilly disobedient subject." It is through roles that you are taught what to do (and not to do) in relation to the nation. And third, the *nation:* this relationship we like to imagine working in the obverse—the nation granting citizenship—but that idea turns the actual relationship on its head. There would be no nation, after all, without its citizens. Citizenship is the engine of national identities, the distributor of political functions, and the maker of the nation itself. Everything flows from the productive site of citizenship.

That's why the criteria used for granting citizenship are so important. Citizenship criteria set the process of national production into motion, not only recognizing identities but articulating the roles. Because these things have to do with meanings—what it means to be a citizen, what it means to play that role—citizenship criteria say a great deal about the nation's character: what it values, what it believes, and what it promotes. *Citizenship criteria produce the meanings of the nation.* Like identity, they prioritize some attributes over others; like role, they prioritize certain functions. Because the citizen is always a combination of both identity and role, the criteria we use to recognize it always ask the two crucial questions that citizenship answers: "Who are you?" and "What should you do?" Different nations have different answers in mind, of course, but all nations ask the two questions when establishing their criteria for citizenship. Because if they do not, if they divorce identity from role, then we are talking about some other kind of institution and not really a nation at all. It would be more like a club. With members. Probably "enrolled."

Blood and Soil in Theory and Practice

What are the most common criteria for citizenship? Today most nations employ a combination of three international legal principles to distinguish insiders from outsiders: (1) *jus sanguinis* (Latin: "right of blood"), which speaks of ethnicity or descent; (2) *jus soli* ("right of soil"), referring to place of birth or residence; and (3) *naturalization,* the granting of citizenship to individuals regardless of blood or soil (for instance, through marriage). *Jus sanguinis* privileges ethnic or "racial" identity, *jus soli* values national territory, and naturalization circumvents both. These three concepts are universally recognized as the standard criteria for establishing citizenship, and they have ancient and ascriptive roots, as William Safran explains:

> Since the biblical period and the era of the Greek city state, membership in a "national" community was (as the term itself implies) determined largely by ascription—birth, descent, and religion—because community was defined in organic terms: it was believed to have evolved from extended families or tribes held together by blood ties and other inherited connections.[18]

This ancient, organic understanding of community is well reflected in the Old Testament, which in the book of Genesis tells how Adam was created literally out of the soil and given dominion over creation; the rest of the Torah describes how Adam's progeny eventually became the nation of Israel. The same holds for ancient Greek society, which posited the idea that the progenitors of Athens emerged from the soil; in fact, it was the Greeks who gave us a synonym for "indigenous": that terrifying mouthful of a word, "autochthonous" (*khthonous,* "under the earth"), referring to both rocks and people. It goes without saying that this logic explains the constitutive myths of many an indigenous *ethnie* too. It's all the same story: a political community conceived as a "family" that sprang from the soil long ago.[19] *Jus soli* privileges the soil. *Jus sanguinis* privileges the "family."

But because these communities always pretended to be more organic and natural than they really were, they had to develop creative ways of dealing with problems that dependably emerge whenever groups claim to have direct organic ties to the past through blood and soil. Such mechanisms are called, tellingly, naturalization. Naturalization means making something that isn't quite natural, natural. Of course, none of it was really natural; communities have always played in the realm of mythologies that cannot be taken literally. Nations have always had outsiders coming in through marriage, warfare, and trade, and naturalization is proof that they knew it. They turned outsiders into insiders by manipulating the myths they had at hand, using culture to transform what was ostensibly natural. And sometimes the community just said No. Those unlucky folks who were excluded from membership on the basis of some unmet cultural criterion were just as important to the nation's self-concept as the citizens inside, because their absence demarcated what the nation was *not*. Both naturalization and No produced the same basic effect on the group: maintaining its boundary, clarifying its lines between insiders and outsiders, and reiterating its values.

Ancient history? Hardly. Modern liberal democracies still work with these old ideas, although in complicated ways that will often change with the blowing of political winds. The United States and France have developed what Safran calls a "functional-voluntary" approach to citizenship, recognizing birthright while remaining open to anyone willing to play by their rules, thus recognizing *jus soli* while interpreting *jus sanguinis* fairly loosely as language competence, allegiance, and/or adherence to values. This can be contrasted with nations like Germany whose criteria are founded almost exclusively on *jus sanguinis*. Safran credits Germany's historical tendency to grant ethnic citizenship to a misreading of Herder, that proto-ethnologist discussed briefly in chapter 2 who argued that culture embodied the "spirit of the people" *(Volksgeist)* but who was widely misinterpreted as locating *Geist* in "Aryan" blood. This bad linkage of culture and biology reached a fever pitch in the Nazi regime when Jews, Gypsies, and other "races" were stripped of their citizenships on the basis of their non-Aryan ethnicity, while other Aryans (such as Scandinavians) were not. Racial criteria were abandoned by Germany after World War II, but its general preference for *jus sanguinis* has survived. Today children who are born to "guest workers" do not qualify for citizenship, and basic civil rights are denied to resident aliens. This situation is even more pronounced in Japan, where third- and even fourth-generation Taiwanese and Koreans lack citizenship, and ethnic Japanese born in other countries have no right to naturalization.

One nation that has tried to combine *jus soli* and *jus sanguinis* to account for different identities and goals is Israel, which developed some useful citizenship ideas (for tribes, anyway) in its infancy. Israel was created by the United Nations in 1948 and characterized as a "Jewish state" (a theocracy) and an "ethnic state" (a homeland for Jews). Yet Israel was from the start ethnopluralist, as evidenced in its "Proclamation of Independence," which invites local "Arab inhabitants" to "participate in the upbuilding of the State on the basis of full and equal citizenship."[20] How could a nation be a Jewish state, an ethnic state, and ethnopluralist all at the same time? In keeping with *jus soli,* citizenship was granted to all people born in Israel before 1952, to all Israel-born Jews, and to anyone with a resident Israeli parent or spouse. In accordance with *jus san-*

guinis, the Law of Return naturalized any and all immigrant Jews wanting citizenship, while non-Jewish immigrants were subject to rigid criteria: residency requirements, the renouncement of citizenship in other nations, a declaration of loyalty, and competence in Hebrew.[21] Predictably, these criteria raised questions.

The first is one that indigenous people will immediately recognize: who is a Jew? Based on rabbinical teachings, Israeli law defined Jewishness in two ways, by matrilineal descent and conversion, but those standards proved controversial as the elders often refused to recognize the Jewishness of children born to nonpracticing mothers and questioned the legitimacy of conversions performed by non-Orthodox rabbis. A second question had to do with the status of non-Jews living in the Jewish state, the "outsiders inside," and a third question concerned Jews around the world who do not receive Israeli citizenship but maintain their connection to Israel, the "insiders outside." What status should be given to those groups? To answer all of these questions, the Israeli Supreme Court created what Safran calls "a hierarchy of memberships":

> distinction was made between (purely political) "citizenship" *(ezrahut),* which was available to all kinds of people; (communally defined) "nationality" *(le'umiut)*—such as that of Jews and Arabs; and membership in the Jewish religious community. In terms of that hierarchy, the children of Jewish fathers but unconverted (or improperly converted) mothers were viewed as Jewish by "nationality" (and hence covered by the Law of Return) but were not so regarded from a religious point of view.[22]

Distinguishing between *citizens, nationals,* and *religious members,* Israel's hierarchy of memberships employed different criteria to recognize different kinds of belonging, each with its own rights, duties, and responsibilities. This allowed some folks to be Jewish without claiming Israeli citizenship and others to be Israelis without being Jewish. Most of all, it allowed Israel to be an ethnic and ethnopluralist nation as well as a Jewish state, all at the same time.

It might have worked well had Israel not occupied Palestine in 1967. As a result of that decision, which was rebuked by the United Nations and every human rights organization in the world, Israel's approach to citizenship today is more like apartheid than anything else, with two different classes of citizenship for Jews and Palestinians, who are extremely separate and unequal. In 2002, Israel ceased granting citizenship to spouses and parents of citizens hailing from the occupied territories, later relaxing those restrictions (but not enough to halt criticism by Amnesty International, the United Nations Committee on the Elimination of Racial Discrimination, and many Israeli and Palestinian human rights organizations).[23] Israel's originally innovative attempt to be pluralistic yet predominately Jewish through its hierarchy of memberships is threatened now, it seems, by a rather old-fashioned colonialism.

Allow me to make a crucial point regarding this brief review of the ways nations define and grant citizenship: in every single case, the criteria produce something of value to the particular nation. France and the United States were founded on Enlightenment democratic ideals— shared sovereignty of the people, republican notions of civic virtue, a separation of powers, and a vibrant public sphere—hence they developed criteria that would produce the nations they had in mind: liberal democracies where popular sovereignty and the rule of law would trump ethnicity, religion, and other forms of identity. By contrast, ethnicity was the value in Germany and Japan, so their criteria produced primarily ethnic states. Put another way, the functional-voluntarist criteria used by France and the United States valued roles over identities, while the organic-determinist criteria used in Germany and Japan privileged identities over roles. Of course, no nation disregards identity or role, since citizenship always requires both; it's really a matter of emphasis. But the rule stays the same: citizenship is granted on the basis of criteria that represent certain values of the nation. What each nation "recognizes" is simultaneously *produced*.

The same rule applies to Israel, which originally tried to formulate its character as a "Jewish state," "ethnic state," and ethnopluralist nation through an innovative hierarchy of memberships (although thanks to its present policies, few would hold Israel up as a model of pluralist citizenship now). I think Israel's original laws provide something of value to Native nations now grappling with similar issues of tribalism, religion, and ethnopluralism, especially the idea of a hierarchy of memberships. But before we get to that, let's take a look at some of the citizenship criteria that are articulated and used in Native America today.

Blood, Soil, and Quanta

Indigenous nations located within the boundary of the United States use both *jus sanguinis* and *jus soli* to establish belonging, but the former is far more prevalent than the latter. Nearly all require lineal descent from a base roll and mandate that one parent must be a member, and roughly two-thirds demand a mandatory blood quantum as well. The Blackfeet are not atypical, requiring lineal descent from an ancestor on their 1935 census roll and one-quarter degree "Blackfeet Indian blood," regardless of place of birth.[24] Oglala Sioux recognizes "children born to any member of the tribe who is a resident of the reservation at the time of the birth," and no blood quantum is required.[25] Rosebud mandates a one-quarter blood quantum only in cases where the parental residency requirement cannot be met, recognizing "persons of one-fourth or more Sioux Indian blood born after April 01, 1935 to a member of the Tribe, regardless of the residence of the parent."[26] Lower Sioux grants citizenship to "children of any member who is a resident of the Lower Sioux Reservation at the time of the birth."[27] They also recognize "all nonmembers"—interestingly, no mandatory lineage is specified—who successfully pass a popular vote by their Community Council.[28] That's naturalization, but at Lower Sioux it's called "adoption."

Even here we can already see that the three criteria used everywhere—*jus soli, jus sanguinis,* and naturalization—are also used in Indian country. These are, after all, universal concepts. Where difference exists, it is in the specific ways in which these principles are interpreted and applied. For example, if there is an Indian community out there granting citizenship purely by right of soil *(jus soli),* I haven't found it. Residence, when required at all, usually supplements lineage, but residency requirements of any sort are just not that common. Further, if there exists a Native community defining *jus sanguinis* broadly in terms of language, religion, culture, or a commitment to values—those "ethnic" ways in which *jus sanguinis* is usually understood today—I haven't come across it either. The "right of blood" continues to be interpreted literally in Native America, and there's a blinding preponderance of blood quantum mandates on the books. Finally, as the Lower Sioux example reveals, when a policy resembling naturalization is established, the language used is "adoption."

Is there a problem with any of this? Not inherently. Remember, it depends on what kind of nation you wish to produce. At the moment, however, it seems fair to observe that most Indian nations are producing citizens who (1) descend from ancestors listed on census rolls, and who are (2) related by blood, but also (3) sometimes territory, and, thanks to (4) blood quantum, share some phenotype. That's your standard Indian national product, and there is nothing inherently good or bad about it. But there may be something inherently *American* about it. One can't help but notice how closely our prototypical Native citizen resembles the *Indian* as defined in the Indian Reorganization Act (IRA):

The term "Indian" as used in this Act shall include all persons of
Indian descent who are members of any recognized Indian tribe now
under Federal jurisdiction, and all persons who are descendants of
such members who were, on June 1, 1934, residing within the present
boundaries of any Indian reservation, and shall further include all
other persons of one-half or more Indian blood.[29]

It is that sort of definition of identity that Wub-e-ke-niew and all traditionalists resist, as it has absolutely nothing to say about culture, language, or peoplehood. If that is all that *Indian* means, the argument goes,
then perhaps genocide has already happened by definition, in which case
some sort of resignation might be necessary. Whatever happened to the
Ahnishinahbæó'jibway?

It's true that today's typical Indian citizen resembles the *Indian* as
imagined by the federal government in 1934, and to a limited extent
that means resembling citizens in all nations around the world. After
all, *jus sanguinis* was used in the IRA definition ("Indian descent"), and
so was *jus soli* ("residing within the present boundaries"). That said,
IRA-type definitions do not generally interpret *jus sanguinis* broadly to
include considerations of ethnicity defined by culture or language, so
the traditionalists have a point: there is no peoplehood possible in such
definitions, no privileging of language or traditions, and thus no cultural
survival. Further, on top of its limited view of *jus sanguinis,* there is also a
third criterion present in the IRA definition (hence in most tribal constitutions today) that seems specific to Native communities: blood quantum.
Blood quantum isn't a measurement of blood but the ascertainment of a
fractioned lineage. This is not the same thing as *jus sanguinis* but a recent
idea whose ideological parents met in the nineteenth century (their names
were Scientific Racism and Colonization), and which is now responsible
for turning increasing numbers of "mixed" Native babies into resident
aliens at the moment of their birth. Jack Forbes has traced the roots of
blood quantum back to a 1705 Virginia Colony statute that denied legal
rights to people of mixed races, including but not limited to Indians, so
the idea was conceived for the purpose of securing white racial privilege.[30] I think blood quantum is a terrible idea from a nationalist perspective, for as long as people ask, "How much Indian are you?"—and
trust me, this happens to some of us all the time—or as long as the idea
of a "part-Indian" is still around, the prospects of an Indian *nation* as
an idea are going to be dim. Now, to be clear, I am not saying that *jus
sanguinis* should be abandoned—that would be foolish from a nationalist

perspective too—nor am I arguing that there is no room for an idea of an "Indian race" in the modern world. If nations like Germany or Japan are allowed to use race to establish citizenship, indigenous nations should be too. All I'm saying is that blood quantum is one of the most colonized ideas around. Indeed, those who call it "statistical extermination" make a sound mathematical point.

The federal government's Indian citizen was determined by *jus sanguinis, jus soli,* and blood quantum, but not naturalization. The reasons for this omission are obvious; the last thing the IRA was trying to do was establish real sovereign nations that non-Indian people might actually join. The IRA was the administration of a kinder, gentler colonization that tried to do as little harm as possible, but it was colonization all the same, so its definition of *Indian* comes as no surprise. More surprising is how little these criteria have changed since Indian nations assumed responsibility for them. The 1979 Supreme Court decision in *Santa Clara v. Martinez* was the Americans' first and final word regarding the absolute right of Indian nations to determine their own citizenship criteria, and although it came at great cost to Julia Martinez's children (who were denied citizenship for lack of a Pueblo father), that decision was a correct one. It is absolutely essential that Indian nations devise their own criteria, and it is just as crucial that they do so in ways that do not violate universal human rights. What I find perplexing—and here I am in basic agreement with the new traditionalists—is how most Indian nations have not taken the *Santa Clara* decision as an opportunity to develop citizenship criteria that would require what they want to produce: cultural revitalization, linguistic renewal, resistance to assimilation. Citizenship criteria articulate the meanings of your nation—they allow you to require what you want to produce—but it seems most nations are still producing an "American Indian."

"Western" ideas like citizenship cannot be blamed. The governments who devise specific citizenship criteria can be, however, and that's where activism plays its part. If Native nationalists are serious about building sovereign indigenous nations, they should rightly ask why the old IRA definition of an Indian "under Federal jurisdiction" is still so ubiquitous in tribal constitutions, and they should demand changes. But one shouldn't throw the baby out with the bathwater by blaming "the West" for decisions that are now made by Indian governments; nor should one lose a useful concept such as *jus sanguinis,* which can be interpreted in myriad ways, or *jus soli,* which has the benefit of privileging Indian territory. Naturalization as well should go by its proper name; "adoption," after all, is not a nationalist concept but an ethnological legacy of Lewis Henry Morgan (who was no nationalist). As for blood quantum, if there is some good purpose to it (and, as we saw in our last chapter, Alfred thinks there is), I don't see it at all. The point is, nationalists should seize the universal discourse of citizenship and use it to produce the things that they want, whatever they might happen to be.

Citizenship is a universal concept indissolubly associated with the nation. The IRA was John Collier's attempt to grant more "self-government" to Indians in a manner befitting "domestic dependent nations." If the definitions the IRA employed—definitions that still resound in many tribal constitutions, as I've been saying—don't produce a sovereign Indian national citizen or cultural renewal, what do they produce? Let's take a closer look at the membership requirements articulated in a constitution: that of the Minnesota Chippewa Tribe (MCT). The MCT is a political consortium of six Ojibwe reservations created by treaties in the nineteenth century and then consolidated under the IRA. Originally adopted in 1936 and revised in 1963, MCT's constitution outlines its membership policy as follows:

> Section 1. The membership of the Minnesota Chippewa Tribe shall consist of the following: (a) Basic Membership Roll. All persons of Minnesota Chippewa Indian blood whose names appear on the annuity roll of April 14, 1941, prepared pursuant to the Treaty with said Indians as enacted by Congress in the Act of January 14, 1889 (25 Stat. 642) and Acts amendatory thereof, and as corrected by the Tribal Executive Committee and ratified by the Tribal Delegates, which roll shall be known as the basic membership roll of the Tribe. (b) All children of Minnesota Chippewa Indian blood born between April 14, 1941, the date of the annuity roll, and July 3, 1961, the date of approval of the membership ordinance by the Area Director, to a parent or parents, either or both of whose names appear on the basic membership roll, provided an application for enrollment was filed with the Secretary or the Tribal Delegates by July 4, 1962, one year after the date of approval of the ordinance by the Area Director. (c) All children of at least one quarter 1/4 degree Minnesota Chippewa Indian blood born after July 3, 1961, to a member, provided that an application for enrollment was or is filed with the Secretary of the Tribal Delegates of the Tribal Executive Committee within one year after the date of birth of such children.
> Section 2. No person born after July 3, 1961, shall be eligible for enrollment if enrolled as a member of another tribe, or if not an American citizen.

Section 3. Any person of Minnesota Chippewa Indian blood who meets the membership requirements of the Tribe, but who because of an error has not been enrolled, may be admitted to membership in the Minnesota Chippewa Tribe by adoption, if such adoption is approved by the Tribal Executive Committee, and shall have full membership privileges from the date the adoption is approved.

Section 4. Any person who has been rejected for enrollment as a member of the Minnesota Chippewa Tribe shall have the right of appeal within sixty days from the date of written notice of rejection from the decision of the Tribal Executive Committee to the Secretary of the Interior and the decision of the Secretary of Interior shall be final.

Section 5. Nothing contained in this article shall be construed to deprive any descendant of a Minnesota Chippewa Indian of the right to participate in any benefits derived from claims against the U.S. Government when awards are made for and on behalf and for the benefit of descendants of members of said tribe.[31]

There are three points that I want to make regarding this policy: specifically, *language, techniques of belonging,* and *ownership of perspective.*

First, the *language* used in this policy connotes nothing particularly "national" in character. It defines belonging not in terms of "citizenship" but as "membership," and as we learn in Section 3, membership has its "privileges." "Rights" make their appearance in Section 5, but in fact there the term references nonmember "descendants" who by *jus sanguinis* have a "right to participate in any benefits derived from claims against the U.S. Government." *Non*members have rights. This policy also uses the language of "adoption," not naturalization, which is probably just as well since it wouldn't count as naturalization anyway given its limited contingency on the committing of a clerical "error." MCT itself is described in distinctly nonnational ways: it is a "Chippewa tribe"—the former word archaic, the latter concept anthropological—and distinguished by, well, its location in the state of Minnesota (?!). Obviously, and perhaps predictably, the MCT membership policy indicates nothing about national identity or role.

Second, the specific *techniques of belonging* outlined in the policy are worth noting for their logic and origins. *Jus sanguinis* is exclusively used, limited by a one-quarter MCT blood quantum and birth to an enrolled parent, and asking that a baby be registered within one year of its birth. *Jus soli* doesn't apply here at all, as birthplace and residence are completely irrelevant. Like all nations using *jus sanguinis,* MCT tells a story about the origins of the people. This story begins in 1889 with an old allotment agreement that created the "basic membership roll" finalized in 1941. Lineal descent from the roll established membership until 1961 when the one-quarter blood quantum was created, but only MCT blood counted (to the exclusion of not only non-Indians and non-Ojibwe but also the nearby Ojibwe territories at Red Lake and Wisconsin, Michigan, North Dakota, and Manitoba). This narrative is quite different from the origin story told at ceremonies. Finally, while Section 2's ban on dual citizenship is not that uncommon, MCT's a priori mandate of American citizenship practically turns the MCT into an immigration field office for the Department of Homeland Security. It articulates in no uncertain terms who the actual sovereign nation is: only an American "citizen" can become a "member" of MCT. America, it seems, is the Chippewa's *ethnie*.

Finally, we must remark upon the *ownership of perspective* in this policy; that is, who "looks" when a person is submitted for membership? We have already commented on the implicit story told in MCT's sense of *jus sanguinis;* we must now ask whose story it is. Ojibwe history is characterized exclusively by its political dealings with the United States: allotment, IRA, annuity rolls, acts of Congress, and, of course, that U.S. citizenship requirement. Nothing in the policy acknowledges that Ojibwe people even existed before 1889, so it is actually the American text—the Nelson Act referenced in Section 1—which provides the origin of *jus san-guinis*. This is obviously an American view, and if some question arises regarding one's membership, the Americans look again. Appeals, we are told, go directly to the BIA, and "the decision of the Secretary of Interior shall be final."

As the political philosopher Carl Schmitt once wrote, "Sovereign is he who decides on the exception."[32] The Minnesota Chippewa Tribe's citizenship criteria are an illustration of how sovereignty operates in the wake of colonization, as it defines Ojibwe citizens in purely American terms, tells an American version of the Ojibwe story, and literally hands all of the exceptions to the U.S. Department of the Interior for decision. Earlier we asked what tribal citizenship criteria that seem to resemble the IRA definition of *Indian* produce. The answer is stated in MCT's Mission Statement:

> The Minnesota Chippewa Tribe . . . is a federally recognized tribal government that, through unified leadership, promotes and protects the member Bands while providing quality services and technical assistance to the reservation governments and tribal people.[33]

Does that sound like a sovereign indigenous nation to you? Are "tribal people" the same as citizens? Or might MCT be the textbook definition of a "domestic dependent nation": a colonized community whose people are recognized by no more than their attachment to the provision of "quality services" and "technical assistance"? The language suggests as much, and it finds support in yet another founding document, the Preamble to MCT's constitution, where we discover not only the purpose of this political community, but its ultimate source of power as well:

> We, the Minnesota Chippewa Tribe . . . in order to form a
> representative Chippewa tribal organization, maintain and establish
> justice for our Tribe, and to conserve and develop our tribal resources
> and common property; to promote the general welfare for ourselves
> and our descendants, do establish and adopt this constitution for the
> Chippewa Indians of Minnesota in accordance with such privilege
> granted the Indians by the United States under existing law.[34]

The very existence of this "tribal organization" is a "privilege granted the Indians by the United States." It really doesn't get much clearer than that.

It must be noted that MCT's original boilerplate constitution was literally handed to Ojibwe by the federal government under the IRA and was officially adopted in 1936. It was revised in 1963, mainly to institute the blood quantum mandate, and sanctioned by a member vote of 1,761 for and 1,295 against. But there are more than forty thousand MCT members today who live under this constitution, and it cannot be said that they are generally happy with it. "Constitutional reform!" is a constant refrain one hears among the "member Bands." Why so many calls for reform? It seems to me that dissatisfaction with the constitution is accompanied by a general discontent regarding contemporary Ojibwe life. Few are happy with the status quo. Prominent cultural groups from language activists to religious ceremonialists are concerned about the ongoing decline of heritage language and traditional culture; community action groups are worried about social problems that perennially afflict our communities (poverty, poor health, pollution, crime, violence, addiction, depression, and despair); and tribal councils are constantly frustrated by the jurisdictional intrusions of state and county legislatures. As a "tribal organization" defined by provision of "quality services" and "technical assistance," the MCT has very little to offer by way of preventing an ongoing genocide, but, as a creation of the IRA, it was never intended to do so. It will be up to the Ojibwe Nation alone to solve its problems, and I'm fairly certain that the permanent constitution for that political entity has yet to be written.

Producing Sovereign Indigenous Nations

This book has argued that indigenous nations are produced by nationalists who turn "low" local cultures into "high" national cultures, and that as part of that effort they modernize the *ethnie*. As my reading of MCT's constitution suggests, it must involve decolonization as well, by which I mean dismantling the legacies of colonialism as they appear in our legal terminology, our academic discourse, our constitutions, and other locales where language is used. It does not necessitate a thorough disavowal of the way one thinks, nor does it mean having to radically transform one's culture. Nationalism should not require a religious conversion. The only unbrainwashing required is to refuse the sweet temptations of fatalism and fundamentalism. Cultural resistance is useful, but it can also be transformed into a commodity sold by a protestant ethnic: the spectacle of disillusionment. If not accompanied by realist nationalism, any cultural resistance that calls itself political activism can easily descend into cynicism and indifference. Resignation.

The bathwater should go, but that baby inside is an x-mark we can use. Don't give up on citizenship or constitutions; revise them to produce sovereign indigenous nations. This brings me to my final point. What are the proper criteria for indigenous citizenship? *Require what you want to produce.* If your heritage language is dying, then make fluency a requirement for citizenship. If your territory suffers from brain drain, make residency a requirement for citizenship. If you need capital, make commitment to the nation's laws a requirement for citizenship and level a progressive income tax. If you wish to produce a nation of lineal descendants with a certain blood quantum and little else, you are probably well on your way. The point is, the character and the "doings" of your nation are produced by its citizenship criteria, and the sky's the limit. So require what you want to produce.

Like other nations, you should adhere to international concepts like *jus sanguinis, jus soli,* and naturalization, but you can tailor these in specific ways to produce the nation you want. *Jus sanguinis,* for instance, is usually defined as lineage or ethnicity—birth to another citizen—but it can also refer to the possession of language, religion, and culture. Are any nations offering language fluency exams to prospective citizens? Why not? *Jus soli* should be considered as a possible requirement for citizenship too, as this concept speaks loudest of the importance of land. Are any nations making distinctions between the rights and duties of citizens who live on the territory versus those who do not? If not, is that another way of saying that the territory doesn't matter? Finally, I'd like to speak a word in favor of naturalization, that third important means to citizenship used by the community of nations, but presently all but ignored by Native ones. Can people marry into your nation? Why not? The obvious answers— they are not of our tribe, they're non-Native—speak of identity but not citizenship, and let's not forget that we're trying to build a nation here. There is nothing preventing any nations, ours included, from telling the naturalized citizens what they have to do to be recognized, whether that means learning the local language, practicing a local custom, paying the local income tax, or just marrying the local lonely guy. These are *roles,* and there's nothing in the blood preventing people from playing their roles. As for ethnic identity, now is a good time to separate that from the political identity bestowed by citizenship. This would mean that not all Indians would necessarily be citizens, and not all citizens would necessarily be Indians, but in fact that would be the way that Indians used to think. Mary Jemison lived as a real Seneca after her captivity, but it seems no one forgot she was "white." The same goes for those "black" Cherokee Freedmen. (On the other hand, the Ojibwe historian William Whipple Warren would qualify for MCT membership today, but he didn't consider himself to be one of the *anishinaabeg* he fought for as a Minnesota state senator in the 1800s, because he considered himself American.) Naturalization is one of the boldest statements a nation can make regarding the reach of its sovereignty, so why not naturalize?

Let me close with a final suggestion. Given the politically fraught nature of Native identity and citizenship—really, all our Indian identity controversies—I propose that our nations model Israel's old "hierarchy of memberships" with different rights, responsibilities, and requirements attached to each level. Israel, remember, distinguished between (1) a political sense of citizenship defined by identity and role, (2) an ethnic sense of nationality that signified one's identity as Jewish, and (3) membership in the religious community. That meant non-Jews could become citizens of Israel—which remained a "Jewish state"—while non-Israelis retained a Jewish nationality and the right to return should they desire. One benefit of the category of nationality has been the supporting role played by Jews abroad who, although not citizens, nor necessarily all that religious, have worked to promote Israel's well-being. In this way, the category of nationality has bolstered the nation, and membership has avoided playing a zero-sum game (except, of course, for the Palestinians).

I see no reason why indigenous nations can't establish new hierarchies of membership that could distinguish between (1) *citizenship* constituted by some combination of *jus sanguinis* and *jus soli*, (2) *nationality* comprised by a definition of *jus sanguinis* alone, and (3) *lineal descent* to characterize those who do not necessarily produce anything of value beyond their birth (which is where we all start, remember). Everyone would get a card, but there would be more than one kind of card, because not everyone would share the same responsibilities and rights. *Citizens* would be the most active in the day-to-day affairs of the nation, so they would enjoy the right to vote, hold office, formulate policy, and control material benefits like gaming revenues and housing; this makes sense because material benefits should impact the economy of the homeland more than the diaspora (that is, some other nation's economy). *Nationals* would belong to the nation as cultural or ethnic members possessing the rights to religious freedom, to adopt Native children, hunt and fish in treaty-reserved areas—all the rights guaranteed to Native people through laws, treaties, and agreements—and the right to return should they choose to become citizens. All citizens would be nationals, not all nationals would be citizens, but both would be recognized as part of the nation. As for *lineal descendants* whose identity is no more than an accident of birth, nationality would be attainable, and maybe citizenship too, but only if specific criteria are met. Which criteria? Require what you want to produce.

I am intentionally being nonprescriptive here because I don't want to tell people what they should be producing as a nation; it is really up to the citizens who construct it. My point is simply this: nations are produced by nationalists, but they are *re*produced by citizens who articulate the meanings of their nation in locales like constitutions. Many of us are unhappy with how our nations are working and seek solutions to our problems in myriad different ways. New traditionalists want to be nations unlike any other, yet risk throwing the baby out with the bathwater; cultural resisters simply refuse to play the modern nation game. I have been saying that realist nationalists should work with what we have in order to make an x-mark that delivers something good. If I were to revise a constitution by myself, I would probably adopt some hierarchy of memberships that would actively produce what I think most Ojibwe want: language revitalization, cultural renewal, some privileging of the land and the people who live there, and the most important goal: economic justice. It could be done in several different ways; all that's required are the three international legal concepts—*jus sanguinis, jus soli,* and naturalization—and a little creative thinking. Well, that, and the fact that we have to fight the fatalists, fundamentalists, and fans of the status quo. Hey, no one ever said nationalism would be easy.

Make Your X-Mark

When Wub-e-ke-niew disenrolled himself from the Red Lake Band of Chippewa Indians, he courageously stood against the illegitimacy of American rule and imagined a "new" Ojibwe nation that was actually very old. He reasserted the importance of an *ethnie,* one that had been completely erased by the Americans in the nineteenth century and not reinscribed since, and he tried to modernize it by arguing for an Ojibwe theocracy. He did it through his writing (his book and columns) and by disfiguring writing (his ID card). One text replaces another; and while one text might be called "the oral tradition" and the other text denigrated as "the white man's way," the fact of the matter is: *both are texts.* As texts, they must be inscribed, signed, given an x-mark signifying consent to some way of life. We can choose which texts we will sign, but our choices are never without limits, not even if we claim to be "separatist," not even when our community is "closed." To be closed implies the existence of an opening at some other place and time. These terms are relational, like inside/outside, and as such they belie the prospects of a permanent withdrawal. In a world where inside/outside has become an increasingly difficult distinction to make, tribal nations should assert their *differentiation,* not separatism, and in so doing their right to exist among a community of nations. We do have that right, as Wub-e-ke-niew said, and it's a right exercised by people who seek not only to survive, but to actively participate in our one and only modern world.

NOTES

Introduction

1. The phrase "platonic notions of Indian sovereignty" appears in *McLanahan v. Arizona Tax Commission,* 411 U.S. 172 (1973), and in a U.S. Supreme Court case, *County of Yakima v. Confederated Tribes and Bands of the Yakima Nation,* 112 S. Ct. 687. Although it refers somewhat disparagingly to the "national" status attributed to Indians, it could just as easily refer to any nation's sovereignty, including that of the United States.

2. Ernest Renan, "What Is a Nation?" in *Becoming National: A Reader,* ed. Geoff Eley and Ronald Grigor Suny (New York and Oxford: Oxford University Press, 1996), 41.

3. Edmund Jefferson Danziger Jr., *The Chippewas of Lake Superior* (Norman: University of Oklahoma Press, 1979), 4.

4. Ibid.

5. Gerald Vizenor, *Fugitive Poses: Native American Indian Scenes of Absence and Presence* (Lincoln and London: University of Nebraska Press, 1998), 15.

6. Kimberly Blaeser, "Gathering of Stories," in *Stories Migrating Home: A Collection of Anishinaabe Prose,* ed. Kimberly Blaeser (Bemidji, Minn.: Loonfeather Press, 1998), 3.

7. Henry Rice, "Chippewa Indians in Minnesota," 1890, 51st Congress, 1st session, House of Representatives, Ex. Doc. No. 247, 3.

8. Ibid., 158.

9. Ibid.

10. Vine Deloria Jr. and Clifford M. Lytle, *American Indians, American Justice* (Austin: University of Texas Press, 1983), 10.

11. Stella U. Ogunwole, *We the People: American Indians and Alaska Natives in the United States* (Washington, D.C.: U.S. Census Bureau, Special Report CENSR-2812, February 2006), 12.

12. Indian Health Service, "Trends in American Indian Health, 2000–2001," June 13, 2008, http://www.ihs.gov/NonMedicalPrograms/IHS_Stats/Trends00.asp, 7.

13. Richard H. Carmona, "Suicide Prevention among Native American Youth," statement before the U.S. Senate Indian Affairs Committee, June 13, 2008, http://www.ihs.gov/adminmngrresources/legislativeaffairs/documents/2005-06-15 Carmona.pdf, 2–3.

14. For these and other statistics regarding indigenous language shift, see Gina Cantoni, ed., *Stabilizing Indigenous Languages* (Flagstaff: Northern Arizona University, Center for Excellence in Education, 1996).

15. Ogunwole, *We the People*, 7.

16. Lewis Henry Morgan, *Ancient Society, or Researches in the Lines of Human Progress from Savagery through Barbarism to Civilization* (New York: Henry Holt, 1877).

17. Raymond Williams, *Keywords: A Vocabulary of Culture and Society*, rev. ed. (New York and London: Oxford University Press, 1983), 318–19.

18. Achille Mbembe, *On the Postcolony* (Berkeley: University of California Press, 2001), 3.

19. Ibid., 3–4.

20. Ibid., 4.

21. Ibid.

22. Ibid.

23. Hans Robert Jauss, "History of Art and Pragmatic History," in *Toward an Aesthetic of Reception*, trans. Timothy Bahti (Minneapolis: University of Minnesota Press, 1982), 46–48.

24. Anthony Giddens and Christopher Pierson, *Conversations with Anthony Giddens: Making Sense of Modernity* (Stanford, Calif.: Stanford University Press, 1999), 94.

25. Ibid., 6.

26. Quoted in Cecelia McKeig and Renee Geving, *Bena: Celebrating the Centennial History* (Brainerd, Minn.: Bang Printing, 2007), 2.

27. Gerald Vizenor, *Interior Landscapes: Autobiographical Myths and Memories* (Minneapolis: University of Minnesota Press, 1990), 274–75.

28. McKeig and Geving, *Bena*, 106.

29. See Stephen L. Pevar, *The Rights of Indians and Tribes*, 2d ed. (Carbondale: Southern Illinois University Press, 1992), 16.

30. Ibid.

31. Scott Starr, "Indian Country," August 24, 2007, *Znet*, June 17, 2008, http://www.zmag.org/znet/viewArticle/14649.

32. James A. Clifton, ed. *Being and Becoming Indian* (Chicago: Dorsey, 1989), 24.

33. Arnold Krupat, *Ethnocriticism: Ethnography, History, Literature* (Berkeley: University of California Press, 1992), 5.

34. Louis Owens, *Mixedblood Messages: Literature, Film, Family, Place* (Norman: University of Oklahoma Press, 1998), 26.

35. Michael Hardt and Antonio Negri, *Empire* (Cambridge: Harvard University Press, 2000), 106.

36. Ibid.

37. Ibid., 107.

38. Ibid., 150.

39. Daniel Heath Justice, "'Go Away, Water!': Kinship Criticism and the Decolonization Imperative," in *Reasoning Together: The Native Critics Collective*, ed. Craig S. Womack, Daniel Heath Justice, and Christopher B. Teuton (Norman: University of Oklahoma Press, 2008), 153.

40. Jace Weaver, "Splitting the Earth: First Utterances and Pluralist Separatism," in *American Indian Literary Nationalism*, ed. Jace Weaver, Craig S. Womack, and Robert Warrior (Albuquerque: University of New Mexico Press, 2006), 24.

41. Lisa Brooks, "At the Gathering Place," in Weaver, Womack, and Warrior, *American Indian Literary Nationalism*, 232–33.

42. Joy Harjo, *The Woman Who Fell from the Sky* (New York: Norton, 1996), 68–69.

43. Brooks, "At the Gathering Place," 232.

44. David Wallace Adams, *Education for Extinction: American Indians and the Boarding School Experience, 1875–1928* (Lawrence: University Press of Kansas, 1997).

45. Arnold Krupat, "Foreword," in Roy Harvey Pearce, *Savagism and Civilization: A Study of the Indian and the American Mind* (Berkeley: University of California Press, 1988), xi–xii.

46. Pearce, *Savagism and Civilization*, 41.

47. Krupat, "Foreword," xii.

48. Rey Chow, *The Protestant Ethnic and the Spirit of Capitalism* (New York: Columbia University Press, 2002), 48.

49. Ibid., 49.

50. Daniel Heath Justice, "Seeing (and Reading) Red: Indian Outlaws in the Ivory Tower," in *Indigenizing the Academy: Transforming Scholarship and Empowering Communities*, ed. Devon Abbott Mihesuah and Anglela Cavender Wilson (Lincoln and London: University of Nebraska Press, 2004), 102.

51. Daniel Heath Justice, *Our Fire Survives the Storm: A Cherokee Literary History* (Minneapolis: University of Minnesota Press, 2006), 21, 58.

52. Ibid., 58.

53. Daniel Heath Justice and Debra K. S. Barker, "Deep Surveillance: Tenure and Promotion Strategies for Scholars of Color," *Profession* (2007): 175.

54. Ibid., 176.

55. Ibid., 177.

56. Ibid., 178.

57. Ibid., 180.

58. Alvin M. Josephy Jr., Joane Nagel, and Troy Johnson, eds., *Red Power: The American Indians' Fight for Freedom*, 2d ed. (Lincoln and London: University of Nebraska Press, 1999), 1.

59. Jace Weaver, *That the People Might Live: Native American Literatures and Native American Community* (New York: Oxford University Press, 1997), xiii.

1. Identity Crisis

1. Louis Owens, *Other Destinies: Understanding the American Indian Novel* (Norman: University of Oklahoma Press, 1992), 3.

2. Elias Boudinot, "An Address to the Whites," in *Cherokee Editor: The Writings of Elias Boudinot*, ed. Theda Perdue (Athens: University of Georgia Press, 1996), 69.

3. N. Scott Momaday, "The Arrowmaker," in *The Man Made of Words: Essays, Stories, Passages* (New York: St. Martin's Griffin, 1998), 9–12.

4. Linda Martín Alcoff and Satya P. Mohanty, "Introduction," in *Identity Politics Reconsidered* (New York: Palgrave Macmillan, 2006), 6.

5. Winona LaDuke, "Foreword," in Andrea Smith, *Conquest: Sexual Violence and American Indian Genocide* (Cambridge: South End Press, 2005), xvii.

6. Ibid.

7. See Walter Benn Michaels, *The Trouble with Diversity: How We Learned to Love Identity and Ignore Equality* (New York: Metropolitan Books, 2006), and Todd Gitlin, *The Twilight of Common Dreams: Why America Is Wracked by Culture Wars* (New York: Metropolitan Books, 1995).

8. Clyde Warrior, "We Are Not Free," in *Red Power: The American Indians' Fight for Freedom*, ed. Alvin M. Josephy Jr., Joane Nagel, and Troy R. Johnson, 2d ed. (Lincoln and London: University of Nebraska Press, 1999), 21.

9. Hank Adams, "An Open Letter to the Los Angeles Times and the Washington Post in the Form of a Last Chapter on Jamake Highwater," June 10, 2001, Jamake Highwater Papers (Box 34), New York Public Library.

10. Erik Hedegaard, "Even Showgirls Get the Blues," September 3, 1998, *Rolling Stone*, January 8, 2009, http://www.rollingstone.com/artists/shaniatwain/articles/story/5939944/cover_story_even_showgirls_get_the_blues.

11. Angela Aleiss, "Race in Contemporary Cinema: Part 10. Iron Eyes Cody: 'Wannabe Indian,'" *Cineaste* 25.1 (1999): 30–31.

12. Matthew Fleischer, "Navahoax," January 26, 2006, *LA Weekly*, January 9, 2009, http://www.laweekly.com/2006-01-26/news/navahoax/.

13. Armand Garnet Ruffo, *Grey Owl: The Mystery of Archie Belaney* (Regina: Couteau Books, 1996).

14. Henry Louis Gates Jr., "'Authenticity' or the Lesson of Little Tree," *New York Times Book Review*, November 24, 1991, 26.

15. Donald B. Smith, *Long Lance: The True Story of an Imposter* (Lincoln: University of Nebraska Press, 1983).

16. Indian Arts and Crafts Act of 1990, 101st Congress, 2d session (P.L. 101-644), Washington, D.C.: U.S. Government Printing Office, 1990.

17. Association of American Indian and Alaska Native Professors, "Statement on Ethnic Fraud," January 9, 2009, http://www.uwm.edu/~michael/nativeprofs/fraud.htm.

18. Dennis Fox, "Indian Arts and Crafts Act: Counterpoint," *Native Americas* (fall/winter 1994): 114–18.

19. Mary Annette Pember, "Ethnic Fraud?" January 25, 2007, *Diverse Issues in Higher Education,* January 8, 2008, http://www.diverseeducation.com/artman/publish/printer_6918.shtml.

20. Cornel Pewewardy, "So You Think You Hired an 'Indian' Faculty Member?: The Ethnic Fraud Paradox in Higher Education," in *Indigenizing the Academy: Transforming Scholarship and Empowering Communities,* ed. Devon Mihesuah (Lincoln and London: University of Nebraska Press), 200–217.

21. "In a majority of disenrollment cases . . . tribal officials are, without any concern for human rights, tribal traditions or due process, arbitrarily and capriciously disenrolling tribal members as a means to solidify their own economic and political bases and to winnow out opposition families who disapprove of the direction the tribal leadership is headed" (David Wilkins, "Self-determination or Self-decimation?" *Indian Country Today,* August 25, 2006, A3).

22. Amnesty International, "Maze of Injustice: The Failure to Protect Indigenous Women from Sexual Violence in the USA," February 16, 2008, http://www.amnestyusa.org/document.php?id=ENGAMR510352007%20.

23. According to Buttes, this identity heist happened around 1969, when certain Indian families, now politically powerful, "squatted" on Mdewakanton lands. "Since that time they have illegitimately claimed Mdewakanton identity, using Mdewakanton lands to set up their own 'Mdewakanton' government . . . which now effectively works in opposition to the legitimate Mdewakanton people" (Barbara Buttes, "Beyond Sovereignty: The Great Mdewakanton Identity Heist," unpublished manuscript, 9).

24. *Sheldon Peters Wolfchild, et al. v. United States,* No. 03-2648L, United States Federal Court of Claims, October 27, 2004.

25. *Marilyn Vann, et al. v. Dirk Kempthorne, et al.,* Civil Action 03-1711 (HHK), United States District Court for the District of Columbia, December 19, 2006.

26. Chad Smith, letter to the editor, *USA Today,* December 6, 2006.

27. Eva Marie Garroutte, *Real Indians: Identity and the Survival of Native America* (Berkeley: University of California Press, 2003), 134.

28. Ibid., 134; emphasis in original.

29. Quoted in Gerald Vizenor, *The People Named the Chippewa: Narrative Histories* (Minneapolis: University of Minnesota Press, 1984), 107.

30. Ibid.

31. Another theory attributes the word *Ojibwe* to a corruption of another word meaning something like "those who make pictographs," referring to birchbark scrolls.

32. Bob Jourdain, personal interview, Leech Lake Reservation, November 23, 2000.

33. Charles Trimble, "Iyeska: Notes from Mixed-Blood Country," *Indian Country Today,* May 8, 2008, A3.

34. Elizabeth Cook-Lynn, *Why I Can't Read Wallace Stegner and Other Essays: A Tribal Voice* (Madison: University of Wisconsin Press, 1996), 35–36.

35. Mary Crow Dog and Richard Erdoes, *Lakota Woman* (New York: Harper-Perennial, 1991), 49.

36. Edward Lazarus, *Black Hills, White Justice: The Sioux Nation versus the United States, 1775 to the Present* (New York: HarperCollins, 1991), 307–8.

37. Marge Piercy, *Woman on the Edge of Time* (New York: Fawcett/Ballantine Books, 1976), 104.

38. Ibid., 100.

39. Jack Forbes traces the origins of blood quantum back to a 1705 Virginia Colony statute. See "Blood Quantum: A Relic of Racism and Termination," November 27, 2000, *Native Intelligence,* December 7, 2007, http://www.weyanoke.org/jdf-BloodQuantum.html.

40. Garroutte, *Real Indians,* 14–37.

41. Schneider believed that kinship studies began with Lewis Henry Morgan, the father of ethnology, who initiated a persistent fascination with clanship that would be passed down through generations of ethnologists. In 1972 Schneider argued that the concept of "kinship," being an English word, should exist in American and European societies too, but he found that it did not. Therefore, it followed, *"the way in which Morgan and his followers used it, it does not exist in any culture known to man"* (David Schneider, *A Critique of the Study of Kinship* [Ann Arbor: University of Michigan Press, 1984], 50; emphasis in original). See also David Schneider, "What Is Kinship All About?" in *Kinship Studies in the Morgan Centennial Year,* ed. Priscilla Reining (Washington, D.C.: Anthropological Society of Washington, 1972), 88–112.

42. Garroutte, *Real Indians,* 127.

43. Manuel Castells, *The Power of Identity* (Oxford: Blackwell, 1997), 7. Subsequent references are given in the text.

44. For an introduction to the thought, culture, and biographies of the first post-boarding-school generation of Native intellectuals, see Hazel W. Hertzberg,

The Search for an American Indian Identity: Modern Pan-Indian Movements (Syracuse, N.Y.: Syracuse University Press, 1971). For a critique of this group, see Robert Allen Warrior, *Tribal Secrets: Recovering American Indian Intellectual Traditions* (Minneapolis: University of Minnesota Press, 1995).

45. Quoted in Vizenor, *The People Named the Chippewa*, 62.

46. For Castells, civil society is "a set of organizations and institutions, as well as a series of structured and organized social actors, which reproduce, albeit sometimes in a conflictive manner, the identity that rationalizes the sources of structural domination. This statement may come as a surprise to some readers, since civil society generally suggests a positive connotation of democratic social change. However, this is in fact the original conception of civil society, as formulated by Gramsci, the intellectual father of this ambiguous concept. Indeed, in Gramsci's conception, civil society is formed by a series of 'apparatuses,' such as the Church(es), unions, parties, cooperatives, civic associations and so on, which, on the one hand, prolong the dynamics of the state, but, on the other hand, are deeply rooted among the people" (Castells, *The Power of Identity*, 8–9).

47. Dennis Banks, "Statement by Dennis Banks," in Josephy, Nagel, and Johnson, *Red Power*, 62.

48. Castells, *The Power of Identity*, 10.

49. My use of this term is different from Garroutte's. For her, indigenism was a synonym for traditionalism. I am referring here to the indigenous peoples movement, especially the antiglobalization variant symbolized by the Zapatistas.

50. Winona LaDuke, *All Our Relations: Native Struggles for Land and Life* (Boston: South End Press, 1999), 180.

51. Subcomandante Marcos, *Shadows of Tender Fury* (New York: Monthly Review Press, 1995), 214–15.

52. Quoted in Charlie Cray, "The War against Oblivion: The Zapatista Chronicles," *Multinational Monitor* 22.3 (March 2001): 27.

53. Medea Benjamin, "Interview: Subcomandante Marcos," in *First World, Ha, Ha, Ha: The Zapatista Challenge*, ed. Elaine Katzenberger (San Francisco: City Lights Press, 1995), 69–70.

54. State Indigenous and Campesino Council of Chiapas, "Interview: Indigenous and Campesino Council of Chiapas," in Katzenberger, *First World*, 122.

55. Robert Berkhofer Jr., *The White Man's Indian: Images of the American Indian from Columbus to the Present* (New York: Vintage, 1978), 3.

56. Quoted in ibid., 5.

57. Ibid., 25–26.

58. Gerald Vizenor, *Manifest Manners: Postindian Warriors of Survivance* (Hanover and London: Wesleyan University Press, 1994), 4–5.

59. Ibid., 23.

60. Roger Williams, "A Key into the Language of America," in *The Norton*

Anthology of American Literature, 7th ed., vol. A, ed. Nina Baym et al. (New York: Norton, 2007), 175.

61. Ibid., 77.

62. I'm already on record contesting both racialism and the Nike N7 Air Native. See Scott Richard Lyons, "The Curious Return of 'Race' in 2007," *Indian Country Today,* December 21, 2007, A3.

63. Frell M. Owl, "Who and What Is an American Indian?" *Ethnohistory* 9.3 (summer 1962): 265–66; my emphasis.

2. Culture and Its Cops

1. American Indian Chicago Conference, "Declaration of Indian Purpose," in *Red Power: The American Indians' Fight for Freedom,* ed. Alvin M. Josephy Jr., Joane Nagel, and Troy R. Johnson (Lincoln and London: University of Nebraska Press, 1999), 13–14.

2. Charles Trimble, "Iyeska: Notes from Mixed-Blood Country," *Indian Country Today,* May 8, 2008, A3.

3. Robert B. Porter, "Decolonizing Indigenous Governance: Observations on Restoring Greater Faith and Legitimacy in the Government of the Seneca Nation," *Kansas Journal of Law and Public Policy* 8 (1999).

4. Gregory Cajete, *Native Science: Natural Laws of Interdependence* (Sante Fe: Clear Light, 2000).

5. Gerald R. Alfred, *Heeding the Voices of Our Ancestors: Kahnawake Mohawk Politics and the Rise of Native Nationalism* (Oxford and Toronto: Oxford University Press, 1995).

6. Craig Womack, "Alexander Posey's Nature Journals: A Further Argument for Tribally-Specific Aesthetics," *SAIL: Studies in American Indian Literatures* 13.2–3 (summer/fall 2001): 49–66.

7. Linda Tuhiwai Smith, *Decolonizing Methodologies: Research and Indigenous Peoples* (London: Zed Books, 1999).

8. See Raymond Williams, "Culture," in *Keywords,* rev. ed. (New York: Oxford University Press, 1983), 87–93.

9. Johann Gottfried von Herder, *Reflections on the Philosophy of the History of Mankind* (Chicago: Chicago University Press, 1968), 49.

10. See the "Treatise on the Origin of Language" in *Herder: Philosophical Writings,* ed. Michael N. Forster (Cambridge: Cambridge University Press, 2002).

11. Terry Eagleton, *The Idea of Culture* (Oxford: Blackwell 2002), 11.

12. Ibid.

13. Matthew Arnold, *Culture and Anarchy,* ed. J. Dover Wilson (Cambridge: Cambridge University Press, 1966) 45, 70; emphasis in original.

14. Lewis Henry Morgan, *Ancient Society,* ed. Robin Fox (New York: Transaction Publishers, 2000).

15. For an introduction to scientific race theories, especially in the American context, see Reginald Horsman, *Race and Manifest Destiny: The Origins of American Racial Anglo-Saxonism* (Cambridge: Harvard University Press, 1981).

16. Franz Boas, *The Mind of Primitive Man* (New York: Free Press, 1965); see also his *Race, Language, and Culture*, reprint (Chicago: University of Chicago Press, 1995). For an excellent reading of Boas and other anthropologists in the context of Native studies, see Arnold Krupat, *Ethnocriticism: Ethnography, History, Literature* (Berkeley: University of California Press, 1992).

17. Samuel P. Huntington, "The Clash of Civilizations?" *Foreign Affairs* 72.3 (summer 1993): 22–49.

18. See bin Laden's speech aired on the Al-Jazeera network on October 29, 2004 (http://english.aljazeera.net/News/archive/archive?ArchiveId=7403). In 1997 and 1998, bin Laden granted interviews to CNN Correspondent Peter Arnett and ABC's John Miller, saying in the latter interview, "The call to wage war against America was made because America has spearheaded the crusade against the Islamic nation, sending tens of thousands of its troops to the land of the two Holy Mosques over and above its meddling in its affairs and its politics, and its support of the oppressive, corrupt and tyrannical regime that is in control. These are the reasons behind the singling out of America as a target." In the former interview, he promised to stop attacking America if the United States pulls out of the Middle East: "if the cause that has called for this act comes to an end, this act, in turn, will come to an end." These statements do not indicate a "clash of civilizations" driven by cultural or religious differences so much as a position of violent resistance to specific military assaults, occupations, and support for "tyrannical regimes."

19. Seyla Benhabib, *The Claims of Culture: Equality and Diversity in the Global Age* (Princeton, N.J.: Princeton University Press, 2002), 4.

20. Amartya Sen, *Identity and Violence: The Illusion of Destiny* (New York: Norton 2006), 11; emphasis in original.

21. Benhabib, *The Claims of Culture*, 5.

22. Sen, *Identity and Violence*, 103.

23. Ibid., 112.

24. Williams, "Culture," 87.

25. Hans Johst, *Schlageter* (Berlin: Albert Langen/Georg Müller, 1933).

26. For this collection of words and phrases I am indebted to several people who had discussions with me about this topic, especially David "Niib" Aubid, George Goggleye, and several anonymous subscribers to the Minnesota-based Ojibwe Culture and Language listserv who answered my query, "How do you say 'culture' in Ojibwe?" with many helpful suggestions.

27. There is always a danger in overemphasizing the significance of the animate–inanimate distinction in *Ojibwemowin*, just as there is always a risk in reading too much "gender" into the German language. That said, it cannot be argued that

there is no connection at all to be made between verb inflections and the world-view that produced them long ago.

28. E-mail dated February 27, 2006. I've honored George's preferred spellings here. Written Ojibwe presently still lacks a standardized orthography (although it won't for long thanks to the popularization of the Nichols and Nyholm dictionary and the spread of Ojibwe language classes at tribal colleges and state universities).

29. Vine Deloria Jr. and Clifford M. Lytle, *The Nations Within: The Past and Future of American Indian Sovereignty* (Austin: University of Texas Press, 1984), 8.

30. Winona LaDuke, "Minobimaatisiiwin: The Good Life," *Cultural Survival Quarterly* 16, no. 4 (winter 1992): 69–71. See also Winona LaDuke, *All Our Relations: Native Struggles for Land and Life* (Cambridge: South End Press, 1994), 4, 132.

31. Craig Womack, *Red on Red: Native American Literary Separatism* (Minneapolis: University of Minnesota Press, 1999), 61.

32. Hannah Allam, "Powwow Lawsuit against St. Thomas Dropped," *St. Paul Pioneer Press,* October 15, 2002, B2.

33. Quoted in ibid.

34. "Women at Host Drums," May 10, 2002, *Red News,* November 18, 2005, http://www.orgsites.com/fl/drumming/_pgggl.php3.

35. Ibid.

36. Ibid.

37. "American Indian Women Drop Powwow Lawsuit against St. Thomas," October 14, 2002, *Bulletin News,* September 15, 2003, http://www.stthomas.edu/bulletin/news/200242/Monday/Powwowsuit10_14_02.cfm.

38. Benhabib, *The Claims of Culture,* 186.

39. Ibid., 185.

40. Jack Goody, *The Logic of Writing and the Organization of Society* (Cambridge: Cambridge University Press, 1986) 9.

41. Ibid., 9–10.

42. Ibid., 10.

43. Sen, *Identity and Violence,* 91.

44. Ibid., 89.

45. Gerald Vizenor, *Fugitive Poses: Native American Indian Scenes of Absence and Presence* (Lincoln and London: University of Nebraska Press, 1998), 88–94.

46. Ibid., 91.

47. Ibid., 91, 94.

48. Ibid., 94.

49. As Krupat explains, "Appiah's understanding of patriotism separates it from nationalism. For him, patriotism is a '*sentiment*' that, unlike nationalism, 'can be made consistent with different political ideologies'" (Arnold Krupat, *Red Matters: Native American Studies* [Philadelphia: University of Pennsylvania Press, 2002], 17).

50. Scott Richard Lyons, "Crying for Revision: Postmodern Indians and Rhetorics of Tradition," in *Making and Unmaking the Prospects for Rhetoric*, ed. Theresa Enos (Mahwah, N.J.: Lawrence Erlbaum, 1997), 121–31.

51. Michael D. McNally, *Ojibwe Singers: Hymns, Grief, and a Native Culture in Motion* (New York: Oxford University Press, 2000).

52. Craig S. Womack, "The Integrity of American Indian Claims (or, How I Learned to Stop Worrying and Love My Hybridity)," in *American Indian Literary Nationalism*, ed. Jace Weaver, Craig S. Womack, and Robert Warrior (Albuquerque: University of New Mexico Press, 2006), 136.

53. Womack, *Red on Red*, 65.

54. Ibid., 22, 211.

55. Jace Weaver, "Splitting the Earth: First Utterances and Pluralist Separatism," in Weaver, Womack, and Warrior, *American Indian Literary Nationalism*, 28.

56. David Treuer, *Native American Fiction: A User's Manual* (St. Paul: Graywolf Press, 2006), 64–65. Subsequent references are given in the text.

57. Ibid., 74, 195.

58. Ibid., 5.

59. Ibid.

60. Ibid., 201.

61. Ibid., 81, 24–25, 17–23.

62. Ibid., 23.

63. Ibid., 5.

64. Anton Treuer, *Living Our Language: Ojibwe Tales and Oral Histories* (St. Paul: Minnesota Historical Society Press, 2001), 5.

65. Treuer, *Native American Fiction*, 107, 24–25.

66. Ibid., 19–20.

67. Ibid., 22.

68. Krupat, *Red Matters*, 47.

69. Treuer, *Native American Fiction*, 201.

70. See Edward Said, *Representations of the Intellectual* (New York: Vintage, 1996), 25–45.

71. The Seven Grandfathers have often been represented in art (for instance, in the popular series of paintings by Leland Bell) and even became an exhibit at the National Museum of the American Indian. For more on the Seven Grandfathers' teachings, see Edward Benton-Banai, *The Mishomis Book: The Voice of the Ojibway* (Hayward, Wisc.: Indian Country Communications and Red School House Press, 1988; reprint, University of Minnesota Press, 2010), 64.

3. Nations and Nationalism since 1492

1. Aimé Césaire, *Discourse on Colonialism*, trans. Joan Pinkham (New York: Monthly Review Press, 2000), 52.

2. Ibid., 78.

3. Taiaiake Alfred, *Peace, Power, Righteousness: An Indigenous Manifesto* (London and New York: Oxford University Press, 1999), 36.

4. Taiaiake Alfred, *Wasáse: Indigenous Pathways of Action and Freedom* (Toronto: Broadview Press, 2005), 281.

5. Ibid., 31.

6. Ibid., 54.

7. Ibid., 105.

8. Anthony P. Cohen, "Culture, Identity and the Concept of Boundary," *Revista de antropología social* (1994): 51.

9. Ronald Neizen, "Recognizing Indigenism: Canadian Unity and the Internationalist Movement of Indigenous Peoples," *Comparative Studies in Society and History* 42.1 (January 2000): 140.

10. As Oren Lyons explains, negotiators at the United Nations resisted nationalist language offered by indigenous activists. "At first we were called indigenous 'populations,' then after a lot of battles we finally became 'peoples.' Some of the people we negotiated with—you know who they are—strongly resisted the idea of us being 'nations'" (personal interview, October 8, 2007, Syracuse University).

11. Raymond Williams, *Keywords*, rev. ed. (New York: Oxford University Press, 1983), 213.

12. Ernest Gellner, *Nations and Nationalism* (Ithaca, N.Y.: Cornell University Press, 1983), 18.

13. Ernest Gellner, "Do Nations Have Navels?" *Nations and Nationalism* 2.3 (1995): 368.

14. Gellner, *Nations and Nationalism*, 1. Subsequent references are given in the text.

15. Charles Wilson Hackett, ed., and Charmon Clair Shelby, trans., *The Revolt of the Pueblo Indians of New Mexico and Otermin's Attempted Reconquest, 1680–1682*, 2 vols. (Albuquerque: University of New Mexico Press, 1942), 2:247.

16. Patricia Riles Wickman, *The Tree That Bends: Discourse, Power, and the Survival of the Maskóki People* (Tuscaloosa: University of Alabama Press, 1999), 204.

17. Anthony D. Smith, "Nations and Their Pasts," *The Warwick Debates on Nationalism*, Warwick University, October 24, 1995.

18. Georges Vacher de Lapouge, *Les Sélections sociales* (Paris: Fontemoing, 1896), 9–10.

19. Anthony D. Smith, *The Ethnic Origins of Nations* (Oxford: Blackwell, 1998 [1986]), 22.

20. Ibid.

21. Ibid., 130.

22. Gerald Alfred, *Heeding the Voices of Our Ancestors: Kahnawake Mohawk*

Politics and the Rise of Native Nationalism (Toronto: Oxford University Press, 1995), 9.

23. Petalesharo, "Speech of the Pawnee Chief," in *The Norton Anthology of American Literature,* 7th ed., vol. B, ed. Nina Baym et al. (New York: Norton, 2007), 1256.

24. Francis Paul Prucha, *American Indian Treaties: The History of a Political Anomaly* (Berkeley: University of California Press, 1994), 1.

25. Quoted in ibid., 13.

26. Charles Alexander Eastman, *From the Deep Woods to Civilization* (Lincoln and London: University of Nebraska Press, 1977), 8.

27. Ibid., 28.

28. Ibid.

29. Robert Allen Warrior, *Tribal Secrets: Recovering American Indian Intellectual Traditions* (Minneapolis: University of Minnesota Press, 1995), 123.

30. Elias Boudinot, *Cherokee Editor: The Writings of Elias Boudinot,* ed. Theda Perdue (Athens: University of Georgia Press, 1996), 90.

31. Ibid., 105.

32. Ibid., 107.

33. Ibid., 107–8.

34. Susan Kalter, "Finding a Place for David Cusick in Native American Literary History," *MELUS* 27.3 (autumn 2002): 10.

35. Maureen Konkle, *Writing Indian Nations: Native Intellectuals and the Politics of Historiography, 1827–1863* (Chapel Hill and London: University of North Carolina Press, 2004), 160–61.

36. Ibid., 182.

37. George Copway, *The Traditional History and Characteristic Sketches of the Ojibway Nation* (London: Charles Gilpin, 1850), 53.

38. Ibid., 46.

39. Ibid., 93.

40. Kay B. Warren and Jean E. Jackson, eds., *Indigenous Movements, Self-Representation, and the State in Latin America* (Austin: University of Texas Press, 2002), 27.

41. Robert Warrior, "Native Critics and the World," in *American Indian Literary Nationalism,* ed. Jace Weaver, Craig S. Womack, and Robert Warrior (Albuquerque: University of New Mexico Press, 2006), 202.

42. Ronald Neizen, *The Origins of Indigenism: Human Rights and the Politics of Identity* (Berkeley and Los Angeles: University of California Press, 2003), 17–18.

43. Taiaiake Alfred, public lecture, Syracuse University, spring 2006.

44. Alfred's work is also of interest to young anarchists in Canada. See http://www.anarchistnews.org/?q=node/1320.

45. Alfred, *Heeding the Voices of Our Ancestors,* 14; my emphasis.

46. Ibid., 16.

47. Ibid., 7.

48. Alfred, *Peace, Power, Righteousness*, 59.

49. Ibid., 137.

50. Vine Deloria Jr. and Clifford M. Lytle, *The Nations Within: The Past and Future of American Indian Sovereignty* (Austin: University of Texas Press, 1984), 266–67.

51. Joanne Barker, "For Whom Sovereignty Matters," in *Sovereignty Matters,* ed. Joanne Barker (Lincoln and London: University of Nebraska Press, 2005), 26, 21.

52. In 2004, Peter Gordon captured widespread media interest for his research of the Piraha people in Brazil, who he said couldn't perform basic math because they had only two words to characterize numerical values ("one" and "many") even though he tried teaching them. He also claimed that they had no origin story—indeed, no memories at all beyond two generations—and no art, no words for colors, and no pronouns. He said that they will starve themselves and their children even though food as available, and that they willingly "share their women" with Brazilian traders. The way I see it, Gordon, who is speaking very authoritatively on these matters, even though he does not speak the Piraha language, has essentially represented the image of Piraha "savages." His whole argument rests on conceptual separatism. See Stephen Strauss, "Life without Numbers in a Unique Amazon Tribe," *Globe and Mail,* August 20, 2004, A3.

53. Alfred, *Wasáse,* 20. Subsequent references are given in the text.

54. Edward Spicer, *Cycles of Conquest: The Impact of Spain, Mexico, and the United States on the Indians of the Southwest, 1533–1960* (Phoenix: University of Arizona Press, 1962).

55. Robert K. Thomas, "The Tap-Roots of Peoplehood," in *Getting to the Heart of the Matter,* ed. Daphne J. Anderson (Vancouver: Native Ministries Consortium Press, 1990), 25–32.

56. Tom Holm, Diane Pearson, and Ben Chavis, "Peoplehood: A Model for American Indian Sovereignty in Education," *Wicazo Sa Review* 18 (2003): 7–24.

57. Taiaiake Alfred and Jeff Corntassel, "Being Indigenous: Resurgences against Contemporary Colonialism," in *Politics of Identity IX,* ed. Richard Bellamy (New York and London: Blackwell, 2005), 609.

58. See Deloria and Lytle, *The Nations Within,* 12, 266.

59. See Scott Richard Lyons, "Rhetorical Sovereignty: What Do American Indians Want from Writing?" *CCC* 51.3 (February 2000): 447–68.

60. Gilles Deleuze and Félix Guattari, *A Thousand Plateaus: Capitalism and Schizophrenia,* trans. Brian Massumi (Minneapolis: University of Minnesota Press, 1987), 6–7.

61. Ibid., 21.

62. Smith, *The Ethnic Origins of Nations,* 15.

63. See Steve Charleston, "The Old Testament of Native America," in *Native and Christian: Indigenous Voices on Religious Identity,* ed. James Treat (New York and London: Routledge, 1996), 68–80.

64. Accessed May 15, 2008, at http://www.kevinlocke.com/kevin/bahai.html.

65. Warrior, "Native Critics and the World," 208–9.

66. Ibid., 210.

67. Alfred, *Heeding the Voices of Our Ancestors,* 170.

68. Alfred, *Peace, Power, Righteousness,* 85.

69. Alfred and Corntassel, "Being Indigenous," 611.

70. Alfred, *Wasáse,* 37, 163, 279.

71. Warrior, "Native Critics and the World," 215–16.

72. Eric Hobsbawm, *Nations and Nationalism since 1780: Programme, Myth, Reality* (Cambridge: Cambridge University Press, 1990), 10.

73. Smith, *The Ethnic Origins of Nations,* 19.

74. See John Mohawk, *Utopian Legacies: A History of Conquest and Oppression in the Western World* (Denver: Clear Light Books, 1999).

75. Jace Weaver, "Splitting the Earth: First Utterances and Pluralist Separatism," in Weaver, Womack, and Warrior, *American Indian Literary Nationalism,* 15.

76. Charles Brockden Brown, *Edgar Huntly; or, Memoirs of a Sleep-Walker* (Philadelphia: M. Pollock, 1857), 3.

77. F. O. Matthiesson, *American Renaissance: Art and Expression in the Age of Emerson and Whitman* (Oxford: Oxford University Press, 1968).

78. Quoted in Robert S. Levine and Arnold Krupat, "Introduction," in Baym et al., *The Norton Anthology of American Literature,* 931.

79. Ibid., 932.

80. Sydney Smith, "A Review of Adam Seybert's *Statistical Annals of the United States of America,*" *Edinburgh Review* 32 (January 1820): 69–80.

81. Lydia Howard Huntley Sigourney, "Indian Names," in Baym et al., *The Norton Anthology of American Literature,* 1033–34.

82. Weaver, "Splitting Earth," 3, 14.

83. Craig Womack, *Red on Red: Native American Literary Separatism* (Minneapolis: University of Minnesota Press, 1999), 7.

84. Vine Deloria Jr., "The Red and the Black," in *Custer Died for Your Sins: An Indian Manifesto* (Norman: University of Oklahoma Press, 1988).

85. Malcolm X, "Statement of Basic Aims and Objectives of the Organization of Afro-American Unity" (June 1964), in *New Black Voices,* ed. Abraham Chapman (New York: New American Library, 1972), 563.

86. Hoyt W. Fuller, "Towards a Black Aesthetic," in *Afro-American Writing: An Anthology of Prose and Poetry,* 2d ed., ed. Richard A. Long and Eugenia W. Collier (University Park: Pennsylvania State University Press, 1985), 587.

87. Larry Neal, "The Black Arts Movement," *TDR: The Drama Review* 12 (summer 1968): 39.

88. Stokely Carmichael, "Toward Black Liberation," in *Black Fire: An Anthology of Afro-American Writing,* ed. LeRoi Jones and Larry Neal (New York: Morrow, 1968), 128.

89. Larry Neal, "Afterword," in Jones and Neal, *Black Fire,* 653.

90. LeRoi Jones, *Home: Social Essays* (New York: Morrow, 1965), 10.

91. Ibid., 251.

92. Elizabeth Cook-Lynn, *Why I Can't Read Wallace Stegner and Other Essays: A Tribal Voice* (Madison: University of Wisconsin Press, 1996), 85.

93. Warrior, *Tribal Secrets,* xviii–xix.

94. Womack, *Red on Red,* 6–7.

95. Ibid., 5.

96. Jace Weaver, "Preface," in Weaver, Womack, and Warrior, *American Indian Literary Nationalism,* xvi.

97. Simon J. Ortiz, "Towards a National Indian Literature: Cultural Authenticity in Nationalism," in Weaver, Womack, and Warrior, *American Indian Literary Nationalism,* 254, 257.

98. The phrase "Indians are still Indians" is in Simon J. Ortiz, "Foreword," in Weaver, Womack, and Warrior, *American Indian Literary Nationalism,* xi.

99. Ortiz, "Towards a National Indian Literature," 257.

100. Weaver, "Splitting the Earth," 11.

101. Ortiz, "Towards a National Indian Literature," 258.

102. Vizenor "defines" survivance as "more than survival, more than endurance or mere response; the stories of survivance are an active presence" (Gerald Vizenor, *Fugitive Poses: Native American Indian Scenes of Absence and Presence* [Lincoln and London: University of Nebraska Press, 1998], 15). Interestingly, the word *survivance* has also been used by French-speaking Quebecois since the nineteenth century to characterize Quebec's right to political independence based upon the *la survivance* of Francophone language and culture.

103. Craig S. Womack, "A Single Decade: Book-Length Literary Criticism between 1986 and 1997," in *Reasoning Together: The Native Critics Collective,* ed. Craig S. Womack, Daniel Heath Justice, and Christopher B. Teuton (Norman: University of Oklahoma Press, 2008), 72.

104. "The simulation of the *indian,* lowercase and in italics, is an ironic name. . . . The Indian with an initial capital is a commemoration of an absence—evermore that double absence of simulations by name and stories. My first use of the italicized *indian* as a simulation was in *The Everlasting Sky.* . . . Since then, natives are the presence, and *indians* are simulations, a derivative noun that means an absence, in my narratives" (Vizenor, *Fugitive Poses,* 15).

105. Ibid.

106. Craig S. Womack, "The Integrity of American Indian Claims (or, How I Learned to Stop Worrying and Love My Hybridity)," in Weaver, Womack, and Warrior, *American Indian Literary Nationalism,* 120.

107. Weaver, "Spitting the Earth," 34; "Preface," xviii.

108. Ortiz, "Foreword," xiv, xiii.

109. Marianne Mithun, *The Languages of Native North America* (Cambridge: Cambridge University Press, 2001), 2.

110. Norbert Francis and Jon Reyhner, *Language and Literacy Teaching for Indigenous Education: A Bilingual Approach* (Clevedon, England: Multilingual Matters, 2002), 33.

111. Elizabeth Weise, "Researchers Speak Out on Languages on the Brink of Extinction." *USA Today,* September 18, 2007.

112. See Arnold Krupat, "Nationalism, Indigenism, Cosmopolitanism: Three Perspectives on Native American Literatures,"in *Red Matters: Native American Studies* (Philadelphia: University of Pennsylvania Press, 2002), 1–23.

113. Ortiz, "Towards a National Indian Literature," 259.

114. Michael Hardt and Antonio Negri, *Empire* (Cambridge: Harvard University Press, 2000), xi–xii.

115. Amnesty International USA, March 30, 2007, "Maze of Injustice: The Failure to Protect Indigenous Women from Sexual Violence in the USA," June 5, 2008, http://www.amnestyusa.org/document.php?id=ENGAMR510352007&lang=e. See also David Melmer, "Fire Thunder Impeached," *Indian Country Today,* June 30, 2006, A1.

116. See Lois Romano, "Battle over Gay Marriage Plays Out in Indian Country," *Washington Post,* August 1, 2005, A02.

117. See chapter 1 for a discussion of the Freedmen controversy. For an analysis of labor issues in the context of indigenous sovereignty, see Scott Richard Lyons, "Unionization Can Be an Act of Sovereignty," *Indian Country Today,* July 9, 2004, A3.

118. Mary McCarthy, "My Confession," in *The Art of the Personal Essay,* ed. Philip Lopate (New York: Anchor Books, 1995), 562; emphasis in original.

4. Resignations

1. Wub-e-ke-niew, *We Have the Right to Exist: A Translation of Aboriginal Indigenous Thought* (New York: Black Thistle Press, 1995).

2. Francis Blake Jr. (Wub-e-ke-niew), "Letter to the Secretary of the Interior," *Native American Press/Ojibwe News,* January 9, 1991, 3. Wub-e-ke-niew's columns are collected online at http://www.maquah.net.

3. Ibid.

4. Wub-e-ke-niew, *We Have the Right to Exist,* 97.

5. Ibid., 229.

6. Clara NiiSkaa, "Red Lake Continues to Violate Legacy and Widow of Wub-e-ke-niew," *Native American Press/Ojibwe News,* January 22, 1999, 4.

7. David Treuer, "His Home and Native Land," *Slate,* March 25, 2005. Accessed June 11, 2008, at http://www.slate.com/id/2115289/.

8. Peter R. Breggin, *Reclaiming Our Children: A Healing Plan for a Nation in Crisis* (New York: Da Capo Press, 2000).

9. Sean Teuton, "The Callout: Writing American Indian Politics," in *Reasoning Together: The Native Critics Collective,* ed. Craig S. Womack, David Heath Justice, and Christopher B. Teuton (Norman: University of Oklahoma Press, 2008), 117.

10. Along with "citizenship," Alfred also dismisses "taxation," "executive authority," and "sovereignty." See Taiaiake Alfred, *Peace, Power, Righteousness: An Indigenous Manifesto* (Oxford and New York: Oxford University Press, 1999), xiv.

11. David Wilkins, "Disenrollment in Indian Country: Indigenous Self-Decimation in an Age of Self-Determination," lecture at the International Indigenous Citizenship Conference, Syracuse University, April 27, 2007.

12. Ibid.

13. Manuel Castells, *The Power of Identity* (Oxford: Blackwell, 1997), 6.

14. Ibid., 7.

15. Ibid., 6–7.

16. Ibid., 7.

17. Herman R. Van Gunsteren, "Admission to Citizenship," *Ethics* 98.4 (July 1988): 732.

18. William Safran, "Citizenship and Nationality in Democratic Systems: Approaches to Defining and Acquiring Membership in the Political Community," *International Political Science Review/Revue Internationale de science politique* 18.3 (July 1997): 314.

19. We still think of nations as "families," if mainly on an unconscious or linguistic level. The cognitive scientist George Lakoff has written extensively and convincingly about the familial metaphors and concepts that are used to understand government and leadership. In *Moral Politics* Lakoff argued that American conservativism and liberalism differed in large part by the kinds of "families" and "parents" the different ideologies assumed were best for "children" (citizens): for conservatives, "Strict Fathers"; for liberals, "Nurturant Parents." See George Lakoff, *Moral Politics: How Liberals and Conservatives Think* (Chicago: University of Chicago Press, 2002).

20. Provisional Government of Israel, *Declaration of the Establishment of the State of Israel, Official Gazette,* no. 1; Tel Aviv, 5 Iyar 5708 (May 14, 1948), 1.

21. The Law of Return was originally formulated in 1950 and went through a series of revisions up until 1970. See www.knesset.gov.il/allsite/mark02/h0225697 .htm#TQL.

22. Safran, "Citizenship and Nationality in Democratic Systems," 326.

23. The Association for Civil Rights in Israel (ACRI) and Adalah: the Legal Center for Arab Minority Rights in Israel petitioned the Israeli Supreme Court to strike down the Citizenship and Entry into Israel Law, which they characterize as "racist," "harmful," and a violation of "basic human rights including the right for family life, freedom, equality, dignity and privacy." In May 2006, Israel's Supreme Court upheld the law on a narrow six to five vote. See ACRI's "Citizenship and Entry into Israel Law: Enacted with No Factual Basis" (http://www.acri.org.il/english-acri/engine/story.asp?id=255).

24. "Constitution and By-Laws for the Blackfeet Tribe of the Blackfeet Reservation of Montana," Article 2, Section 3.

25. "Constitution and By-Laws of the Oglala Sioux Tribe of the Pine Ridge Reservation," Article 2, Section 1.

26. "Constitution and By-Laws of the Rosebud Sioux Tribe of South Dakota," Article 2, Section 1.

27. "Constitution of the Lower Sioux Indian Community, Minnesota," Article 3, Section 1.

28. Ibid.

29. "The Indian Reorganization Act (Wheeler-Howard Act)," Section 19.

30. Jack Forbes, "Blood Quantum: A Relic of Racism and Termination," *Native Intelligence,* November 27, 2000. Accessed June 10, 2008, at http://www.thepeoplespaths.net/Articles2000/JDForbes001126Blood.htm.

31. "Revised Constitution and Bylaws of the Minnesota Chippewa Tribe, Minnesota," Article 2.

32. Carl Schmitt, *Political Theology: Four Chapters on the Concept of Sovereignty,* trans. George D. Schwab (Boston: MIT Press, 1985), 1.

33. "Revised Constitution and Bylaws of the Minnesota Chippewa Tribe, Minnesota," Mission Statement.

34. "Revised Constitution and Bylaws of the Minnesota Chippewa Tribe, Minnesota," Preamble.

SCOTT RICHARD LYONS (Ojibwe/Dakota) is assistant professor of English at Syracuse University, where he teaches indigenous and American literatures. He has also taught at Leech Lake Tribal College, the University of North Dakota, and Concordia College, Moorhead. The author of numerous critical and scholarly essays (including "Rhetorical Sovereignty: What Do American Indians Want from Writing?"), he is also a personal essayist and frequent contributor to newspapers such as *Indian Country Today* and *Star Tribune* (Minneapolis–St. Paul). He has worked with grass-roots organizations on issues ranging from Ojibwe language revitalization to Native theater.